聴竹居

日本人の理想の住まい

Chochikukyo　An ideal dwelling in Japan.

はじめに

　京都府・大山崎町の天王山の麓に竹の音を聴く住まい「聴竹居（ちょうちくきょ）」と名付けられた築90年になるひとつの木造平屋建ての住宅がある。この一軒の木造住宅が今、日本を代表する「日本の20世紀遺産20選」（日本イコモス）のひとつにも選ばれ、注目を浴びている。

　京都帝国大学で教鞭をとった建築家の藤井厚二は、明治維新以来日本に導入された欧米の模倣による洋風住宅に疑問を投げかけるとともに、元来、日本人が営んできた、気候風土に適合した暮らしと比較し、さらに学術的に解き明かすことで、真に日本の気候風土と日本人の感性に適合する近代的な住宅とは何かをとことん追求した。そして、藤井の5回目の自邸「聴竹居」は、藤井が生涯追い求めた「日本の住宅」の理想形の全てが集約され、実現されている。

　2017年夏、昭和の住宅として初めて国の重要文化財に指定された「聴竹居」は、21世紀に生きる我々が忘れかけている、日本人にとって住み良いとはどういうことか、住まいにとって何が大切か、さらにそうした視点で住まいを考えることの大切さを、時代を超えて今も静かに語り続けている。

INTRODUCTION

　At the foot of Tennozan, Oyamazaki-cho, Kyoto Prefecture, there is a 90 year-old single story independent wooden house, named Chochikukyo. For a residence the meaning of the name, Chochikukyo, is listening to the sound of bamboos. This free-standing wooden house is among Selection 20, 20th century cultural legacy in Japan, and is attracting the attention.

　The house was designed by Japan's 20th century architect Koji Fujii, who also taught at Kyoto Imperial University. Fujii is famous for the liberal ideas that enabled him to create Chochikukyo in a blend of Japanese and Western modern styles. Koji Fujii questioned the suitability of Western style buildings, which copied the houses in the West since Meiji Restoration (1870), for a climate such as Japan's. Western style buildings had been easy to see in Japan since Meiji Restoration. Fuji compared the Western house in Japan to the Japanese traditional house and scientifically analyzed the wisdom of Japanese architects in their insights to comfortable living with the Japanese climate, and features of nature. He thoroughly pursued models of modern house in Japan, which fit the climate and natural features of Japan as well as the sense and taste of the Japanese people. In the end, Chochikukyo, Fujii's 5th house, realizes all of the ideal elements of Japanese dwelling-house.

　In the summer of 2017, Chochikukyo was the first Residence of its kind, built in Showa era (1926-1989) to be designated as a national important cultural asset of Japan. Chochikukyo, over time, has told us and is telling us of the importance of living together in harmony with the environment; a fact that many of us today, living in the 21st century, tend to ignore. However, it is very important to think as we move into the future and we must design buildings that can cope with changing climates caused by global warming. Chochikukyo and Fujii give us pause for thought.

玄関
Exterior side of Vestibule

凡例

＊本文中の書名・雑誌名の指示には『』を用いた。
＊本文中「」内に示した藤井厚二の言葉は、『日本の住宅』（1928年　岩波書店）または
　『THE JAPANESE DWELLING-HOUSE』（1930年　明治書房）より引用したが、旧仮名遣いなどは改めた。
＊「小上がり」以外の室名は藤井厚二作成の図面上の表記に従った。（実測図集の図中を除く）
＊日本文に併記した英文は基本的に全訳としたが、写真説明などでは要約されている箇所もある。

NOTES: ＊ The original language of the book is Japanese, which is translated into English, provided that some captions are in summary in English form.
＊ Citations from the book entitled THE JAPANESE DWELLING-HOUSE, which Koji Fujii published in English, are in italic font. The other citations in English from books/publications in Japanese are unofficial translation and are indicated with quotation marks:" ".

目次

はじめに	003	INTRODUCTION
写真集	006	PHOTOS
一屋一室	023	One Room under One Roof
閑室と茶室	049	Kanshitsu and Chashitsu
共生と調和	061	Symbiosis and Harmony
藤井厚二が手掛けた調度品	085	Furniture & Furnishings designed by Koji Fujii
八木邸	097	The Yagi Residence
藤井厚二の生涯	107	A Life of Koji Fujii
〈木造モダニズム〉の原点　藤森照信	118	Origin of Wooden Modernism　by Terunobu Fujimori
聴竹居　行為に相即する家　深澤直人	122	Chochikukyo—Residence in Perfect Interfusion with Behavior　by Naoto Fukasawa
聴竹居が伝えるもの　堀部安嗣	126	What Chochikukyo Conveys　by Yasushi Horibe
「聴竹居」の歩み　松隈 章	132	The Course of Chochikukyo　by Akira Matsukuma
参考 ―『日本の住宅』各論概説	149	Reference: Brief of *Nippon no Jutaku*
実測図	157	Drawings based on Field Survey
年譜	258	Chronological Record
あとがき	262	Concluding Remarks

CONTENTS

新緑の「聴竹居」
Spring

南西側から見た縁側

Verandah viewed from south-west side

居室側から見た縁側

Verandah viewed from the living-room

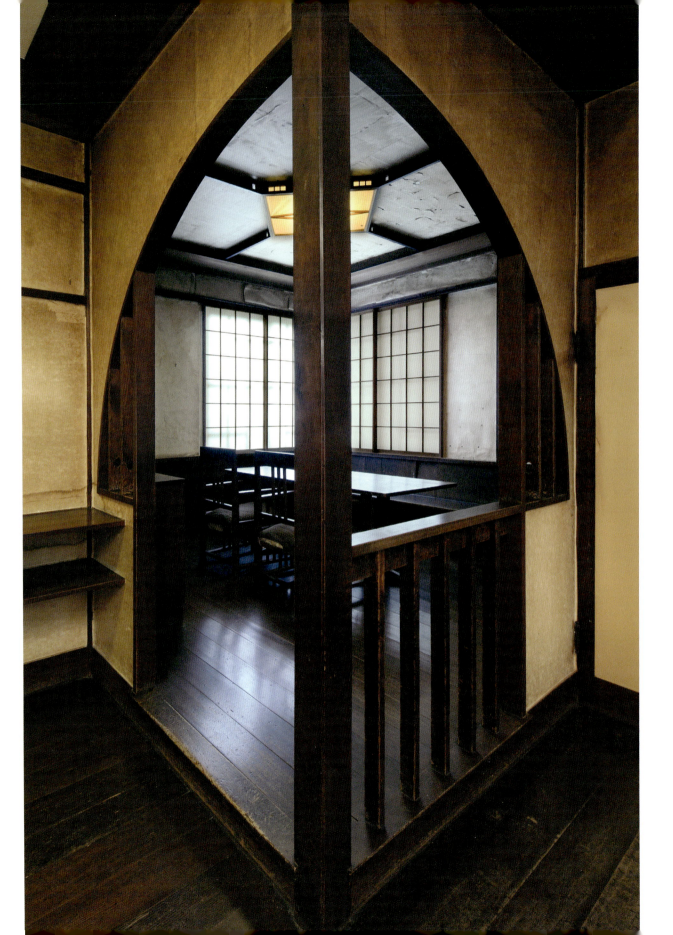

食事室
Dining-room

朝日を浴びる縁側
Verandah under the morning sunlight

「聴竹居」が建つ京都府南部の大山崎。木津川、桂川、宇治川の三川が淀川へと合流する
Chochikukyo stands in Oyamazaki, the southern area of Kyoto prefecture, where The Kizu, Katsura & Uji Rivers become the Yodo River.

縁側の掃き出し窓
Floor level windows through which dirt is swept

縁側
Verandah

紅葉の「聴竹居」
Autumn

縁側の南西側のコーナー
South-west corner, verandah

雪景色の「聴竹居」
Winter

深い軒につららが下がる
Icicles hanging from deep eave

十三夜の月夜の「聴竹居」
Under the moon on the 13th night of its cycle

一屋一室

「一屋一室」とは、襖や障子を開ければ、ひとつの屋根の下、住宅一軒がまるで一室となるような間取りのこと。四季とともに暮らした日本人は、住まいでも四季の変化に寄り添い、夏季には屋内を風が通り抜け、冬季には短い日差しを存分に利用できる工夫をした。「聴竹居」は、こうした昔ながらの日本の住宅の良さに、洋風の暮らし方を取り入れるべく設計された。居室を中心に主な部屋が隣接し、戸を開ければ大きな一室となる「聴竹居」は、四季折々の自然の光や風の恵みがもたらされる住まいである。

One Room under One Roof

"One Room under One Roof" refers to the layout where once fusuma sliding doors/shoji screens are opened several rooms can be transformed into one big room under one roof. Japanese people lived with four seasons around the year, so houses corresponded to the transition of four seasons: a house was designed that breeze would freely flow through the interior during summer-time and during winter-time the shortened hours of sunlight could be available throughout the house for the maximum possible time. Chochikukyo is designed so as to apply Western mode of living in what is good in conventional Japanese house. In Chochikukyo, the living-room is in the center with main rooms attached to it and, when doors/screens are opened, all the rooms are connected to one large room. Chochikukyo is a residence which is blessed with natural light and breeze throughout four seas.

玄関

　道路から直接、門のない敷地内に入り、ゆっくりと右にカーブする石段を上ると玄関が現れる。北側を柱で南側を腕木で支えた庇も、格子柄の明かり窓も非対称の意匠。面取りガラスのついた内開き扉の北側の腰板から出る3本の杉丸太は、濡れた傘を立てかけるためのもの。玄関内部の土間には下駄箱と、極めてシンプルな傘・杖立てが造り付けられた。板間に上がってすぐ北側には手洗い場を一体とした客用トイレがある。南側には靴を履くときに使えるベンチ。その下部はスリッパ入れとしても利用できる。藤井は外部に出入りする部分と客室や居室に出入りする部分を分けるべきと考え、結界として半円形のモチーフの木製スクリーンを設け、スクリーン裏には傘入れを設けている。

Front Entrance

There is no gate at the site boundary from the access road. Walking up the stone steps which make a nice right curb, there is a front entrance door. The canopy is supported by a column to the north and a bracket to the south as well as a skylight in an asymmetrical lattice pattern design. Three *sugi* (Japanese ceder) logs attached to the wainscot, in the north of inward-opening doors with tempered glass panels, are to rest wet umbrellas. On the naturally compacted soil floor area inside the entrance, there is a fixed shoe cupboard and a fixed simple stand to hold umbrellas/canes. When you step up to the wooden floor, to the immediate north is a restroom for the guest, providing toilet with washbasin. To the south a bench is provided so that guests may sit while putting on their shoes. Slippers may be kept beneath the bench. Fujii thinks that the area with access to and from the house exterior should be divided from the area with access to and from drawing-room/living-room. The boundary is marked with a wooden screen in semicircular motif. The back of the screen is furnished with an umbrella pocket.

玄関外側

Exterior side of Vestibule

左：玄関内部
left: Interior of Vestibule

下：玄関の板間。和風住宅では土間と畳の部屋を障子で分かつが、その役割を木製スクリーンで表現している
bottom: Wooden floor in the vestibule: In the Japanese style house, *shoji* paper screens divide soil floor space and tatami-mat rooms while the wooden screen is serving the dividing function in Chochikukyo.

居室

　玄関板間の正面の開き戸を開けると、建物内で最も広く、中心をなす居室に通じる。居室は、食事室や「小上がり」と呼ばれた三畳間と緩やかにつながり、読書室、客室、縁側との境は引き違い戸や障子で、その開閉により続き間のようにもなる。またそれぞれの引き違い戸の上部には開け閉めができる欄間を設け、常に風が通り抜け新鮮な空気で満たされるように工夫されている。3つある円形の照明器具は、それぞれのエリアの天井の広さにより大きさが異なっている。

Living-room

Opening the swing door in front of the wooden floor of the vestibule, one can see that the space is connected to the living-room, which is the largest room and the center of the residence. The Living-room is open to the dining-room and the raised tatami-mat seating area, which is about 5 square-meters. The family reading-room, the drawing-room, and the verandah are divided by sliding doors/ *shoji* screens, so once the doors/screens are opened, those rooms are somewhat connected to the living-room. The sliding doors are furnished with overhead transoms which can be opened/closed to allow constant wind/air flow so that the rooms are filled with fresh air. Size of three circular lighting fixtures differs in proportion to the area of each ceiling.

上：食事室側から見た居室
above: Living-room viewed from the dining-room

右頁：縁側側から見た居室。円形の照明器具は、黒漆塗りのフレームに薄美濃紙を貼り、外側に金揉と銀揉の鳥の子紙を貼っている
right page: Living-room viewed from the verandah: Circular lighting fixture has thin *Mino* washi craft paper applied to the black lacquer-painted frames, pasted gold- and silver-crumpled *torinoko* paper on the outer shade.

右頁：居室から縁側を見る。右手は読書室、左手は客室に続く
right page: View the verandah from the living-room: family reading-room in right and drawing-room in left.

居室北側。藤井がデザインした時計（スコットランドの建築家マッキントッシュのデザインした時計を真似ている）と、床の間の役目を果たす造り付けの飾り棚。上部の両開きの小さな引き戸の中に神棚が収まっている。左の開き戸は調理室に続く
North side of the living-room: Clock which Fujii designed (following the clock designed by Mackintosh, Scottish architect); built-in display shelf which functions as an alcove. Kamidana, a Shinto home altar, is housed in the overhead cabinet behind the small double sliding doors. The sliding door on the left leads to the kitchen.

食事室

　居室の一部としても使えるように、食事室は居室の北側45度の位置に設けられ、4分の1円のデザインが施された間仕切りで、食事室と居室は穏やかに連続している。食事室の窓下にある造り付けベンチの隅に座り、居室側を眺めると、間仕切りの弧が半円形を描く。天井は、周囲を杉板張りにして折りあげた内側を金砂子鳥の子紙張りにして、藤井がデザインした照明の側部から漏れる光が柔らかく反射するようにできている。造り付け戸棚は、配膳用と調味料入れの2箇所で、調理室からも使える構造になっている。床は居室より15cm高く、窓も他室の窓より床面から5cm高くなっているのは、窓の外を通行する人の視線をかわす工夫。食事室は本屋の北東の隅に位置するので、朝日が入り、夏は縁側に次いで涼しい。

Dining-room

Dining-room is on the north-side of the living-room at 45 degrees. Dining-room and the living room are divided by a partition in quarter circular form. Both rooms are naturally connected as one space. When seated on the corner of the bench which is fixed beneath the window of the dining-room looking towards the living-room, one can view the arch profile of the partition depicting a circle. As for the ceiling, the peripheral is in *sugi* board, and the coffered ceiling area is pasted with golden sand *torinoko* paper, which gently reflects light coming through the sides of a lighting fixture which Fujii designed. Built-in cupboard can be accessed both from the dining-room and the kitchen, which are used for serving dishes and holding condiments. The floor is 15 cm higher than the living-room, and the height from the floor to the window is 5 cm higher than the windows of the other rooms: this is designed so as to avoid being seen from the window by outside passers-by. Dining-room is on the north-eastern corner of the house, which allows the morning sunlight to come in and during summer time it is cool next to the verandah.

左頁：調理室開き戸前から見た食事室。ベンチ横の造り付け台上部には花籠を吊し、季節の花を楽しんだ
left page: Dining-room viewed from in front of the swing door of kitchen: hanging flower basket over the counter next to the bench enabled to enjoy flowers of the season.

下：藤井による透視図「食事室から見た居室」
bottom: Fujii's perspective drawing: Living-room viewed from the dining-room

右：食事室。奥は居室と小上がり（畳の部分）
right: Dining-room, Living-room and Raised tatami-mat seating area in the back

食事室は面積約9㎡で、窓下に造り付けの
ベンチが設けられている
Dining-room is about 9 square-meters. The bench seat is fixed under the window.

左頁：右側にあるのが食事室戸棚。左中段が配膳用、右上の開き扉が調味料入れで、調理室側とつながる
left page: Cupboard in the dining-room, which is connected to the kitchen: left middle shelf is used to serve dishes while a sideboard with a swing door in top right holds condiments.

読書室

居室と引き戸でつながる読書室。四畳（7.5㎡）余りの空間に藤井と子ども用の造り付け机、本棚がコンパクトかつ機能的に設えられている。二人の子ども用机は縁側に面して障子で仕切られ、縁側越しに庭を望む。西側の窓の横に設けられた藤井の机からふり返ると、開け放たれた読書室と客室の引き戸越しに客室の床の間を見ることができる。

Family Reading-room

Reading room is connected to the living-room once the sliding door is opened. In the space about 7.5 square meters, desks and bookshelves for Fujii and his children are built-in satisfying the functional needs in the compact configuration. Desks for two children face the verandah, divided by *shoji* paper screens. Looking back from Fujii's desk next to the window on the west, one can view the alcove in drawing-room when the sliding doors of reading room and those of drawing-room are opened.

読書室の子ども用机

Family Reading-room: Children's desks

左：読書室全体。天井は竹の皮の網代張り
left: Family Reading-room, ceiling is in wickerwork with bamboo sheath.

右：藤井の机上部に設えられた違い棚
right: Staggered shelves installed over Fujii's desk

縁側

「南に面する部屋の外部には、長く細長い縁側が付いている。夏季には直射日光の当たらない部屋が主に使われ、冬の晴れた日には、縁側で針仕事やその他の家事が行われる。縁側は日光に対して開かれているため、囲炉裏と火鉢の必要がない。この家庭生活の一般的な方法は、日本特有の気候によく適合している」。そう記した藤井は、昔ながらの日本の住宅にある縁側の冬の「サンルーム」としての機能に加え、夏季には地窓から涼しい外気を取り込み涼しい風が流れる工夫を加えた。さらに3面をガラスで囲むことで三川合流の大パノラマを満喫できる空間とした。

Verandah

Fujii states as follows: *outside the rooms facing south a long, narrow verandah is attached. In summer, those rooms free from direct sunlight are mainly used, while on fine winter days, needlework and other kinds of household chores are carried out on the verandah, which is open to the sun, thereby dispensing with the need of "irori" (hearth) and "hibachi" (braziers). This general way of domestic life is in conformity with the peculiar climate of the country.* In addition to the conventional function of a verandah, in a Japanese house, as a sunroom in the winter, Fujii has provided floor-level windows for the intake of cool fresh air during summer months so that cool breeze may flow throughout. Three sides of verandah are covered in the glasses to allow the panoramic view over the conflux of three rivers.

左：縁側西側の嵌め殺し窓とコーナー棚
left: Verandah, Fixed windows and the corner shelving in the west

右頁：南側には二つの地窓が設けられている
right page: In the south, two floor-level windows are provided.

床上60cmの高さに3つのガラス窓と、両隅の嵌め殺し窓が連続し、風雨を防ぎつつ眺望や日差しを楽しめるようにしている。窓下2つの地窓は、庭からの涼しい外気を取り込むためで、その空気は天井に設けられた排気口から屋根裏に抜ける。夏季は居室や読書室への直射日光を防ぎ、冬季は居室の奥まで日光が届き、晴天の昼間は暖房が必要ないほどであった。

For the verandah, 3 glazed windows are followed by the fixed transparent windows at both ends. They are 60 cm high above the floor, enabling both protection of the house from wind/rain as well as panoramic views and plenty of sunlight. The 2 floor-level windows beneath the large windows are for the intake of chilled fresh air from the garden. The chilled fresh air is led to the loft by the exhausts on the ceiling. During summer, direct sunlight to the living-room and the family reading-room is screened. During winter, sunlight reaches the end of the living-room, as a result heating is not required during daytime on the fine days.

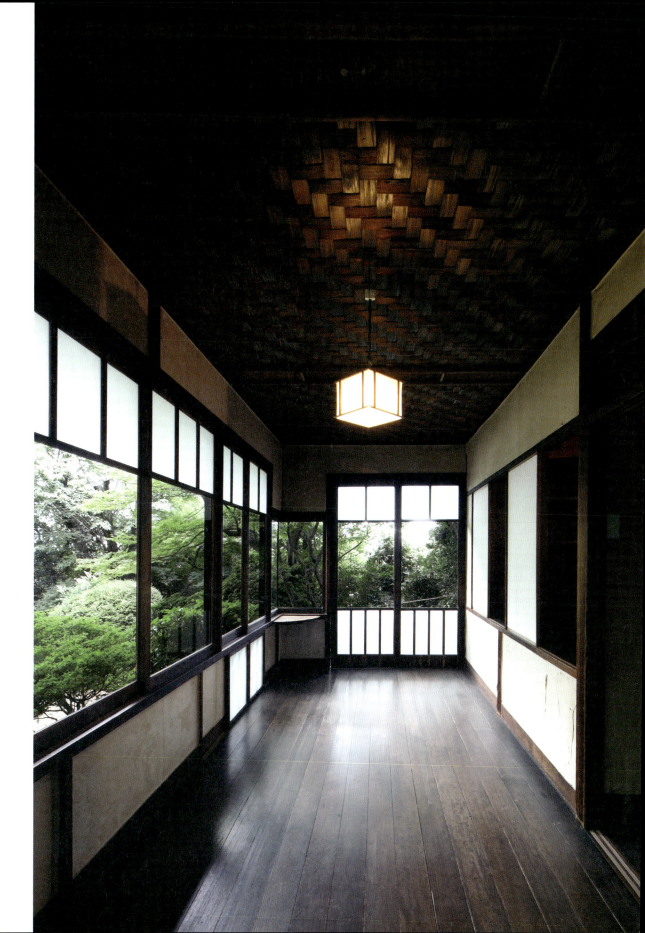

右：西側は掃き出し窓。右側の紙障子で仕切られた部屋は読書室
right: On the west wall is the floor-level window for sweeping out dirt. On the right divided by *shoji* paper screen is the family reading-room.

左頁：大きな開口部を通じて日差しが居室奥にまで届く
left page: Sunlight reaches the end of the living-room through large opening.

左頁：天井は杉へぎ板網代張りで、開閉可能な排気口が2箇所ある
left page: Ceiling is in wickerwork with sugi shingle boards and equipped with two opening/closing air exhaust pits for improving air quality.

幅2m20cm、長さ6mの縁側床面
Floor of the verandah: 6 meter-long and 2.2 meter-wide

客室と床の間

　玄関の板間からも引き戸で出入りできる客室は、両引き戸で居室とつながる。10.5㎡の広さだが、最もデザインが凝らされた空間。板間に椅子とテーブル、造り付けベンチが置かれ、窓には紙障子、居室との境の両引き戸の上には弧を描く欄間がある。天井は中央が杉の一枚板で両脇を網代としている。椅子式の洋風としながらも、ディテールには和の自然素材が駆使されている。

Drawing-room & Alcove

Access to the drawing-room can be also gained by stepping up onto the wooden floor of the vestibule and going through the sliding door. It is connected to the living-room by double-sliding doors. Drawing-room is 10.5 square meter-area, but the most detailed attentions are paid among all the rooms. On the wooden floor are a table and chairs, and the fixed bench. Window is installed with *shoji* paper screens. Above the double-sliding door dividing the room from the living-room is a transom with arched opening. The center of the ceiling is in single *sugi* board, with wickerwork on both sides. The room is in the Western style with table and chairs, but Japanese natural materials are widely used in the details.

左：造り付けベンチと床の間の間に設けられたスクリーンは、杉の柾目板と細竹のたて子、竹の床柱で構成され、繊細な素材使いで小宇宙を形成する
left: Screen between the fixed bench and the alcove consists of sugi quarter-sawn board, thin bamboo poles, and bamboo alcove column. Delicate and fine material creates small cosmos.

右頁：居室との境は布張りの両引き戸。欄間の桐の板の小口には赤漆が塗られている
right page: Fabric-upholstered double-sliding doors divide the drawing-room and the living-room. Side edge of kiri (Japanese paulownia) board at the transom is painted in red lacquer.

椅子とテーブル、美濃紙の照明も藤井による。床の間は、椅子座に合わせて床から34cmの高さ。窓の紙障子は、右側の戸棚上の壁面に引き込むことができる

Fujii designed a table & chairs, and the lighting fixture in *Mino* craft paper. Alcove is 34 cm-high from the floor to match the height of the chair seat. *Shoji* paper screens installed along the window can be stored by sliding them in the wall over the right sideboard.

床の間は椅子に対応した目線の高さを採用しており、幅が約3mあるのは引き違い戸を開けて居室と一体化して使う場合が多く、また読書室から眺めることも考慮に入れているからである。ベンチ横にも小さな床が設けられ、書画の大きさによって使い分けられるようにしている。

The height of the alcove is designed to match the view line of the guests sitting on chairs. Alcove is about 3 meter-wide, as the sliding door is opened to use the drawing-room with the living-room as an integrated space. It is also considered that the alcove may be viewed from the family reading-room. Small aclove area is provided next to the fixed bench, which allows use of the smaller space and the alcove space depending on the size of paintings.

客室から居室越しに読書室が見える
The family-reading room is visible from the drawing-room via the living-room.

小上がり

　椅子に座った人と畳に座った人が同一空間で心地よく過ごすために、藤井が居室に設けた「小上がり」と呼ばれた三畳の畳間。居室のソファに藤井夫妻が座り、畳間には母親が正座し、子ども達はそこに腰掛けていた。みなの目線が合うよう、畳の面の高さが工夫されている。小上がりの奥には和室が続き、寝室に当てられていた。

Raised Tatami-mat Seating Area

Fujii provided a raised tatami-mat seating area in the living-room so that the people on the chairs and those on the mat floor in the same room would spend time pleasantly. Mr. & Mrs. Fujii sat on the sofa in the living-room while Fujii's mother kneeled formally on the raised seating area, and daughters sat on the raised area just as sitting on chairs. Height of tatami-mat area is so designed that all the people in the living-room can have direct eye contact. At the back of the raised seating area is the tatami-mat room, which was used as a bedroom.

北側の壁面には飾り棚と仏壇、天袋が造り付けられた。西を向いて拝むように設えられた仏壇の扉は片開きで斜めになっており、居室からも仏様が見える

The north wall has a built-in display shelf, family Buddhist altar, and overhead storage. Family Buddhist altar is so placed to pray in the west direction. The altar door is diagonally-installed with a single leaf swing door, which allows viewing of the Buddha figure in the altar from the living-room.

右頁：居室より32.7cm高い小上がり。段差を生かしてクールチューブ（導気口）が隠されている。小上がり右隣の開き戸は、寝室、浴室などに続く
right page: Raised mat seating area, 32.7 cm higher than the living-room. The air intake cool tube is hidden in the gap of the floor level. Swing door on the right is followed by the passage leading to bedrooms and bath-room

小上がりから時計と神棚のある壁を見る

View from the raised tatami-mat seating area to the wall with a clock and *kamidana* (a Shinto home alter)

閑室と茶室

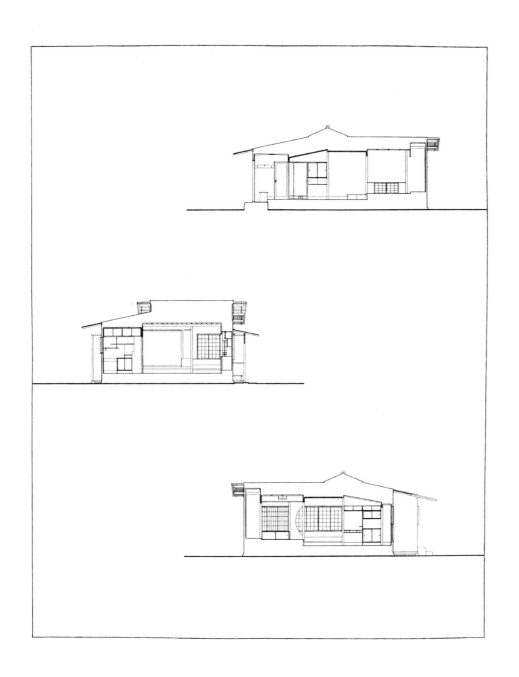

藤井厚二は、茶道の古い伝統に拘泥したり囚われたりせずに「和敬清寂」を楽しむ部屋を望んだ。「聴竹居」には、2つの離れが設けられている。「閑室」は本屋の北側に建てられた、藤井が一人で考え事に没頭できる書斎的な空間。また、本屋の南側にある「茶室」は、藤井や妻が親しい人を招いて茶会やお花の会を催す空間であった。

Kanshitsu and Chashitsu

Koji Fujii wanted to make a room to enjoy harmony, respect, purity, and tranquility without being bound by and restricted by the old tradition of the Way of Tea. Chochikukyo has two pavilions which are separated from the main building. Kanshitsu, Room of Quiet, to the north of the house proper is something like a study space where Fujii could devote himself to thinking or study. Chashitsu, a tea room, to the south of the house proper, was the space for Fujii and/or his wife to host a tea ceremony or a gathering featuring flowers.

閑室

「閑寂を楽しむと云う意味で閑室」と藤井が名づけた44㎡の建物は「聴竹居」と同じ1928(昭和3)年に完成した。「茶室より広い用途に向けていることは事実だが、どちらも概念は同じである」と藤井は記す。道路から石段を登り、飛び石を上ると玄関。その引き戸は、柱を挟んで東と南の2面に設けられている。玄関横には洗面と便所を備え、板敷きの洋間風の造りの「下段の間」と小上がり一間半の床の間を持つ三畳の「上段の間」、流しなど水回りも備えた「次の間」から構成されている。藤井はこの閑室を「日本独特の建築的趣味を体現しており、私は瞑想的な気分のときや、親しい来客との会話や食事の際にここへ通う」と記した。

Kanshitsu (Room of Quite)

The building of 44 square meter-area, which Fujii named as "Kanshitsu to enjoy tranquility" was built in 1928, at the same time as Chochikukyo. Fujii states that "it is true that use of Kanshitsu is wider than the tea room, but that the concept is the same". From the access road, ascending the stone steps and following the stepping stones leads to the front entrance. The sliding doors are on double surface, in the east and the south of the entrance post. The restroom containing wash basin and toilet is located next to the vestibule. Kanshitsu has 2 sections, namely upper and lower. The lower section has a wooden floor in the Western style. The upper section is about 5 square-meter with a further 2.5 square-meter alcove plus an anteroom with pantry including the sink. Fujii refers to Kanshitsu as follows: "Kanshitsu represents the architectural taste unique to Japan. I come to Kanshitsu when I feel like meditating or I talk to and dine with close friends and visitors".

左:閑室・下段の間
left: Lower floor, Kanshitsu (Room of Quiet)

右頁:下段の間から上段の間を見る(照明器具は藤井デザインのものではない)
right page: View the upper section from the lower section. (the lighting fixture is not designed by Fujii)

東側から見た閑室。待合の席の右は下段の間の窓。
右奥の窓が上段の間
Kanshitsu viewed from the east side, a window in the bottom right of the waiting
seating is the window of the lower section.
The window deep in right is for the upper section.

左頁：下段の間。柱に丸太を用い、飾り棚を設けるなど、数寄
屋風の造りになっており、腰掛式の茶室としても使われた
left page: Lower section is in *Sukiya*-style with columns in log with
display shelf. It was also used as a tea room with table/chairs.

下段の間の窓に沿って造り付けられたベンチシートは革製。角には幅25cm、奥行き56cmの違い棚も造られた
Bench seating built-in along window of the lower section is in leather. At the corner is 25 cm-wide and 56 cm-deep staggered shelves.

下段の間の天井。左は皮付き丸太を押さえに使った竹皮の網代張り。右は萩を組み、押さえに竹を組んでいる
Ceiling of the lower section: left is in a wickerwork of bamboo sheath, held with a barked log, and right is in braid of *hagi* (Japanese bush clover), held with bamboo braid.

下段の間の造り付けの机は、柱に丸太、竹を用いるなど、床の間風の設え
Built-in desk, the lower section, is alcove-like arrangement with log/bamboo for columns.

閑室の玄関へ続く飛び石。右の枝折戸の向こうが待合の席
Stepping-stones are arranged up to the entrance to Kanshitsu.
Over the swing door in battle twigs is the waiting seating.

茶室

　従来、茶室は茶人が数寄屋大工に建てさせるのが一般的だった。建築家として茶室を設計したのは、藤井が初めてだと言われている。1930（昭和5）年頃に完成したと見られるこの茶室は、閑室よりひとまわり小さく、本屋からの視界をさえぎらないよう、南東に4mほど低い位置に設けられた数寄屋風の真壁造りである。南東角の足元には滝口があり、滝から流れ落ちる水はその下の池に注ぎ、やがて小川に続いていた。

　ブルーノ・タウトはこの茶室を訪れ、1933年5月9日の日記に「この茶室は茶室建築の革新である」と記した。

Tea Room

Conventionally, it was usually the case that a master of tea ceremony asked a carpenter of *Sukiya* style of architecture to build a tea room. This tea room, which is assumed to have been built in 1930, is a size smaller than a pavilion (Room of Quiet). It is a tea room surrounded by walls with exposed timber pillars in *Sukiya* style, which is built to the southeast of the house proper, lower by about 4 m in order not to block the view from the house proper. Beneath the southeast corner of the tea room is the top of the waterfall. Water flowing down the waterfall reaches the pond below, which then flows into a stream.
Bruno Taut visited the tea room. He wrote in his diary on May 9, 1933: "This tea room is an innovation in architecture of tea rooms".

右：東側から見た茶室。外観は数寄屋風の真壁造り
right: Tea room viewed from east side; exterior is in walls with exposed timber pillars in *Sukiya*-style

右頁：南側から見ると、各室ごとに屋根の形状を切り替えている様子がわかる
right page: When viewed from south side, it is clear that the roof profile is different for each room.

茶室・板の間。造り付けの机の上部には市松模様にデザインされた窓があり、障子の開け閉めにより多彩な表情が楽しめた
Wooden floor of Tea Room: Above the built-in desk is the checkered pattern window, which enables to enjoy the wide-ranging expression by opening/closing *shoji*-screens.

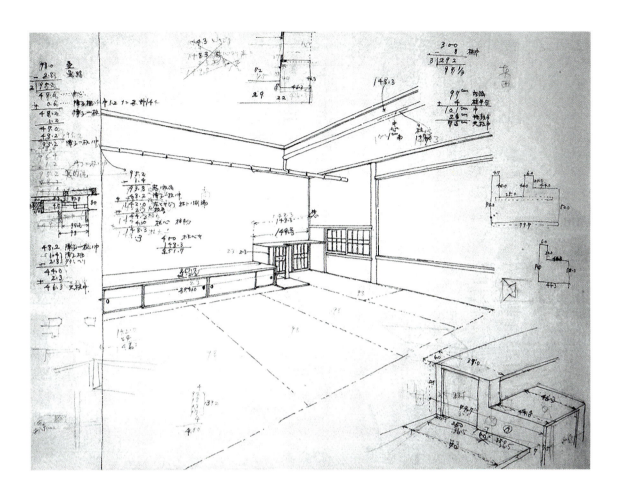

藤井が大工に設計意図を伝えた透視図（茶室内の閑室）。床の間、天井、窓の構成を空間としてイメージしながら設計を進めた

Perspective drawing (of Kanshitsu, main room in the Tea Room) which Fujii prepared to share his design intent with the carpenter. Fujii preceded the design by visualizing the space configuration of alcove, ceiling, and windows.

茶室・座敷の復元図
Main Room of Tea Room (reconstruction)

共生と調和

住まう土地の気候風土に適応させることが、住宅の最大の必要条件であるとした藤井は、和風住宅と洋風住宅の長短を比較し、その長所を取り入れた。「聴竹居」では、和と洋の暮らしがバランスよく共存し、日本の夏を心地よく過ごすことができる。

Symbiosis and Harmony

Fujii was of the opinion that the most necessary condition for houses was that they adapt to the nature and climate of the site. He compared advantages/disadvantages of Japanese and Western style houses and applied advantages to Chochikukyo. In Chochikukyo, Japanese and Western ways of living are well balanced in harmony and residents/visitors can comfortably spend summer days in Japan.

条件

藤井は、「聴竹居」を建てるまでに4軒の自邸を実験住宅として建てた。その経験から理想的な住宅について五つの条件を考えた。

1. 8人の人間が快適に住むのに充分な大きさとする（当時、藤井家は母・元と妻と二人の子ども、女中一人の6人家族だった）。
2. 来客の応接用に当てる空間は可能な限り減らし、家族の居住空間の快適さを第一に目指す。
3. 腰掛式（椅子式）生活を主として、坐式（畳式）生活を混用する。
4. 木造平屋の建物とし、その大きさは可能な限り小さくするため、調理と暖房のための電気器具を取り付ける。
5. 夏季の生活の快適性を第一に考慮する。

Conditions

Fujii built four personal houses as experimental houses before building Chochikukyo. Based on prior experience, Fujii came up with 5 conditions for an ideal house:

1. *To make it large enough for eight persons to live in comfortably (although the present inmates number six, namely, the master, his wife, three children and a maid servant).*
2. *To reduce the space devoted to rooms for the reception of visitors as far as possible so that the comfort of the family may be chiefly looked to, though it is usual in a Japanese dwelling-house to reserve a spacious room for the reception of guests.*
3. *To make the **tatami** mode of life subservient to the carpet mode of life.*
4. *To make it a one-storied wooden building and to reduce the size of the building as far as possible by installing electric apparatus for cooking and heating purposes.*
5. *To give primary consideration to comfort in summer life.*

南側の庭の樹木も今では本屋を包み込むように生長している
Trees planted in the garden, south of the house, are grown up to envelop the main house.

気流

　日本では昔から「住まいは夏を旨とする」と言われてきた。藤井は日本各地の気候を調べ、さらに外国の気候と比較して「室内環境を快適に保つには、著しく不快となる夏場の対策が大切だ」とあらためて説いた。その実践である「聴竹居」では、家の中の空気が流れる状態になるよう、「一屋一室」にすることにより通風を確保すること、室内の空気を速やかに排出する方法、床下と天井裏をつなぐ通風（通気筒）、自然の冷気を取り入れる「クールチューブ（導気口）」といった工夫を実践した。また外壁の断熱性能にも着目し、「聴竹居」では土蔵壁を採用した。和紙を壁面や天井に採用したのも、調湿に優れているからであった。

Air Current

In Japan, from ancient times, it was said that houses should prioritize the living during the summer time. Fujii surveyed the climate throughout Japan, and compared with the climate abroad. He re-stated that "in order to maintain the room interior environmentally comfortable, measures taken to counter extreme discomfort during summer time are important". Fujii applies this approach to Chochikukyo to allow constant airflow throughout the house: ventilation is maintained by arrangement of "one room under one roof" method. Interior stale air is extracted by air tube connecting under-the-floor and the loft, and an intake of cool air is possible using the cool tube. Fujii also paid attention to insulating performance of exterior walls in soil. He applied *washi* craft paper to wall and/or ceiling as it is excellent in controlling humidity.

上：縁側の天井排気口
above: Ceiling exhaust at verandah

右：調理室の天井排気口
right: Ceiling exhaust at kitchen

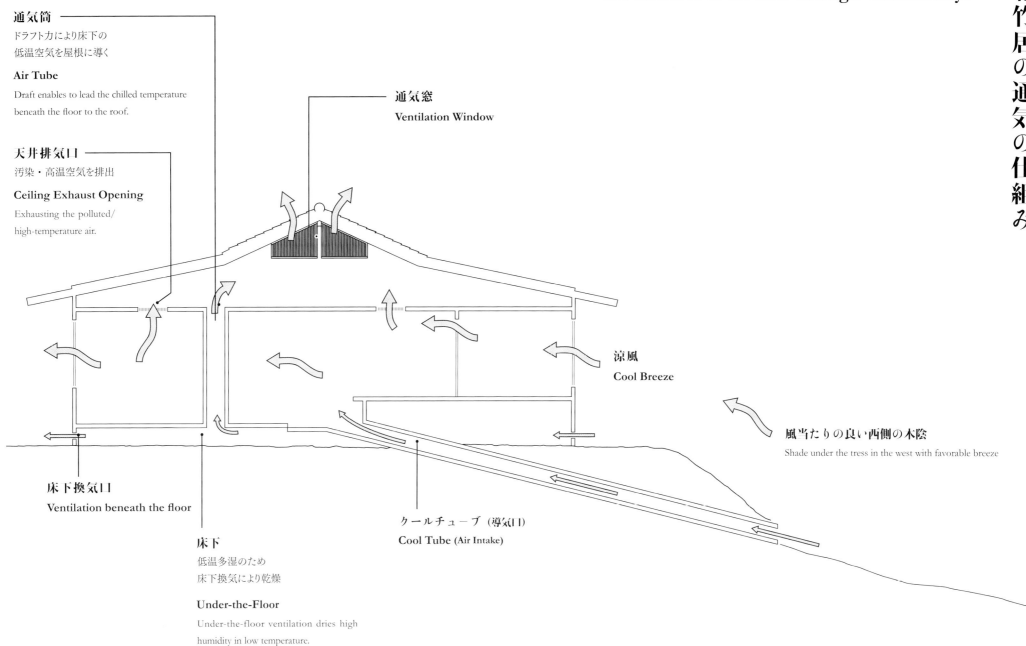

Mechanism of air flow through Chochikukyo

聴竹居の通気の仕組み

屋根妻面に設けられた通気窓は、夏季には開放する
An air ventilation opening provided at the gabled roof is opened during summer.

左：調理室の通気筒（写真の中央壁背後）
left: Air Tube (in the back of center wall, kitchen in the picture)

下：床下換気口
bottom: Ventilation opening under the floor

小上がりに設けられたクールチューブ（導気口）
Cool Tube installed beneath the raised floor area (outlet)

軒と庇

　藤井は、「日本の気候という観点からすると、庇と大きく突出した軒を備えることは必須である。これらは夏季に直射日光を防ぐ役に立つだけでなく、雨季（6月中旬から7月初旬）にも有効である」と記した。「聴竹居」でも深い軒と庇が採用され、強い夏の日差しをしのぎ、少々の雨ならば窓を開け放つことができる。

Eave and Canopy

Fujii states that *in view of the climate of Japan, it is very necessary to provide pentice and far-projecting eaves. They are not only useful in averting the direct sunlight in summer but are of much avail in the rainy season (which occurs between the middle of June and early part of July).* Chochikukyo is also furnished with deep eaves and canopy eaves to relieve the strong sunlight during summer time and also allow for windows to be open in case of light rain.

軒を深くするために、屋根の素材は、銅板が用いられた
To make eaves deep, copper plates are used for the roof.

屋根

　藤井は屋根に適した素材も研究した。「屋根は軒の出を深くするためにも、建物の外観を環境に調和させるためにも緩やかな勾配とする必要があるため、葺き上げ材料には主に銅板を」用いた。一方、中央の棟部分は、屋根裏の換気を良くするために勾配を急にし、大きな通風窓を設けて瓦葺きとした。

Roof

Fujii also studied the suitable roofing material. "As it is necessary for the roof to have an easy pitch, not only for the purpose of providing far projecting eaves but of harmonizing the outward appearance of the building with the surroundings", he largely used copper plate. On the other hand, the ridge at the center of the house is with a sharper inclination for sufficient ventilation of the loft, and is tiled provided with a large air ventilation opening.

銅板部分の屋根の勾配は 21/100 と緩やか。軒など以外は、断熱を考え、二重にしている
The pitch of copper plated roof is 21/100, easy pitch. Besides eaves, the sheathing board is laid double for insulation.

右頁：中央の棟部分の勾配を 45/100 にすることにより、切妻部分に大きな通気窓を設けた
right page: By taking pitch of 45/100 in the ridge at the center of the house, a large air ventilation opening is provided at the gabled area.

天王山の麓に位置する聴竹居の全景。右手奥に赤い屋根の大山崎山荘と宝積寺の三重塔が見える
Bird's eye view of Chochikukyo located at the foot of Tenozan: right end are Oyamazaki Villa (in red roof) and three-story pagoda of Hoshakuji.

平屋

木造の軸組工法が大半であった昭和初頭まで、住宅は平屋または2階建ての家が一般的で、2階建てでも階下と同等の広さの2階を上げることはまれだった。藤井は、「平屋建は生活の能率上に著しく有利なるのみならず、住宅の外観を自然と融和せしめて気持ちよきものと為すに適当」と記し、さらに1923 (大正12) 年に起きた関東大震災から教訓を得て、「地震に対する予防上より見るも平屋を推奨」するとした。ただし、従来の日本住宅が「すべてが直線のみなので、単調を破るために平面にして区割した種々の凹凸を設けることが有効」と記し、居室に対して食事室や読書室を出っ張らせるなどの工夫をしている。

Single-storied House

Up until early Showa, most Japanese houses were of wooden frame construction. Moreover, houses were either one or two story constructions. Furthermore, even in two story houses, it was very rare that the lower and upper floor was equal in area. Fujii stated that a one-story house was conducive to much greater efficiency of life "and is suitable to harmonize exterior appearance of a house with nature". Fujii learned lessons from 1923 Great Kanto Earthquake and stated that a single story house is advisable from the point of view of precaution against earthquakes, but he stated that "a conventional Japanese house consisted of only straight lines, and that it is effective to provide a variety of irregularities changing the planes to break the monotony". Fujii therefore projects the dining room and the family reading-room from the living-room.

調和

「我々(日本人)は、住宅の中で、色彩を多く用いることを好まない。それは、色彩が神経を興奮させる傾向があるためで、むしろ出来る限り刺激となる効果を排除し、静かで簡素なものとすることを好む」と藤井は言う。土や紙、木など、自然の素材そのものの美しさを活かし周囲の自然に溶け込ませること。また外側にある縁側や大きくせり出した軒により、建物の内部と外部の境界線が曖昧となるため、季節や時間により多彩に変化する光や影、風を感じられるようにすること。これらの、日本人の感性に寄り添った繊細なデザインが「聴竹居」に散りばめられている。

Harmony

Fujii stated that *we do not like much coloring in our dwelling-houses, as it tends to excite our nerves, and prefer to make them as quiet and plain as possible so as to preclude any stimulant effects*. Chochikukyo is filled with delicate and sophisticated design details following the sense of the Japanese people; beauty of natural material such as earth, paper, or wood is used so that the house blends in with the surrounding nature; and the verandah in the peripheral of the house and largely-projected eaves blur the boundary between the exterior and the interior, which, in turn, enables inhabitants to feel light/shade and breeze which vary by the season or by the time of the day.

食事室のベンチ横には花台兼用の戸棚が設けられた
In the dining-room, next to the bench is a sideboard, which may also used as a floor display counter.

窓

　藤井は、窓を設けるのは「光を内部に入れ」「換気を促進すること」、そして「変化に富んだ自然の美しい風景を内部から見ること」だとし、機能面だけでなく、窓を「自然と室内を繋ぐ大切な装置」と位置づけた。窓の形は、西洋建築の上下窓や開き窓よりも、古来、日本建築が採用してきた引き違い窓が、景色を眺めるにも、換気量の調節にも適しているとした。縁側では大きく水平に連続した窓割りとし、ほかの窓は単調さを嫌って、桟の割付けに工夫が凝らされ、正方形に近い形や細長い長方形を組み合わせた意匠などを凝らした。

Windows

Fujii states that windows are to let in light and to facilitate ventilation. Besides functional requirements, he further states that "windows enable inhabitants to look out the diversified and beautiful surrounding scenery". With regard to window profile, he prefers horizontal sliding windows to sash windows or casement windows which are often found in Western architecture. Horizontal sliding windows have been conventionally used and, in Fujii's view, are the best for inhabitants to view the scenery as well as to control ventilation. The verandah windows have large horizontal frames while other windows are in unique frames to break monotonous rhythm and come in well-thought out designs, such as combining almost square or long rectangular profiles.

縁側の窓。光と内から見える風景を切り取るため、床から60〜170cmの部分は透明ガラスに、上下はすりガラスとしている
Windows in the verandah: Clear glass up to 60cm - 170cm from the floor and the frosted glass above as a result of calculating light and view from the inside of house.

縁側の東面（左）と西面。西面は外部から出入りできるように掃き出し窓になっている

East (left) and west side of the verandah: The west side has the floor level windows which allow the access from outside and sweeping dirt.

和紙と障子

日本建築における紙障子を透した日光が身体にも心地よく、その拡散光が美的にも魅力的な空間を浮かび上がらせるとした藤井は、障子に使う和紙の素材特性を実験により分析、光拡散の割合を数値化するなど、機能面を確かめた。その結果、藤井は、光を透過し、室内に拡散させるためには、和紙が最も適しているという結論を得た。

Japanese *Washi* Paper and *Fusuma* Sliding Doors

Fujii assumes that sunlight passed through paper *shoji* screens is comfortable for the human being's body and the diffused light is aesthetically beautiful in the interior space. In experiments he checked the properties of *washi* paper as a material, and the quantified rate of light-diffusion. He concluded that *washi* paper, Japanese translucent paper, is best suited for letting light pass through and diffusing it inside the room.

客室の窓。ガラス戸の格子や庭の木々の陰が
紙障子に映り込み、刻々とその様相を変える
Windows of drawing-room: Ever changing shadow
of glass lattice and trees in the garden reflect on the
paper shoji screens.

縁側と居室の開口部を開放すれば、冬季も日差しが居室に届く
Sunlight reaches the living-room, even during winter, when the openings on the verandah side and those on the room side are opened.

居室から縁側側を見る。紙障子を通した拡散光で室内が優しく照らされる
View through the verandah side from the living-room: Diffused natural light passed through paper shoji screens illuminates the room interior dimly.

調理室

　高い天井と大きな窓を持つ清潔で明るい調理室は、棚建具と天井は白ペンキ、壁面は白漆喰、水回りは白タイルで仕上げられている。大正から昭和初期にかけての生活改善運動の高まりを反映して機能性も追求し、当時の最新式電気冷蔵庫（スイス製）や電気コンロ（アメリカ製）などを取り入れ、当時は珍しいオール電化を実現している。煮物台は部屋の中央に置かれていたが、その上部には排気口を設け、天井が織り上げられている。流しの左脇にはダストシュートが造り付けられ、水とともに排出された生ゴミは、網で水と分けられ、水は排水管へ、生ゴミは堆肥として再利用した。また勝手口の外にある煉瓦の窯で湯を沸かし、風呂や洗濯用の流しのほかこの調理室でも使えるようになっていた。

Kitchen

The clean and light kitchen has a high ceiling and a big window. Cabinets including shelving and ceiling are all painted white, walls are in white plaster, and the wet area is in white tiles. Reflecting the movement to improve the mode of living during Taisho to early Showa period, functional equipments were used: an imported up-to-date electric refrigerator (made in Switzerland) and an electric heater (made in America); electric utilities were quite rare at that time. Cooker was put in the center of the kitchen. Vent is provided above the area of the cooker. Ceiling is coffered to accommodate vent opening. To the left of sink is a waste disposal shoot where perishable waste and water can be collected and filtered. Waste water is sent to exhaust pipes and the perishable waste is reused as compost. A brick-made kiln is installed outside of service entrance for hot water of the bath and water for laundry & for the kitchen.

流しは当時、人造石研ぎ出しだった。その右が調理台で上方の小さな開き扉が食事室と共有の調味料棚

When the sink was first built it was in polished artificial stone. To the right of the sink is a cooking worktop. The small swing door over the worktop is a sideboard for condiment which can be opened from either the kitchen or the dining-room.

右がスイス製の電気冷蔵庫。上部にコンプレッサーをのせている。時計の下が、冷蔵庫付属の電流計と電圧計。この壁面手前に、電気コンロが置かれていた。壁の奥には床下と天井裏を結ぶ通気筒がある。左は食器や調理器具などの棚
Right is the electric refrigerator made in Switzerland attached with compressor on the head. Below the clock is an ammeter and voltmeter attached to the refrigerator. Electric heater was placed in front of this wall. At the back of the wall is an air tube connecting under-the-floor and loft. The cabinet in left houses chinaware and cooking utensils.

食事室の棚とつながる配膳口。その引き戸の引手を左側に置いて使いやすくしたり、引き出しの引手金物は配膳カウンターより奥にするなど、細部まで使い勝手に配慮している
Service opening connected to the shelving in the dining-room
Details are also well designed with consideration for easy to use: pull of the sliding door is on the left side for easy opening/closing and metal handles of the drawers are set back from the side surface of the service counter.

ディテール

住宅は、単に堅牢性や安全性、衛生面などの機能だけでは不十分であると考えた藤井は、「精神上にも慰安を与え、各人の性情に適応したる愉快なものである」べきとした。気持ちよく住む家のために、藤井は細部にもこだわった。

Detail

Fujii claims that it is not enough for dwelling-house to meet functional requirements such as solid structure, safety, and hygienic arrangement. He states that "dwelling-house should provide mental comfort/relaxation and be of pleasure suitable for sense/feel of inmate". Fujii paid detailed attention to realize an intimate and comfortable house.

幾何学的なデザインが施された玄関。はめ込まれたカットグラスが美しい
Entrance in geometric design: Cut glass panel inserted is attractive.

上左：食事室の弧を描く間仕切り
above left: Partition in arch profile, dining-room

上右：窓のビスの溝の向きが揃えられている
above right: Groove of window screws are all in uniform direction.

下左：居室と玄関の間にある扉のドアノブ
bottom left: Door knob between the living-room and the vestibule

下中：縁側の引き違い窓。冬のすき間風を防ぐために柱は凹に、戸は凸に削り、気密性を高めた
bottom middle: Double sliding windows; in order to avoid draft during winter posts are cut in concave & door leaf in convex for higher air-tightness.

下右：タオル掛けバー。滑り落ちにくいようにバーは45度傾けられている。
bottom right: Towel bar; a bar is angled by 45 degrees so that towel does not slip off.

083

藤井厚二が手掛けた調度品

　藤井は、茶道、華道、陶芸を嗜み、家具、照明、敷物、書籍の装本など、身の回りのあらゆるものを、自らが考える理想の「日本の住宅」に合わせてデザインした。そこには藤井独自の美学が表されている。

Furniture & Furnishings designed by Koji Fujii

Fujii enjoyed Way of Tea, flower arrangement, and making pottery. He designed all the personal items to match ideal Japanese Dwelling in his mind including furniture, lighting fixtures, carpet/mat, binding of his publications, which represented his aesthetics.

ベンチ・椅子

　藤井は、設計した住宅用に日本人のための本格的な家具デザインに取り組んだ。造り付けの家具では、機能性や合理性とともに、部屋全体の統一感も重視した。なかでも、椅子式の客室などには、高くした「床」を設え、それと一体感のあるベンチを造り椅子やテーブルと組み合わせるなど、欧米で吸収した最先端のデザインと日本の古建築や茶室の感性を融合させた。

Bench and Chairs

Fujii designed the furniture which fit the Japanese people living in the houses which he designed: built-in furniture prioritized sense of consistency of the room interior besides functional and rational requirements. Especially drawing-room with table/chairs has built-in bench which is integrated into the raised floor setting. He designed chairs/table to complete the room: the most advanced design Fujii absorbed in the West is in harmony with Japanese ancient architecture and sense of tea room.

客室の造り付けベンチ（W160.0 × H45.0 × D50.0cm）は、本来は閑室の下段の間と同じ仕様で、スプリングが入り緑の革が張られていた。椅子は、背に枕がついた肘掛け椅子が置かれた

The original built-in bench in drawing-room (W160.0 × H45.0 × D50.0cm) had the same specification as the lower area of Room of Quiet: green leather-upholstered with (seat) spring. Armchairs with cushioned seat back are placed.

上左：肘掛椅子（八木邸）　シオジ
革張り（緑・張り替え）
W57.0 × D51.5 × H88.7cm　SH（座面高）44.0cm
left above : Armchair (The Yagi Residence) in Shioji (Fraxinus platypoda) upholstered with green leather

下左：肘掛椅子（八木邸・食堂）　シオジ
革張り（緑・張り替え）
W48.4 × D50.8 × H86.4cm　SH48.0cm
left bottom: Armchair (Dining Room at The Yagi Residence): Shioji upholstered with green leather (Green lethers in both photos are not original ones)

上中：小椅子（八木邸・応接間）　シオジ
W44.5 × D44.5 × H87.5cm
middle above: Chair (Parlor, The Yagi Residence): Shioji

下中：安楽椅子（八木邸・居間）
W66.0 × D68.0 × H79.0cm　SH31.1cm
middle bottom: Easy Chair (Living Room, The Yagi Residence)

上右：肘掛椅子（聴竹居・食事室）
W55.5 × D51.8 × H90.5cm　SH43.5cm
当初は緑の革張り。細い角材を使用。
right above: Arm Chair (Dining Room, Chochikukyo: with fine rectangular timbers, originally upholstered in green lether

下右：枕付肘掛椅子（聴竹居・客室）　チーク
W49.0 × D64.0 × H90.5cm
着物の帯が枕に、袖が肘掛けに当たらないようにデザインされた
right bottom: Arm Chair with cushioned seat back (Drawing-room, Chochikukyo): The chair was so designed that neither cushioned seat back rest disturbs the tie of kimono nor arm rest disturbs the long sleeves of kimono.

机・テーブル・台

「聴竹居」本屋の食卓の天板は杉一枚板だが、裏を補強しているので経年による反りがない。客室にはオーストリアの建築家のヨーゼフ・ホフマンが設立したウィーン工房がデザインしたものに似た糸巻き形のテーブルがある。閑室には撥足(ばちあし)のついた和風デザインのテーブルのほか、2種類の角テーブルがあり、並べても使えるようになっている。

Desk, Table, & Pedestal

Chochikukyo Single *Sugi* (cedar) piece table top of dining table in the house proper (main house), has not warped with from age to the reinforcement in the back. In the drawing-room is a thread bobbin-shaped table, which resembles the design by Wiener Werkstëtte which Josef Hoffmann, an Austrian architect, founded. Room of Quiet has two types of square tables besides a table in Japanese design with flip legs, which can be lined up side by side.

食事室では、L字型のベンチを窓下に造り付け、独立したテーブルと椅子を組み合わせた
In the dining-room, L-shaped bench is fixed beneath the window with a free-standing table and chairs.

上左：丸テーブル（八木邸）
left above: Round Table (The Yagi Residence)

下左：拡張台付きレコードキャビネット（八木邸）
W52.7 × D40.7 × H76.4vm
left bottom: Cabinet for gramophone with Extendable Top (The Yagi Residence)

上中：机（八木邸）
center above: Desk (The Yagi Residence)

下中：電話台（八木邸）
W34.0 × D34.0 × H46.7cm
center bottom: Telephone Table (The Yagi Residence)

上右：テーブル　シオジ（八木邸・居間）
W79.8 × D79.8 × H63.5cm
right above: Table in Shioji (Living Room, The Yagi Residence)

下右：糸巻き形テーブル（聴竹居・客室）
W60.5cm × D60.5 × H65.3cm
right bottom: Three Bobbin-Shaped Table (Drawing-Room, Chochikukyo)

照明・暖房器具

「紙を通した光は高雅なる落ち着いた成を与える」と藤井は考え、障子だけではなく照明器具もほとんどが和紙、薄美濃紙を張ったデザインとした。藤井は、薄美濃紙の散光実験もし、光を散らす工夫を凝らした。

Lighting Fixture & Heater

Fujii thought that light passing through paper creates refined and calm feeling, so he not only uses *shoji* screens but also most of lighting fixtures which he designed had thin Mino paper pasted on. Fujii conducted light-diffusion experiment with Mino paper and did more to diffuse light.

「聴竹居」居間のシーリングライト
Ceiling Light: Living Room, Chochikukyo

左：スタンド（八木邸・居間）　H151.0cm（シェード部分 W42.6 × H22.7cm）
left: Floor Standing Lamp (Living Room, The Yagi Residence)

上右：ブラケット（聴竹居・客室）
right above: Ceiling Bracket Lighting (Drawing-room, Chochikukyo)

下右：卍井桁型ペンダント　薄美濃紙張り
同様のものが閑室、下段の間に使われていた。
right bottom: Pendant Lighting Fixture in 卍 shaped double crosses pasted with thin *mino* paper. The similar fixture was installed in the lower area of Room of Quiet.

左：電熱器　暖房器具　銀鼠釉（八木邸）W24.7 × D24.7 × H27.7cm
カバーは、陶器と鉄製（写真）のものがある
left: Electric Heater in silver gray glaze (The Yagi Residence)
Either ceramic or steel (photo)-made heater was placed in each room of Chochikukyo.

右：青海波　暖房器具（聴竹居）
「聴竹居」の各室に備えていた電熱器。
right: Heater with seigaiha (blue ocean wave) design motif, Chochikukyo

藤焼

「陶板類のみならず、日常の生活に使用する陶磁器をも、其の建物の内容に調和するもの」を作りたいと考えた藤井は、敷地内に窯をつくり、陶工・川島松次郎などの協力の下、「藤焼」と称して作陶を重ねた。陶器小屋では水車で捏ねられた陶土を足回転のろくろで成形し、素焼きの花器や茶碗、香合などに絵付けをし、それらを窯で焼いた。藤焼は、藤井が設計した住宅の竣工の際の施主への贈り物にも使われ、それらの作品は、1932年に発刊された『聴竹居作品集　二』（田中平安堂）にまとめられた。

Fuji Pottery

Fujii wanted to make not only ceramic panel but also pottery for daily use which are in harmony with the building. He built the kiln on the site and made pottery labeled as Fuji Pottery under the cooperation of Matsujiro Kawashima, a potter. In the working hut, Fujii formed the clay, worked with water mill, by rotating potter's wheel with his feet. He then painted unglazed flower base, tea pot, incense container among others and baked them in the kiln. Fuji Pottery was also presented to the client upon the completion of a house which Fujii designed. Fuji Pottery was complied in *Chochikukyo Sakuhin-shu II* (Work Collection) *Tanaka Heian-do* published in 1932.

「聴竹居」に残された藤焼の茶碗

Fuji Pottery: Tea cup remained in Chochikukyo

「飛鶴」(釣香炉)
釣香炉で、「聴竹居」客室の床の間に飾られた。また、藤井の遺作「扇葉荘」の客間にも飾られていた

Flying Crane: This pendant incense-burner in the shape of a crane is suspended from the ceiling of the alcove, drawing-room, Chochikukyo. This piece was also suspended in parlor of The Senyo-so, Fujii's last work.

上左：平鉢　四角　黒釉
left above: Square Pan with black glaze

上右：平鉢　四角　掛け分け
right above: Square Pan with multi-color glaze

下左：平鉢　八角　淡黄釉
left bottom: Octagonal Pan with pale yellow glaze

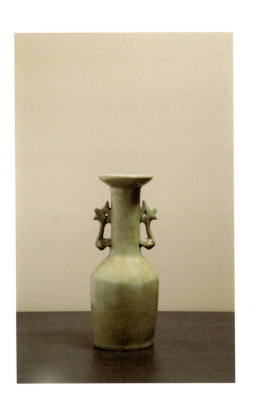

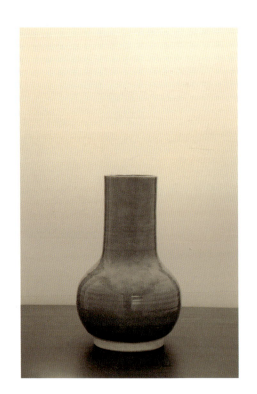
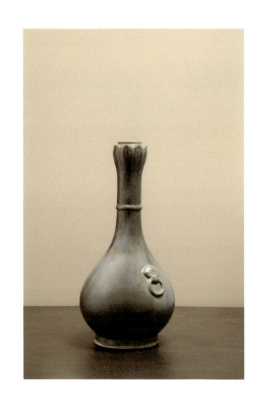

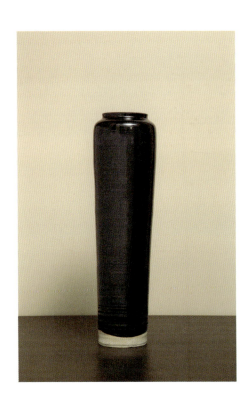

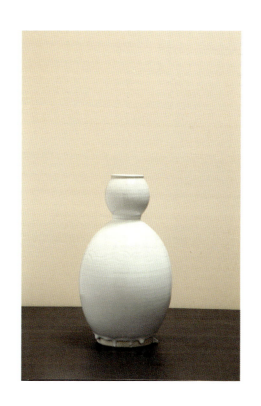

左頁：上段左より、耳付花器（黄茶釉）、花器（黄茶釉）、花器
下段左より、花器（黄茶釉）、花器（黒釉）、花器、花器
left page
top from left to right: Flower Vase with Handles (yellow-brown glaze),Flower Vase (yellow-brown glaze), Flower Vase, Flower Vase
bottom from left to right: Flower Vase (yellow-brown glaze), Flower Vase (black glaze), Flower Vase, Flower Vase

上段左より、花器（染付）、花器（染付）、花器（白釉）
下段左より、花器（染付）、花器、花器（白釉）
top from left to right: Blue and White Ceramic Flower Vase, Blue and White Ceramic Flower Vase, Flower Vase (white glaze)
bottom from left to right: Blue and White Ceramic Flower Vase, FlowerVase, Flower Vase (white glaze)

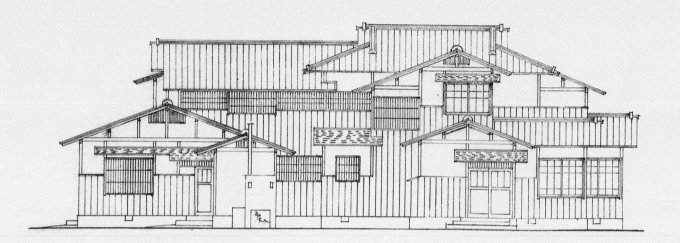

実験住宅「聴竹居」の完成後、初めて依頼を受けたのが注文住宅「八木邸」だ。新興住宅地に実現した実業家のための個人住宅も、心地よい空間を目指した藤井の住宅思想や実験を今に伝えている。

The Yagi Residence

After Fuji built Chochikukyo, the experimental house, the first house he commissioned as a custom design was The Yagi Residence. This residence, built for an entrepreneur, in the emerging residential area, also conveys Fujii's idea for houses and his experiments, aimed at the comfortable and intimate space.

板堀越しに見た八木邸。藤井は平屋を理想としたが、客人の多い八木邸では家族の個室を2階としてプライベートな空間を独立させた
The Yagi Residence viewed from the front of board fence: Fujii's ideal is single-floor while in case of the Yagi Residence with many visitors, 2nd floor with family rooms is defined as a private space.

1910(明治43)年、大阪・天満橋と京都・五条を結ぶ京阪電気鉄道が開通した。その沿線にある香里園は土地の利便性から神戸・六甲や大阪・北摂地域のように住宅地としての開発が目論まれていた。しかし、大阪城から見て北東の鬼門に当たるという伝えが災いし、宅地開発は遅々として進まなかった。そこで、京阪は鬼門解消のために千葉の成田山不動尊別院を誘致し、文化的なイメージを向上させるために大阪市玉造にあった聖母女学院の移転を計画した。それに先立って上下水道も敷設され、1928(昭和3)年に造成された宅地が大々的に売り出された。ちょうど「聴竹居」竣工の年のことである。

この年、京都・嵐山に居を構えていた八木市造(重兵衛)が、香里園駅にほど近い4区画(約400坪)を入手した。3区画が自宅、残る1区画が妹夫婦の宅地とされた。京都八木商店は「船場八社」に数えられた有力糸商「八木商店」に繋がる血筋で、当時、神戸と大阪に店を構えていたので通勤に便利な香里園を選んだ。

市造に藤井を紹介したのは、市造の両親、八木商店先代の重兵衛夫妻であった。夫妻は茶の湯を通じ藤井との知己を得ていた。市造から設計依頼を受けた頃、藤井は同じ香里園の宅地を購入した喜多愿吉からも設計を依頼されている(喜多邸は現存しない)。香里園の藤井設計の2邸もまた、聴竹居と同じ大工棟梁・酒徳金之助が手がけ、棟梁は同地に住み込んで建築に携わった。

竣工の1930(昭和5)年、施主の市造は33歳で、この時家族は妻と長女の3人であった。しかし市造は会社経営者であり、また馬主でもあったため、この木造2階建ての個人邸は多くの客をもてなす必要もあった。そのため、3〜4名の使用人が住み込みで働いていた。

「夏を過ごしやすい家」という思想は、八木邸でも貫かれ、屋根裏に導く通気筒や、床下の涼しい外気を室内に取り入れるハッチ式の扉(1階の納戸と女中部屋の入り口下)が設けられた。また、離れにお茶を楽しむ空間「閑室」(現在は解体された)が設けられたのも聴竹居と共通する。

八木邸には、藤井オリジナルの家具や照明、電熱器などを含むインテリアも数多く残されている。

In 1910, Keihan Electric Railway started service between Tenmabashi in Osaka and Gojo in Kyoto. Korien, a small town/village, which is along the line, was expected to be developed as a residential town such as Rokko in Kobe or Hokusetsu area in Osaka. However the old saying that Korien is in the northeastern quarter, unlucky direction, of the Osaka Castle blighted the development. Keihan invited Naritasan Fudoson Branch Temple (Buddhism) to bless the area in order to frighten away the unluckiness. Furthermore, in order to enhance cultural image, Keihan planned to relocate Seibo Jogakuin (missionary school originally in Tamatsukuri in Osaka city center) to this new area. Prior to these establishments, a potable water supply and sewage system were put in place. In 1928, when Chochikukyo was built, Keihan started extensive sales of housing lots.

In 1928, Ichizo (Jubei) Yagi, who was living in Arashiyama, Kyoto, bought four lots (about 1,320 square meters) of land near Keihan Korien station: three lots for his house and the one lot for his younger sister's couple. Ichizo was managing Kyoto Yagi Shoten, which is related in blood to Yagi Shoten; the leading thread/textile dealer which was among the top eight thread/textile dealers in Senba, merchants' quarter in Osaka. As Ichizo's shops were in Kobe and Osaka, he purchased land in Korien, which was convenient for him to commute to either his shop in Kobe or his shop in Osaka.

Ichizo's parents, Mr. & Mrs. Jubei Ichizo, and the previous proprietor of Yagi Shoten referred Fujii to Ichizo. They knew Fujii through the occasion of The Way of Tea. When Ichizo asked Fujii to design a new house, Fujii was also approached by Keikichi Kita to design a new house on the site Keikichi he had bought also in Korien. (The Kita residence is no longer standing.) Two houses designed by Fujii in Korien were built by Kinnosuke Sakatoku, a master carpenter who also worked on Chochikukyo. Sakatoku lived in Korien while he was working on the houses.

In 1930, when The Yagi Residence was built, the client, Ichizo was 33 years' old. He lived with his wife and their first daughter. Ichizo owned racehorses besides managing the company, two-storied house was also to serve guests. Three or four maids lived in the house.

The idea that houses prioritize the comfort during summer was also applied to The Yagi Residence: air tubes acting as exhaust pipes to carry hot summer air to the attic were provided and a hatch door to intake cool fresh air from under the floor and to supply to the rooms was installed (beneath the entrance of storage and that of maids' room on the 1st floor). Kanshitsu, a tea-house, to enjoy The Way of Tea in the annex was built (no longer standing), similar to Kanshitsu in Chochikukyo. Furniture, lighting fixtures, electric heaters which Fujii designed and other interior decor is left in The Yagi Residence.

引き違い戸の八木邸玄関
The Yagi Residence entrance with sliding doors

門扉(表札は後補)
Gate doors (Name plate was installed later)

右頁：配膳兼用のカウンターハッチが備え付けられた独立型の食事室。南側の大きな窓と東側の小さな窓から光が差し込む
right page: Independent dining-room with counter hatch, also used for serving. Natural light comes through a big window in south and a small window in east.

1階居間。床の間は椅子の視点に合わせている。和紙張りのコードペンダント照明とピアノ横のスタンド照明も藤井デザイン
Living-room (1/F): An alcove is in line with view line when seated on the chair. Code pendant lighting with Washi and a flloor standing lamp next to the piano are Fujii's design.

書斎。玄関を入って右にある応接室の奥に続いている
Study room: next to the parlor in the right of the entrance.

左頁：約20㎡の調理室。食事室と雁行するように隣接するため南側（流し側）と東側に窓がある。「聴竹居」同様、オール電化の家として建てられ、中央テーブルの横に電気オーブンが置かれていたのでその上部天井に排気口がある
left page: Kitchen (about 20㎡) : Windows in the south (sink-side) and east to align the kitchen and dining-room in a staggered formation. Alike Chochikukyo, all the utilities are in electric: electric oven (was next to the center table) with overhead ceiling exhaust.

食事室のカウンターハッチを通じて配膳ができるのも「聴竹居」と共通
Dishes are served through the counter hatch, as in the case of Chochikukyo.

調理室の造り付けの戸棚、配膳台、調理台。戸棚の開き戸は網戸仕様になっている
Built-in cupboard with screen swing opening, serving counter, and cooking counter

階段下の広間。階段の手すりと袖壁に幾何学デザインが施されている
Saloon under the staircase with geometric design on handrail and side wall

2階の主寝室
Master Bed Room, 2/F

踊り場が階段の2箇所に設けられ、高く広い窓がある。階段が光と風の取り入れ口として活用されている
Half-landing, at two points of the staircase, with tall/wide windows to intake light/wind into stairs.

1階の浴室前の脱衣室。ガラス棒の簀の子とタオル掛け
Dressing space in front of Bathroom (1/F): with grates and towel bar made out of glasses.

2階の洗面室。洗面室の鏡なども造り付け
Vanity-room (2/F) with built-in mirror

30歳頃の藤井厚二
Koji Fujii, around 30 years' old

藤井厚二の生涯

40歳で聴竹居を完成させた藤井厚二。その生涯を追う。

A Life of Koji Fujii

Koji Fujii built Chochikukyo at the age of 40 years old. This chapter summarizes his life.

福山から東京帝大へ

1888（明治21）年12月8日、藤井厚二は現在の広島県福山市宝町に11代続く造酒屋「くろがねや」の次男として生まれた。父・与一右衛門（幼名廣一）は金融業や製塩業なども堅実に営み、傍ら円山応挙「瀑布亀図」、竹内栖鳳「薫風行吟」など一級の絵画や書、茶道具などに親しみ、藤井も幼い頃からそれらに触れて育つ環境にあった。その父は1898（明治31）年に突然、他界。2歳年上の兄・祐吉が12歳で12代目を継いでいる。この兄は藤井の「実験住宅」建設や『日本の住宅』をはじめとする出版など、生涯を通じて藤井の取り組みを評価し、経済的に支え続けた。

1907（明治40）年、かつて藩校であった福山中学（現在の県立福山誠之館高等学校）を卒業。岡山の第六高等学校を経て、1910（明治43）年、東京帝国大学工科大学（現在の東京大学工学部）建築学科に入学。東京小石川に四歳年下の学習院に通う妹・快と母・元と共に暮らす。2年後、快は大阪・寝屋川市の素封家に嫁いでいる。

大学の講義では「法隆寺建築論」を発表した日本初の建築史家・伊東忠太（1867－1954）に教わっている。建築家としての代表作品には「平安神宮」や「築地本願寺」「祇園閣」があり、西洋化一辺倒から脱して日本の新しい建築様式を生涯追い求めた。その伊東の思想に藤井は大きく影響を受けた。西本願寺の別院「真宗信徒生命保険会社」（現在の「西本願寺伝道院」）に置かれている伊東デザインの「怪獣」の彫刻が「聴竹居」に置かれているのもその現れだ。帝大の卒業設計はドーム状の屋根が特徴的な新古典主義を志向した「A Memorial Public Library: 記念公共図書館」であるが、建築手法は西洋に学びながらも日本的なものに対する思いが芽生え始めていた。

「聴竹居」にある伊東忠太デザインの「怪獣」（石像）
Stone image of "monstrous animal" by Chuta Ito at Chochikukyo

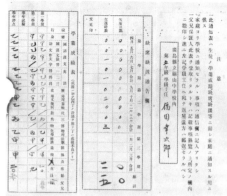

左：福山誠之館高校記念館
left: Memorial Hall of Fukuyama Seishikan High School

上：藤井の福山中学時代の「通知表」
above: Fujii's report card, Fukuyama Junior High School

From Fukuyama to Tokyo Imperial University

On December 8, 1888, Koji Fujii was born in Takara-machi, Fukuyama city in Hiroshima prefecture. He was the second son of the master of the Kuroganeya, Japanese sake brewery, which at that time had been in operation for eleven generations. His father, Yoichiemon, (his childhood name by Koichi), was involved in sound and diversified businesses: he was managing finance and salt manufacturing business as well as the sake brewery. Yoichiemon was fond of the leading arts such as Bakufu-kame-zu by Ookyo Maruyama, Kunpu-yugin by Seiho Takeuchi, Japanese calligraphy, and tools of tea ceremony among others. Fujii was brought up in this refined environment to appreciate first-class arts. His father suddenly passed away in 1898. Yukichi, two-years senior to Koji, succeeded in taking over the brewery as the 12th generation at the age of 12 years' old. Yukichi appreciated Koji's works and financially supported Koji in building experimental houses and publishing books such as The Japanese Dwelling-house among others.

In 1907, Koji graduated from the then Fukuyama Junior High School, prefectural school; a predecessor of the current Hiroshima Prefectural Fukuyama Seishikan High School. He continued his studies in the 6th High School in Okayama and was enrolled at the Department of Architecture of College of Engineering, Tokyo Imperial University; a predecessor of the Faculty of Engineering, Tokyo University. He lived in Koishikawa Tokyo, with Kokoro, his sister four years junior, who was attending Gakushuin and, his mother, Gen. Two years later, Kokoro married into a wealthy family in Neyagawa, Osaka.

At the Tokyo Imperial University, one of his lecturers was Chuta Ito, the first Japanese historian of architecture, who published a book on the architectural theory of Horyuji-temple. The major works by Chuta Ito, as an architect, include Heian Shrine, Tsukiji Hongwanji Temple and Gion-kaku. Ito left the pro-Westernization, and pursued the new architectural style in Japan throughout his career. Fujii was largely influenced by Ito's idea. This can be clearly seen by the fact that sculpture of "Monstrous Animal" which was designed by Chuta Ito and placed in Shingon Believers' Life Insurance Company, a branch of Nishi-Hongwanji Temple (currently, Nishi-Hongwanji Dendoin) is set in Chochikukyo. Fujii's work upon graduation from Tokyo Imperial University was A Memorial Public Library, which was in Neoclassicism with the remarkable feature of dome-shaped roof. While Fujii was learning the architectural techniques from the West, attention to something Japanese was emerging in his mind.

竹中工務店での記念写真（1914年）。最後列中央やや右寄りに前年入社の藤井の姿が見える
Takenaka & Co. staffs including Koji Fujii (1914): Fujii stands in the rear row a little right from the center.

大阪朝日新聞社社屋（1916年竣工）。昭和40年代まで大阪・中之島の景観を代表する建物だった
Osaka Asahi Shinbun Corporate Office (1916) : the land mark building in Nakanoshim, Osaka up to around 1965

竹中工務店時代

1913（大正2）年7月に東京帝大を卒業した藤井は、この年の10月に竹中工務店に入社。神戸で勤務に就いた。1899（明治32）年、創立以来、設計技術の近代化を急いでいた竹中藤右衛門は「三顧の礼」で藤井を迎え、合名会社竹中工務店にとって最初の帝大卒の社員となった。すぐさま「大阪朝日新聞社社屋」と同社主の住まい「村山龍平邸・和館」を手掛けている。前者は東京帝国大学で学んだ欧米の建築技術と様式的なデザインを遺憾なく発揮してできあがった先進的な「オフィスビル」であり、一方、後者は起伏ある広大な敷地の形状を存分に生かしたランドスケープが特徴的だ。江戸時代の京都・西本願寺の飛雲閣を思わせる外観で、書院や数寄屋を近代化した細部意匠へのこだわりが随所にみられる「住宅」である。藤井は、国家の「西洋化」＝「近代化」の意志の表出の求められた「オフィスビル」よりも、欧米に萌芽したモダニズム建築の中でも、よりデザインの自由度を増しつつあった「住宅」に魅力を感じたのだろう。

竹中工務店を辞めた後は「住宅」と環境工学に没頭することになる。さらに、藤井の人生にとって大きな出来事は、大阪朝日新聞社のプロジェクトを通じて関西建築界の雄、建築家・武田五一に出会っていることだ。当時「大阪朝日新聞社社屋」プロジェクトの新聞社側の顧問を務めていたのが武田だった。

竹中には6年足らずの在籍であったが、他に「橋本汽船ビル」「明海ビル」「十合呉服店」などの設計を担当、黎明期の同社設計組織の基礎を築いている。その緻密で繊細なデザインは、現在の設計部に脈々と受け継がれている。

A Period Working for Takenaka & Co.

Fujii graduated from Tokyo Imperial University in July 1913. He, then, joined Takenaka & Co. in October and started working in Kobe. Ever since Toemon Takenaka established Takenaka & Co, the first official establishment, in 1899, he accelerated the modernization of design technologies. Toemon Takenaka earnestly persuaded Fujii to work for his company. Fujii was the first employee of Takenaka & Co., who graduated from the Imperial University. Immediately after joining the company, Fujii was involved in the design work of Osaka Asahi Shinbun (Newspaper) Corporate Office and the residence of its founder, Japanese House, Murayama Ryuuhei Residence. The former was a modern office building that made best use of the Western architectural techniques and style-dependant design Fujii studied at the Tokyo Imperial University. On the other hand, the main feature of Japanese House, Murayama Ryuuhei Residence, is the landscape which makes full use of the profile of the site which is rich in peaks and valleys. The exterior appearance of this house reminds us of Hiun-kaku in Nishi Hongwanji Temple, Kyoto. It is a residence where Fujii's care with the detailed interior design, which modernized the *shoin* or *skiya* style of architecture, is demonstrated. Fujii must have been attracted by Modernism architecture emerging in the West, especially by residences that had more freedom in design, rather than office buildings, which were required to reveal the national will of Westernization, which was equivalent to Modernization.

After Fujii left Takenaka & Co., he devoted himself to the design of residences and environmental engineering. Moreover, what was important in Fujii's career was that on the occasion of Osaka Asahi Shinbun project Fujii met Goichi Takeda, who was the great leading architect in Kansai area. Takeda served as adviser to The Asahi Shinbun for the Osaka Asahi Shinbun Corporate Office project. Although Fujii worked for Takenaka & Co. for less than six years, he was in charge of design of many other projects such as the Hashimoto Shipping Building, Meikai Building, Sogo Department Store. At its dawn, Fujii established the foundation of Takenaka's Building Design Department. His detailed and delicate design has been passed down from generation to generation to the current members of the Department of Building Design of Takenaka Corporation.

明海ビルヂング（1921年竣工）。神戸・旧居留地の一角に建っていた。
下は藤井によるスケッチ（実現したものとデザインは異なる）
Meikai Building (1921)　built in the former foreign settlement of Kobe.
Bottom is Fujii's sketch. (The sketch was prepared for study and is different from what was built.)

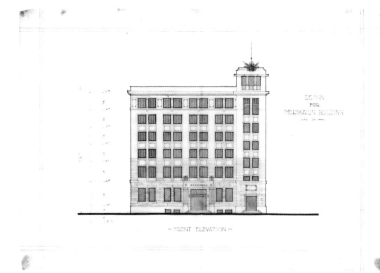

橋本汽船ビルヂング（1917年竣工）。神戸の海岸通りに面して建てられた。
下は藤井によるスケッチ（実現したものとデザインは異なる）
Hashimoto Kisen (Line) Building (1917) built along the Kaigan-dori, Kobe.
Bottom is Fujii's sketch.(The sketch was prepared for study and is different from what was built.)

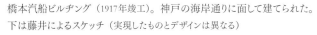

大阪朝日新聞社社屋を設計する際に描かれた藤井のスケッチ。時計塔、階段、エントランス
Fujii's sketch prepared in designing Osaka Asahi Shinbun Corporate Office: clock tower, stair case & entrance

欧米視察旅行。そして京大へ招かれる

「くろがねや」を若くして継いだ兄の与一衛門（祐吉）の恵まれた財力による援助を受け、藤井は自邸を5つの「実験住宅」として建てている。その最初は竹中工務店に在籍していた1917（大正6）年、神戸市の熊内（現在の新神戸駅近く）に建てた第1回自邸で、ここには母・元と住んだ。1918（大正7）年、出雲大社大宮司の娘・千家壽子と結婚した。

藤井は同年5月に竹中工務店を退社するが、翌1919（大正8）年11月初めまでは残務整理と引き継ぎで出社している。それを終えた藤井は、11月8日に横浜港を出港し、1920（大正9）年8月14日に帰国するまでの約9か月間、「建築に関する諸設備および住宅研究」のため、欧米に私費で出かけている。藤井の海外視察日記によると、訪問地はアメリカ（サンフランシスコ、ニューヨーク、シカゴ、フィラデルフィア、ワシントン、セントルイス、デトロイト、ボストンなど）とヨーロッパのイギリス（ロンドンなど）、フランス（パリなど）、イタリア（ローマなど）、スイス（チューリヒなど）、ベルギー（ブリュッセル）の計6か国。この視察には当時住宅改良会の顧問をつとめていた武田五一の助言があったとされ、藤井は欧米のモダニズムデザインの萌芽と最先端の建築設備に触れ、大きく影響を受けた。

帰国した藤井は1919（大正8）年に創設された京都大学工学部建築学科の講師として武田五一より招かれ、勤務することになる。武田は藤井と同じく広島県福山町に生まれ、16歳ほど年上であった。京都高等工芸学校（現在の京都工芸繊維大学）の図案科教授だった武田は、「京都府記念図書館：1909年」「芝川又右衛門邸」などヨーロッパで生まれたアール・ヌーボーやゼツェッションなど近代主義の建築に向けた新しいデザインの潮流を積極的に吸収した作品を次々に発表。藤井は意匠製図を担当し、その後、京都帝大の中央大講堂の設計などを嘱託され、翌年、助教授となっている。

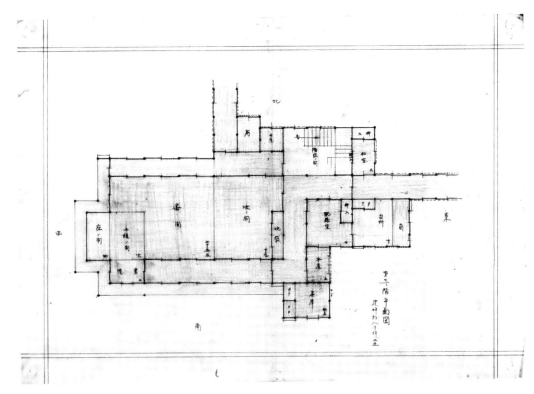

村山龍平邸・和館（書院棟）。下は藤井による村山邸平面プランのスタディ
Japanese House, The Murayama Ryuuhei-Residence
Bottom is the floor plan by Fujii.

京都帝国大学建築学教室の教員と学生。
前列左から2番目が藤井。その右が、天沼俊一（日本の建築史家）、さらに右が武田五一

Teachers and students of the Architectural Study Department, Kyoto Imperial University.
Fujii is in the front row second from the left. Shunichi Amano (historian of Japanese Architecture) is the right side of Fujii. Goichi Takeda is on the right side of Amano.

大正8（1919）年発行のパスポート
Passport issued in 1919.

「外遊アルバム」より。
左頁、アメリカ・フロリダ州セント・オーガスティン。
右頁、イギリス船カルメニヤ甲板にて
left page: St. Augustine, Florida, USA
right page: On the deck of the British vessel

Visited Europe/America & Invitation to Kyoto Imperial University

Fujii's elder brother Yoichiemon (Yukichi), who succeeded as master of Kuroganeya, was young and inherited a fortune. He rendered financial support for Fujii to build five experimental houses for himself. His 1st House was built in 1917 while he was working at Takenaka, in Kumochi, Kobe (near Shinkobe station), and lived with Gen, his mother. In 1918, he married Ms. Hisako Senge, daughter of the chief priest of Izumo Taisha (shrine). Fujii left Takenaka & Co. in May 1918, but he kept in close contact with the office to do the follow-up work and to hand over the pending projects to people in charge until early November in 1919. After completing his work at Takenaka & Co., on November 8th, he left Yokohama by ship returning on August 14, 1920; nine month-stay abroad on his own money. He visited the Western countries to research various equipments of architecture and houses. According to his travel journal, he visited six countries: America (including San Francisco, New York, Chicago, Philadelphia, Washington, St. Louis, Detroit, and Boston) and England (London, etc.), France (Paris, etc.), Italy (Rome, etc.), Switzerland (Zurich, etc.), and Belgium (Brussels, etc.) . It was said that Goichi Takeda, then adviser to the Association of Residential Improvement, advised Fujii to see the West. Fujii saw the emerging Modernism design and the most advanced architectural equipments in the West. He was largely influenced by them.

After returning to Japan, Goichi Takeda invited Fujii to join the Department of Architecture, Faculty of Engineering, Kyoto Imperial University, which was founded in 1919. Takeda like Fujii was born in Fukuyama, Hiroshima, and 16 years senior to Fujii. Takeda was a professor of the Design Course in Kyoto Polytechnics, a predecessor of the Kyoto Institute of Technology, and released works such as Kyoto Memorial Library (1909) and The Shibakawa Mataemon-Residence. He was actively absorbed with the new design trends that were emerging in Europe such as Art Nouveau and Sezession, heading towards Modernism architecture. When Fujii joined Takeda as a lecturer he was teaching interior design drawing classes, after which he was commissioned to design the Central Grand Auditorium of Kyoto Imperial University. Following this he became an assistant professor in 1921.

実験住宅*の試み

京都帝国大学への勤務が始まった1920 (大正9) 年、藤井は京都府乙訓郡大山崎町に居を移した。第2回目の実験住宅が現在のJR山崎駅の東、京都と大阪を結ぶ西国街道沿いにできあがったのである。なぜ藤井が大山崎を選んだかは不明だが、しばらく、神戸から京都まで通っていたとき、桂川、宇治川、木津川の三川が合流して淀川へと続くその雄大で広々とした風景が気に入ったに違いない。淀川の対岸には石清水八幡宮が鎮座する男山を望み、背後には豊臣秀吉が明智光秀を倒した天王山が迫っている。自然の恵みを享受するには申し分のない土地だった。山麓には清冽な湧き水があり、1923 (大正12) 年にサントリーのウイスキー工場がここに設けられたのも、清冽な水と三川から立ち上る冷涼な霧がウイスキーの熟成には欠かせなかったからだという。

また大阪と京都、そして大和を河川で結ぶ要衝の地にあった大山崎は、古くから灯明などに使われるエゴマ油を扱う油座が組織され、西日本一帯の油を扱う地として繁栄した。その名残りか、現在も西国街道一帯には豪商の端正な家並みが僅かに残っている。

山崎駅前の妙喜庵・待庵の存在も茶の湯を嗜む藤井には、この地を選ぶ大きな要素になっていたにちがいない。待庵は大山崎の戦いの際、秀吉のために利休が戦場近くで茶の湯を楽しめるよう移築した茶室とも、また、現在地より西に住まいしていた千利休が移築した茶室ともいわれている。実際に待庵は日本最古の茶室といわれ、千利休の影響を色濃く反映した現存する唯一の茶室で、国宝に指定されている。茶室建築にならう閑室の建築を志していた藤井には、自然環境も歴史的背景も、これ以上の適地はなかったのだろう。

*実験住宅という言葉を藤井自身は使ってはいない。『日本の住宅』などの著書には第1回住宅、第2回住宅、第3回住宅、第4回住宅という言葉が使われている。

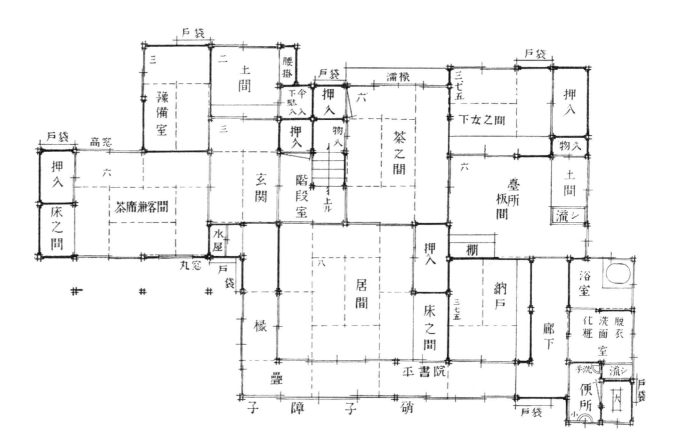

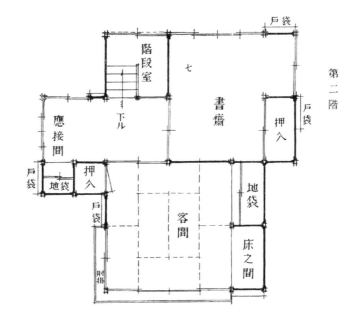

第1回住宅 (1914年竣工)。神戸市熊内に建てられた。基本は和風プランで、南側に縁側を置く日本の農家の間取りを参照した
The 1st House (1914) at Kumochi, Kobe: Japanese style in general and Fujii referred to the floor plan of Japanese farmer's houses with verandah on the south side.

A New Attempt - Experimental Houses *

In 1920, when Fujii started working for Kyoto Imperial University, he moved to Oyamazaki-cho, Otokuni-gun, Kyoto prefecture. His 2nd experimental house was built to the east of JR Yamazaki station, along the Saigoku Road, which connected Kyoto and Osaka. The reason for Fujii deciding to live in Oyamazaki is not known, but he must have been pleased with the magnificent open view of rivers Katsura, Uji, and Kizu, coming together with the Yodo, which he watched while he was commuting from Kobe to Kyoto. From Oyamazaki, on the other side of the Yodo, he could view Otokoyama with Iwashimizu Hachimangu. Beyond there is Tenno-zan mountain, where Hideyoshi Toyotomi killed Mitsuhide Akechi. Oyamazaki, for Fujii, left nothing to be desired but to enjoy the benefits of nature. At the foot of the mountain, crystal-clear spring water surfaced. In 1923, Suntory built its whisky factory in Yamazaki as the crystal-clear spring water and cool mist from three rivers nurtured the maturing whisky. Oyamazaki was a strategic point connecting Osaka, Kyoto, and Yamato (Nara) by rivers. The Oil Merchants' Union was organized and dealt in wild sesame oil, which had been used for a light offered to a God for a long time. Oyamazaki prospered as the place that dealt in oil, which was distributed throughout Western Japan. A few rows of decent houses for the wealthy merchants still remain in the Saigoku Road area, which can be seen as a vestige from the past prosperity.

Taian (Tea Room) of Myoki-an Temple located in front of Yamazaki station must have been a major factor for Fujii to select Oyamazaki for his residence, as he enjoyed the Japanese tea ceremony also known as The Way of Tea. Tea-room Taian is said to be a tea hut which Sen no Rikyu relocated to this location, close by the battle field of Oyamazaki, so that Hideyoshi could enjoy tea. It is also said to be a tea hut which Rikyu, who was living further west from the current house of the Sen family, relocated for himself. Taian is referred to as the oldest tea room in Japan. It is the only tea room under the rich influences of Sen no Rikyu which was left until now and is designated as a national treasure. For Fujii, who intended to build a pavilion named a room of quiet, following the architecture of tea rooms, there was no other suitable site for his house either in the context of natural environment or historical background.

*Fujii did not use the term as an experimental house. In his publication, Nihon-no-Jutaku (Houses in Japan), the terms such as the 1st House, 2nd House, 3rd House, and 4th House were used.

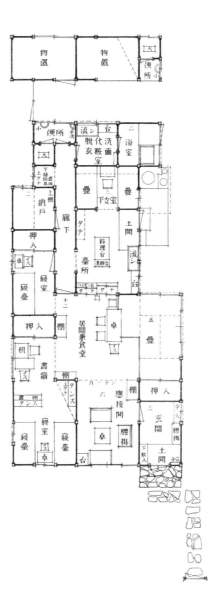

上：第2回住宅（1920年竣工）。京都府・大山崎の西国街道に面した平屋建て住宅。畳と椅子の空間の同居を試みはじめる
above: The 2nd House (1920) in Oyamazaki, Kyoto: one-story house facing Saigoku Road. Fujii introduced a technique to equip a space with both mats and chairs.

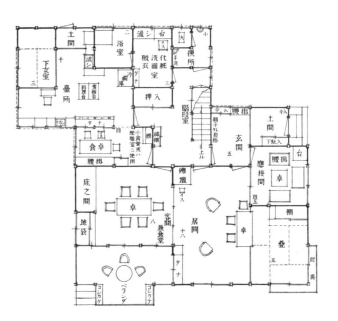

右上・右：第3回住宅（1922年竣工）。「聴竹居」の東南の一段下がった土地に建てられた2階建て住宅
right above/right: The 3rd House (1922): two-story house on the site in the southeast, one step lower, from the potential site for Chochikukyo

大きな転機となった関東大震災

第2回実験住宅に住み始めると、藤井は大山崎の天王山の麓に約1万2000坪の土地（山林）を購入。そこに三回目の実験住宅を完成させると気候に関するデータなどを採り始めた。

ちょうどその時期、近代化に邁進していた日本を大きな災害が襲う。1923（大正12）年9月1日に起こった関東大震災である。明治維新以降、日本は欧化政策のもと、数多くの洋風建築を建ててきたが、その多くがこの震災で一瞬にして倒壊してしまった。その光景を藤井は震災後3週間、まだまだ大混乱の続いていた時点で視察し、関西建築協会（現在の日本建築協会）の機関誌『建築と社会』に一文「関東の震災を見て」（1924年1月）を記している。

> 「平素建築上に抱いている考を一層深くした。（中略）吾々の建築は他を模倣したものでなくて、我国の気候、風土、習慣に、ピッタリと適合したものでなければならない」「無条件で外国の建築を受けいれたものが、我国の気候風土に対して、如何なる結果を齎すかは、申迄もなく明らかなことです」「吾々が建築上に手本として、参考として居る国々、米国も、英吉利（イギリス）でも、独逸（ドイツ）でも、何れも日本よりは余程北に在って、冬を主として考えなければならないし、我国は夏を主として考えなければならないと云う様に、全く反対です」

欧米視察を終え、京都帝国大学に招かれた藤井が、着任して間もなく「関東大震災」で洋風建築の被害を眼のあたりにしたことは、より深く「日本の建築」を意識するきっかけになっていった。日本の伝統的な住まいで経験的に行われてきた気候風土にあわせる建築方法を科学的な眼で捉え直し、理論化し、環境工学の知見を設計に盛り込み、居住し実証・改善を加えながら、自邸を「実験住宅」とする作業を次々と進めた。2階建ての第3回（1922）、平屋建ての第4回（1924）、そして最後に平屋建ての第5回住宅（1928）の「聴竹居」で藤井の理想は一つの完成形を見ることになった。

上・左上：第4回住宅（1924年竣工）。「聴竹居」の北側。実際には住まず、温度測定などの計測をした
above/left above: The 4th House (1924): in the north of Chochikukyo. Fujii never lived in this house and took temperature and other measurements.

左：第5回住宅（1928年竣工）。完成当時の「聴竹居」
left: The 5th House (1928): Chochikukyo upon completion

下：1930年頃の三川合流部を聴竹居側から眺めた風景
bottom: View from Chochikukyo around 1930

Kanto Earthquake, Major Turning Point for Fujii

After Fujii moved to the 2nd experimental house, he bought about 46,280 square meters of land at the foot of Tennozan, Oyamazaki for his next house. At the time of completion of the 3rd experiment house, when Fujii had started to collect the climatic data, and Japan, which had been proceeding with the modernization, was hit on September 1, 1923 by the major disaster, the Great Kanto Earthquake. During and after the Meiji Restoration (late 19th century), many Western buildings were built under the national policy of Westernization, and many collapsed because of the quake. Fujii, three weeks after the quake, observed that the disaster-hit area was still suffering under major confusion and posted an article entitled Looking at Aftermath of Kanto Earthquake in *Kenchiku-to-Shakai* (Architecture and Society), a journal published by the Architectural Association of Kansai, a predecessor of The Architectural Association of Japan. His article includes the following comments: my thought on architecture which is always in my mind was reassured…Our architecture should not copy the one of other countries, instead it should fit climate, natural features, and habit. In the Japanese climate, the result of applying architecture of foreign countries without conditions is clear cut. We are referring to architecture abroad such as America, England, or Germany, located further north of Japan, which prioritizes the climate in winter while we should prioritize the climate in summer.

Fujii came back from Europe/America, and was invited to Kyoto Imperial University. He saw the damage to the Western buildings caused by the Great Kanto Earthquake immediately after assuming the teaching position. This made him even more conscious of architecture for Japan. Fujii, from the scientific point of view revisited the empirically tested architectural methods used in the Japanese traditional houses, which corresponded to the Japanese climate. The resulted theory and the findings in the environmental engineering were accommodated in the design efforts of the house in which he lived. He repeated the verification and improvement while he was preparing for his houses as experimental houses, one after another; the 3rd House (two-story) in 1922 and the 4th House (one-story) in 1924. Fujii's ideal was somewhat completed in his 5th House (one-story), namely Chochikukyo in 1928.

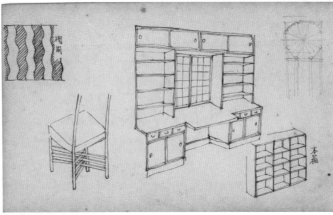

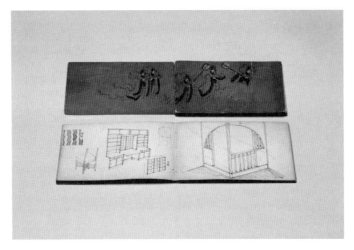

藤井のスケッチブックより。「聴竹居」食事室（上）、読書室（中）
Fujii's sketch book on Chochikukyo: Dining-room (above), Family Resding-room (middle)

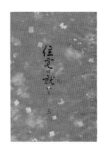  

上段左から、住宅プラン集の『住宅に就いて 三』（1931年・石版刷り）、藤焼についてまとめた『聴竹居作品集 二』（1932年）、写真入り冊子の『床の間』（1934年）。下段左から、『鐵筋混凝土の住宅』（1931年）、藤井の遺作をまとめた『扇葉荘小景』（藤井壽子著、1938年）
From top left: Jutaku-ni-tsuite III (1931 in lithography, floor plans of houses), Chochikukyo Sakuhin-shu II (1932, on the Fuji pottery), *Tokonoma* (1934, leaflet on alcove with photos), Tekkin-konnkurito-no-jutaku (1931, Houses in reinforced concrete), & *Senyo-so Shokei* (1938, Yoshiko Fujii published, compiling Fujii's last work).

下：『住宅に就いて 三』より「15坪のプラン例」
Example of floor plan of about 50 square meter-house, Jutaku-ni-tsuite III

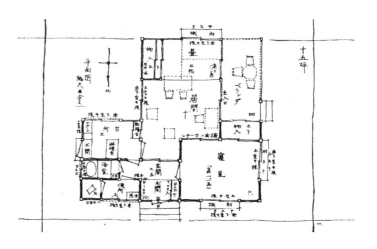

藤井厚二の多彩な才能

「実験住宅」の実践の中から、藤井は日本の住宅についての強い思想を表現できるようになっていった。1928（昭和3）年、真に日本の気候風土に適した住宅のあり方を環境工学の点から科学的に考察した理論書『日本の住宅』を著し、さらに翌年、住宅設計の集大成・完成形として写真と図面で構成された『聴竹居図案集』(1929年)、『続聴竹居図案集』(1932年)を著し、理論と実践の成果を世に発表している。そして1930（昭和5）年には、この三つの書物を統合・英訳した「THE JAPANESE DWELLING-HOUSE」（明治書房）を著し、「二五〇〇年以上の歴史を持つ日本の住宅は、世界中の同種の建築の中でも、無類の優れた特色を有している。日本の住宅の顕著な特色は影響を受けずに残っている。これらの特色を世界へと紹介することにより、多くの建築家にとって参考となる貴重な素材を提供できるばかりか、日本の生活や文化に深い関心を持つ人々にとっても、興味深い研究の主題を提示することができるだろう。」と記して「日本の住宅」を世界へ発信している。

世界的な建築家ル・コルビュジエ (1887 - 1965) と1歳違いの藤井が世界の潮流に沿っていたことを示す一つのエピソードがある。1933年、同じく世界的な建築家ブルーノ・タウトのあの「桂離宮」訪問から1週間もたたない5月9日、彼はなんと「聴竹居」を訪れている。その日の日記に「極めて優雅な日本建築」「気持ちのよい階段」「この茶室は茶室建築の革新である」と率直な感想を記している。

藤井はその後も多くの住宅（住宅以外の建物を含めると50軒以上）を設計したが、1937（昭和12）に完成した京都の中田邸「扇葉荘」が遺作となる。

1938（昭和13）年7月17日没。京都・嵯峨野の二尊院で、自ら病床でデザインした墓所に眠っている。完成形とした自邸「聴竹居」に住んでわずか10年、49年の短い生涯であった。

茶道、華道、陶芸を嗜み、家具、照明、敷物、書籍の装丁など身のまわりのあらゆるものを「日本の住宅」にあわせるべくデザインした。「其の国の建築を代表するものは住宅建築である」という考え方を貫き、生涯を住宅設計に専念した。

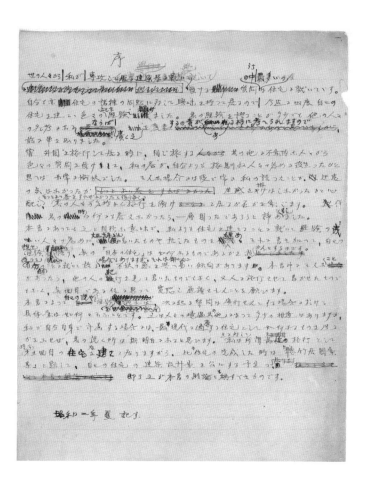

上：『日本の住宅』の原稿
above: manuscript of *Nihon-no-jutaku* (Dwelling-house in Japan)

下：藤井自らが墓標をデザインした二尊院（京都市）にある墓
The Tomb of Koji Fujii with Fujii designed-gravepost, Nison-in Temple, Kyoto

Fujii's Diversified Talent

In design practice of experimental houses, Fujii could express his established ideas on the houses in Japan both in theory and in practice. In 1928, he wrote a theoretical book, Nihon-no-Jutaku, which scientifically examined the way of houses fit for the Japanese climate from the view of environmental engineering. He published Chochikukyo Zuan-shu (Collection of Design Document) in 1929 and Zoku Chochikukyo Zuan-shu in 1932 with pictures and sketches, which compiled a complete set of documents on residential design. In 1930, Fujii combined the afore-mentioned three books in Japanese and published as THE JAPANESE DWELLING-HOUSE from Meiji-shobo. Fujii states: The architecture of the Japanese dwelling house, which boasts a history of over 2,500 years, has excellent features unrivalled by any other architecture of its kind in the world…its prominent features have remained unaffected. By introducing these characteristics to the world, not only can valuable materials for reference be furnished to many architects but an interesting subject for study can be suggested to those persons who are deeply interested in Japanese life and culture. Fujii released Japanese dwelling-houses to the world.

How Fujii, one year senior to Le Corbusier, who was the world renowned architect, was centrally positioned in the global trend of architecture is proofed by the fact that Bruno Taut, another world famous architect, visited Chochikukyo. On May 9, 1933, less than a week after his visit to the famous Katsura Villa, Taut visited Chochikukyo. Taut wrote down his straightforward impressions of Chochikukyo in his diary: "very elegant Japanese architecture"; "pleasant stairs"; "this tea hut is the innovation of architecture of tea rooms". Fujii designed over 50 buildings including many houses. The Senyo-so, a residence of the Nakata family in Kyoto, built in 1937 was his last work. Fujii died on July 17, 1938. He rests in a tomb in Nison-in Temple in Sagano, Kyoto, which he designed while he was sick in bed. It was only ten years after Fujii built Chochikukyo, a completed form of his idea and ideal that his short life of 49 years ended.

Fujii enjoyed the Way of Tea, flower arrangement, and ceramic art. He designed everything around himself such as furniture, lighting fixtures, floor coverings, and binding of books so that they complemented the houses in Japan. He kept to his values that domestic architecture represents architecture of the country and he devoted himself to the residential design throughout his career.

〈木造モダニズム〉の原点

藤森照信（建築家・建築史家）

　聴竹居を初めて訪れた時、このモダンさはどこから来たんだろうかと考えた。

　20世紀における世界のモダンな建築の動きは二段階を経たことが知られ、まず最初は、アール・ヌーヴォーと呼ばれる一群が世紀末のヨーロッパに現れ、それまでの、やれゴシック・リヴァイヴァルだネオクラシックといった歴史主義からの離脱を開始し、この動きは1930年前後にバウハウスに行き着き、建築は白い箱に大きなガラスのはまる世界共通（インターナショナル）の表現となる。

　アール・ヌーヴォーに始まる最初の40年間をモダンデザインといい、1930年以後をモダニズムと分けて考えると、わが聴竹居は最初のモダンデザインの一つに入る。ここまでは分かりやすいが、謎はこの先にある。

　アール・ヌーヴォーの建築は日本にも大量に出現しているが、聴竹居は明らかにそれらとは違い、どう見ても日本の木造住宅の伝統をベースにしている。モダンデザインとしての和風建築。こんな例は、モダンな側にも伝統の側にもない。モダンな例はヨーロッパと同じ姿のモダンデザインを作っているし、一方、伝統の側はそれこそ昔ながらの書院造や数寄屋造を作り続けるなかで、突如、両者の中間に聴竹居が誕生した。もしそれが中間ゆえの野合ぶりと混乱を示していたなら出来損ないとして無視すれば済むが、聴竹居はそうはいかず、スーッと見る人の気持ちの中に入り込むばかりか、住みついてしまう。

　戦後のモダニズム建築家は、鉄とガラスとコンクリートで作られた機能主義的、合理主義的造形ばかりに馴染んできたから、木造だけならまだしも、「木造にしてモダニズムとは異質な建築」に住みつかれては、厄介というか、心は千々に乱れるというか、いったいこれは何なんだ、どこから来たのか、と問いたくなる。

　建築家のそんな問いに答えるのは建築史家の仕事の一つだから、初めて聴竹居を訪れて以来、けっこう長いこと考え続けてきた。考え続けて、少し前にやっと答えに行き当たったので、ここに書いておきたい。

　答えの手がかりを見つけたのは、聴竹居の問題とは別に、茶室について本を書いている時、いわゆる建築家と呼ばれる明治の辰野金吾以後に生まれる職能人たちのうち、だれが初めて茶室を手がけたのかを調べていて、意外な事実に気付いた。辰野金吾は「あんな脂っこいもの」（"女っぽい"の意で、唐津の言い方）と否定的だったのは知っていたが、その直弟子たちも茶室の設計をしていない。孫弟子の世代もやらないなかで、例外的に藤井厚二が神戸市に建てた1914（大正3）年の第1回住宅の中で「茶室兼客間」として初めて試みていることが分かった。

　そこで藤井と茶の関係を探ると、ただごとではない。藤井は広島県福山の生まれで、藤井家はこの地方きっての豪商として知られ、家を挙げて茶を嗜み、茶道具の収集にも力を注ぎ、慶長年間の御所丸茶碗「藤井」を所有していたが、福山の発展のため私費で発電所を作るべくこの「藤井」をはじめ骨董や書画を売って建築費の足しにしている。なお、現在は大阪の湯木美術館に入り、「由貴」と銘されている。

　藤井は生涯茶を嗜み、広大な自邸の一画に窯を築き、職人を抱え、茶碗をはじめ焼き物制作を楽しみとし、吉村順三によると、学生時代に事前の連絡もなく訪れると、辻留から弁当を運ばせ、もてなしてくれたという。それくらい茶の世界とは深かった。

　日常的に茶を嗜むため、聴竹居の敷地の一画に茶室を作ってはいても、しかしそれだけで聴竹居の独得の建築表現に茶と茶室の影響があるとはいえない。

　突破口を開いてくれたのは、聴竹居のよく知られた特異な食堂の作りだった。食堂は四畳半を取り、その一部が主室の角から張り出し、その角には四分円のアーチがかかり、聴竹居の中で最も印象深い一画となっている。

　これのどこが特異なのか。主室である居室は縁側の側を背にして長方形を取り、長方形の突き当たりが室内の正面となっているから、普通の和室ならここが床の間となるが、もちろん床の間を付けない代わりに、ここが正面であることを示すものとしては、それと分からないように神棚が置かれ、中央上部にはマッキントッシュのデザインを模した時計がはめ込まれている。その正面の右手の角から唐突に食堂の一画が突き出す。人々の目が自ずと向く正面に四角な別の部屋の一部が突き出すなんて、平面は左右対称を旨とする世界の室内にはあり得ないし、左右非対称を許容する日本の伝統木造にあっても、こと正面については無い。ただの一つの例外を除いて。

　その例外とは茶室。それも普通の茶室ではなく〈残月亭〉と呼ばれる特別な茶室である。

利休の茶室を介して

　利休は、京の聚楽第の利休屋敷の中に〈色付九間〉と呼ばれるきわめて特殊な間取りと作りをした茶室を作っている。まず面積が広く三間四方の九間（三間四方の部屋のことをこう呼ぶ）を取るのも異例なら、床の間状に一段上がった上段（の間）が設けられるばかりか、その上段の右手角にさらにもう一段上がった上段が設けられる。その上々段の角には床柱のような独立柱が立つ。上段を二重にしたのは、聚楽第への天皇行幸の時、上々段には天皇の、上段には秀吉の座を想定したにちがいない。行幸の時、天皇が利休屋敷を訪れたという記録はないが、秀吉はしばしば訪れ茶を楽しんでいる。

利休没後4年して聚楽第は取り壊されて色付九間も消えるが、新たに移った地に利休の子の少庵は色付九間を三坪減じ、二重の上段を一段にして〈残月亭〉を新築する。これも普通ではなく、秀吉専用で、上段には秀吉が座して少庵の呈する茶を喫み、柱にもたれて突き上げ窓から残月を見て利休を偲んだことから残月亭、角の独立柱は"太閤柱"と呼ばれる。

色付九間に始まり残月亭で定着した特異な平面構成に想を得て、藤井は主室の角に食堂を突き出したにちがいない。角の独立柱も食堂が一段上がっていることも、そう考えると納得がゆく。

このことに気付いて、やっと、聴竹居の背後には利休の茶室があることを確信できた。

というと、そんなことはたとえば応接間など随所にみられる茶室的作りから確認できたろうに、と思われるかもしれないが、"茶室的作り"があったからといって茶室の影響とも言えないところが建築史家のつらいところで、茶室ではなく数寄屋造の影響と考えるほうが普通だからだ。

数寄屋造とは、書院造が利休の茶室の影響を受けて変化して成立したスタイルだから、当然のように"茶室的作り"が込められており、"茶室的作り"が観察されたからといってそれが茶室と数寄屋のどっちの影響なのかははっきりしないが、残月亭の上段は数寄屋造に例はなく残月亭に固有の特徴だから、これがあれば茶室の、それも利休の茶室の影響と特定することができる。

なお、残月亭の上段がもたらす非対称の空間には近代的建築家の感性を魅せる力が秘められ、藤井も最後の作の〈扇葉荘〉（1937年竣工）の伝統的な広間の茶室（座敷を兼ねる）でも採用しているし、村野藤吾は自邸の座敷で、堀口捨己は八勝館の皇后用和室で取り込んでいる。

聴竹居と利休の茶室につながりがあることを知ると、正面の右手下の残月亭的突き出しに隣接して床から四本脚で立ち上がる不思議な小さな棚の由来も推察できよう。利休の待庵の水屋の名高い吊り棚が発想の源だろう。待庵は聴竹居のすぐ近くにあり、茶の好きな藤井には手のうちにある建築であった。

利休の創案になる茶室は、伝統の木造建築でありながら、定形化した既存のスタイル（書院造）にとらわれない自由なデザインを最大の特徴としていたが、この特徴に深く学ぶことにより、藤井は、伝統的な木造住宅の中に自由なデザインを導入することに成功する。この自由なデザインという特徴こそ、ヨーロッパのアール・ヌーヴォー以後のモダンデザインの勘所に他ならなかった。

利休の茶室を介して、藤井は1928（昭和3）年、聴竹居によって伝統木造とモダンデザインを繋ぐことに成功した。

この影響は大きく、後続の若い世代が木造でモダンを試みるようになり、堀口捨己、アントニン・レーモンド、吉村順三、前川國男、丹下健三などが、木造のモダニズム建築を次々に手がけてゆく。

当時、世界においては、モダニズム建築は鉄筋コンクリート造もしくは鉄骨造と決まっていたが、例外的に日本では伝統の木造技術を駆使してモダニズム建築が実現した。これらを現在では〈木造モダニズム〉と呼ぶ。鉄筋コンクリート造や鉄骨造にはない木造ならではの温かさとシャープさが看取されるから、誇りを込めてそう呼ぶ。

現在も日本の建築家たちは、木造によりモダンでオシャレな住宅を作り続けているが、その源をたどると聴竹居に行き着く。

Origin of Wooden Modernism

Terunobu Fujimori (Architect/Historian of Architecture)

When I visited Chochikukyo for the first time, I was thinking where its modernity came from.

It is known that in the 20th century modern architecture around the world experienced two phases. Phase 1 began with a group of Art Nouveau movement, which emerged in Europe at the turn of the century, leaving Historicism such as Gothic, Revival, or Neo-classic architecture. This Art Nouveau movement led to Bauhaus Design, which around the 1930's resulted in the expression of Internationalism of architecture in the creation of buildings like white boxes enveloped in glass. If the first 40 years started in Art Nouveau is referred to as Modern Design, followed by the Modernism around 1930, our Chochikukyo is among the former Modern Design. It is easy to understand up until this point, but then there is the point which cannot be easily explained.

In Japan many buildings in Art Nouveau design emerged, however Chochikukyo is clearly different, and is based on the tradition of wooden Japanese houses in every aspect. Architecture in Japanese style as Modern Design cannot be found either among the Modern Architecture or among the Japanese Traditional Architecture. Modern examples in Japan were in the Modern Design the same as those in Europe while the Traditional examples continued to produce the *shoin* or *sukiya* style of Japanese architecture. Chochikukyo was created all of a sudden between the Modern and the Japanese Tradition. If Chochikukyo is unprincipled or displays chaos due to being inbetween the two, we can just ignore it. However, this is not the case with Chochikukyo. It not only naturally immerses itself in the mind of people who view it, but also stays in their mindset.

Post-war architects of Modernism have been familiar only with the realization of Functionalism and Rationalism in steel, glass, and concrete. It is therefore disturbing to our emotions when we see that Chochikukyo is not only simply in wood, but also is a heterogeneous architecture, both in wood and in Modernism. We cannot stop asking what on earth it is and where it comes from.

One of the jobs as a historian of architecture is to present an answer to the questions raised by architects, so I have been looking for answers for quite a long time since I visited Chochikukyo for the first time. Just recently, at last I found the answers, so I would like to share them with my readers.

I found a clue when I was writing a book on Japanese tea rooms, separate from the issue of Chochikukyo. Kingo Tatsuno, who practiced in Meiji era (1868-1912), was the first person to be labeled as an architect in Japan. When I was looking into the professionals to find out who designed a tea room for the first time after Kingo Tatsuno, I identified an unexpected fact. I knew that Kingo Tatsuno had a negative view of tea rooms as he states "how come I was involved in such a feminine stuff" (in a dialect of his birth place, Karatsu). None of his immediate followers designed tea rooms. Though none of his followers in the immediate next generation did the tea room, as an exception, Koji Fujii tried a tea room also used as a drawing-room in his first experimental house in Kobe built in 1914.

Then I found out that the relationship between Fujii and The Way of Tea was not ordinary. Fujii was born in Fukuyama, Hiroshima prefecture. The Fujii family was known as a leading wealthy merchant in the region. The family was interested in Japanese tea, and directed efforts to collect relevant tea tools. They owned a *goshomaru* tea cup dated back to Keicho era (1596-1615) which is signed by Fujii. However the Fujii family sold it and other antiques, paintings/calligraphic work to supplement with their private fund to construct the power generation plant for the development of Fukuyama. The *goshomaru* tea cup, with a signature of Yuki, is now kept in Yugi Museum in Osaka.

Fujii himself enjoyed The Way of Tea throughout his life. He built a kiln in a part of the huge site of his residence, kept the artisan and enjoyed baking tea cups and other pottery. According to Junzo Yoshimura, when he visited Fujii's residence without prior notice during his student days, Fujii extended warm hospitality with a lunch box from Tsujitome, the catering service specializing in tea ceremony. This indicates how Fujii was deeply related to the world of The Way of Tea. Even if he set a Tea Hut on the site of Chochikukyo to enjoy The Way of Tea in his daily life, this alone cannot explain that the architectural expressions unique to Chochikukyo are affected by The Way of Tea and tea rooms.

A breakthrough came from the well-known form of the dining-room in Chochikukyo, which is quite special and unique. A part of the dining area, four-and-a-half mat wide space, is projected out from the corner of the main room. The transition corner has a one quarter arch-shaped opening, which is an impressive and the best scene in Chochikukyo.

Which part of the afore-mentioned arrangement is special and unique? The living-room, which is the main room in the residence, is a rectangular shape with the verandah at the back. The other end of the verandah in the rectangle is the front wall in the living-room. In the usual Japanese room, an alcove is set in the front, but in this residence, needless to say there is no alcove, instead a *kamidana* (Shinto altar in the home) is discretely placed to indicate the front wall. A clock modeling a Mackintosh design is embedded in the upper part of the center of the front wall. From the corner in the right of the front wall, a part of the dining-room is projected out unexpectedly. Namely, a part of the other area in square shape extends out in the front wall, where people's attention is directed. This never happens in the room interior in the international style, which is based on symmetry. Even in the Japanese Traditional wooden house, which allows asymmetry, the afore-mentioned design never happens in the front wall with one exception, which is not a usual tea room but a special tea room called Zangetsu-tei.

Using Rikyu's Tea Room as an Interface

Rikyu built a tea room, called Irotsuke-kokonoma, in an extremely special room arrangement with interior decor at Rikyu Yashiki (or Rikyu residence) in Jurakutei (Hideyoshi Toyotomi's public/private house) in Kyoto. Firstly, it is unusually spacious, with *kokonoma*, which was 3 mats x 3 mats wide room. Furthermore, the room had a one-step elevated floor, which is something similar to an alcove. On top of that one-step a further elevated floor area was provided in the right corner. The independent column, which was comparable to an alcove pillar, stood on the top floor. The double elevated floor must have been provided, for the occasion of the Emperor's visit, so that a seat on a highest elevation can be offered to the Emperor and Hideyoshi could sit on the lower elevation. Though there was no record that the Emperor stopped by at Rikyu Yashiki upon his visit, Hideyoshi visited this tea room from time to time to enjoy tea.

Four years after Rikyu's death, Jurakutei was demolished, and so was Irotsuke-kokonoma. Rikyu's son, Shouan, newly built Zangetsu-tei on the new site: Irotsuke-kokonoma was reduced by about 10 square meters and the double elevated floor was cut to a single elevated floor. This was also not a usual tea room. Hideyoshi sat on the elevated floor, enjoyed the tea served by Shouan, leaned against the column, and thought of the past Rikyu by viewing the moon at dawn through the overhung windows. This was why the tea room was named as Zangetsu-tei, or the room with the moon at dawn. The independent column in the corner was called *Taikoo-bashira* or a column for Hideyoshi. Fujii must have been inspired by the special floor layout/elevation, which originated from Irotsuke-kokonoma and was well established in Zangetsu-tei. Accordingly, he projected the dining-room at the corner of the main room. I am convinced that the independent column in the corner and the one-step elevated dining floor in Chochikukyo followed the design of Zangetsu-tei. At last, I am confident that the backbone of Chochikukyo is Rikyu's tea room.

My reader may wonder why I, in my first visit, could not confirm such influence of the tea room type-like design/decor which is found in the Drawing-room and other places in Chochikukyo. As a historian of architecture, I cannot jump to the conclusion that it is influenced by tea rooms only with tea room type design. It is normal to consider that it is under the influence of *sukiya* style, not that of tea room. *Shoin* style of architecture was transformed with the influence of Rikyu's tea room and, as a result, *sukiya* style was established. Accordingly, *sukiya* style has certain elements of tea room-like design /decor. Even if tea room-like design/decor is observed, it is not clear whether it is under the influence of tea room or that of *sukiya* style. In case of Chochikukyo, I can confirm that it is influenced by tea room, specifically Rikyu's tea room; the single elevated floor cannot be found in *sukiya* style and is a feature unique to Zangetsu-tei. Asymmetric space created by the elevated floor in Zangetsu-tei has the potential to charm modernistic architects; Fujii introduced asymmetric space in a traditional tea room (also used as parlor) in Senyo-soo, his last work in 1937; Togo Murano introduced it in the parlor in his residence; and Sutemi Horiguchi in the Japanese tatami room for an Empress.

Once we know that Chochikukyo is something to do with Rikyu's tea room, we can guess the origin of the mysterious small shelf which stands on four legs at the bottom right of the front wall in the living-room, next to the room in Zangetsu-tei style. Fujii must have been inspired by the famous hanging shelf in the pantry of Rikyu's Taian. Taian is in the neighborhood of Chochikukyo. For Fujii, who loved The Way of Tea, Taian was familiar architecture. The most important feature of tea rooms, originally created by Rikyu, was the liberal design, not bound by then existing standardized style (namely, *shoin* style) even if they were traditional wooden architecture. Fujii fully learnt the style of such tea rooms, and as a result succeeded in applying a liberal design into the traditional wooden house. This feature of liberal design was vital to Modern Design in Art Nouveau and the following design trends.

Fujii successfully correlated traditional wooden architecture and Modern Design in Chochikukyo, built in 1928, by using Rikyu's tea room as an interface. This case has largely influenced architects of younger generations to try Japanese wooden architecture in Modern style. Sutemi Horiguchi, Antonin Raymond, Junzo Yoshimura, Kunio Maekawa, and Kenzo Tange among others built wooden architecture in Modernism one after another. At the time of Fujii, Modernism architecture around the world was always in reinforced concrete of frame structures. As an exception, in Japan, the techniques of traditional wooden structures were fully utilized to realize the Modernism architecture; this is referred to as Wooden Modernism nowadays. This reference is given with pride that the warmth and sharpness are not felt in reinforced concrete structures or steel structures but only in wooden structures. Even now, Japanese architects are producing modern and refined wooden houses, the root of which dates back to Chochikukyo.

聴竹居
行為に相即する家

深澤 直人（プロダクトデザイナー）

「アフォーダンス」というのはアメリカの認知心理学者ジェームズ・ギブソンが生み出した言葉で、人間が環境の中に見出す意味の事である。例えば椅子の背にジャケットを掛けたり、駅のホームにある柱に身体をもたせかけたり、電車の肘掛けに傘を引っ掛けたりするような、その状況と環境に合わせて人間が無意識にピックアップする意味を指す。それは、その場で自覚せず見出した価値ととることもできるし、また環境が提供する価値とも言える。私は、「状況とその場と人の行為が溶け合った瞬間のこと」と捉えている。もしその駅のホームの柱や電車の肘掛けや椅子の背が、そこで発生する行為を予測してデザインされていたとしたら、それを「行為に溶けるデザイン（Design dissolving in behavior）」ということもできる。その行為とはあくまでもその場で立ち現れる顕著な行為であり、さりげなく差し伸べられた環境の自明の価値のことである。

藤井厚二はその自明の価値をその場に住みながら、そしてその場に居る人の姿と行為を繰り返し思い浮かべながら検証し、聴竹居を生み出したのではないだろうか。現に藤井は聴竹居に先だって平屋の家（第4回住宅）をその北側に建てた。実際には住まなかったが、そこで聴竹居を構想したに違いない。藤井が差し出した家の中に溶け込んだ細かな配慮は、生活してみて初めて気付くものであるようにも思う。その場で生活しながらデザインしないとたどり着かない細かな配慮である。

まずはこの場に家を建てようと思い立った理由があると思う。この場を決めた動機には「ここに住みたい」という直感的な願望、つまり住まう本人の目線と、「ここが建てるのに適した場所だ」という建築家としての経験による知識の集積からくる分析の目線が重なり合っている。「眺め」はここに建てようと思った動機の最初にくるものである。どういう場所に家を建てるのが生態的に適しているかという考察の末に見つけた場であることは言うまでもない。南に下って行く高台に佇み、180度開けた視界を見ながら考えたに違いない。思えばその場に佇み、住みながらそこに建てるべき建物の概念を考え出そうとする建築家が現代にどれくらいいるだろう。ただ奇抜な箱を建てようとしているとしか思えないような建築ばかりがはびこる現代から比べれば、藤井はそこに腰を据えてその場で営まれる生活の行為・行動の細部に身体感覚を繰り返し合わせていったに違いない。

その場に居て考えるということが、如何に生理的に適したものを建てるのに重要か。図面を渡されて考え始めるのとは大きく異なる。建物を考えるのではなく、その場の持つ雰囲気を感じ取るのである。どの位置に佇むか、である。

私は1000坪ほどの渓谷の雑木林を買ってそこに小屋を建てた経験がある。まず地形は俯瞰できない。草ぼうぼうでどこまでが自分の土地かもわからない。まずは草むらに分け入り、3本の高い木の根本にある小さくやや平らな場所にテントを張った。そこに寝て夜の星を見、朝の光や夕暮れの日差しを味わった。火を起こしてコーヒーを入れたが、そのカップを置く平らな場所がない。ごろついた石の上のわずかな平らな部分にコーヒーカップを置いた。最初に見出したアフォーダンスである。その隣の石に腰掛けた向きは、自然に少し前に下った南の方角だった。左に川のせせらぎの音が聞こえた。自分の身体の感覚を研ぎ澄まし、環境が差し伸べたその場の価値を探しながら小屋を建てる場所を決めていった。この土地を切り開いた後にわかったのは、この小屋を建てた場所が如何に適正な場所だったかということである。そこから見える遠目の視界と近くにある木々や垣根、さらに近くの窓の縁など、目は視線を遠ざけたり近づけたりしながら居心地のバランスを読み取って行く。その場に佇んで住む場を決めるということは、そういう行為の積み重ねだ。前に降り、視界が開け、背に山を置くという場は、極めて生態的な居場所の定義である。

藤井が大山崎の天王山の麓に1万2000坪の土地を購入したのは、環境が差し出す価値をアフォーダンスとして読み取ったからだろう。坂の上の高台から南の眼下には、木津川、桂川、宇治川が合流して淀川となる三川合流部が広がる。これを見、窓越しに180度の視界を確保するために、建物の縁側の両角までをガラスにして角に桟を入れなかったのも、庭を扇型にして木を植えず芝を植えたのも、聴竹居がここに建つべくして建った必然の成り立ちのような気がする。ここにこれだけの広さの土地を購入したのは、住居のデザインの実験場となる思いにかなった条件が揃っていたからに違いない。何を建てるかの前にどこに建てるかが思いの始まりで、ひいては人がどこに、どの向きに立つか、佇むかの点から聴竹居の構想が広がっていったと思う。

藤井の考える「住まう」

建築家というのは外から見た建物の形を気にするあまりにその場に佇むということを怠っている場合が少なくない。建物がまだ建ってないわけだから空想するしかないが、外観はアフォーダンスの集積によって自然に成るものである。場という自己の周囲が建物に成って行くという概念は、藤井が最も大切にしていたことに違いない。藤井は身体が環境から受け取る価値を感じ取るセンサーの感度が人一倍高かったといえよう。そこで環境が差し伸べている価値を受け取ることができない場合は、建てようとするものや作ろうとするもののイメージが先行して場の力との間に誤差が生まれ、その場に相応しくない、あるいはそぐわないものができてしまう。これに人は違和感を感じる。

相即とは華厳思想で「万物が互いに他の全事物を含みこんで、一体として存在していること」をさす。「居る」という行為に相即することが建物を建てるということである。この「自然に成る」ということがものづくりでは難しい。自分の思い描く通りにものを作りたくなってしまい、「相即」ということを怠ってしまうのだ。ものづくりには「通例」というのがあって、それに靡いてしまうから同じような住宅がたくさんできてしまう。例えばそれは和風とか洋風といった形式のことである。和洋を問わず過去の形式に影響を受けないということはないが、藤井はこの通例とか形式というものを疑ったのではないかとも思う。むしろ行為の流れを薄切りにし、それに従って立ち現れてくる自然な行為からくる機能との相互作用(インタラクション)に重きを置き、それを見逃さなかったのだと思う。その椅子に座り目をやる先に何があればいいか、玄関で傘をたたみどこに立て掛けるように身体が動くか、といったようなことを連続して読み取っていったに違いない。夏を主体に考えねばならない日本の建築の条件も気候風土が差し出す調和の意味である。そのために自然の空調として地下を通した冷気を取り入れる「導気口」を設置していることも、軒を長くしていることも見逃せない。

　聴竹居はとかく和風に洋風の感覚を取り入れたとか、「なになに風」という評価をされがちであるが、現実にはこれは純粋に住宅の在り様を突き詰めた家の提案で、藤井自らの実験空間である。生活は時代背景を反映しているから聴竹居もその時代の背景に溶け込んでいることは間違いないが、単純に和様式とか洋様式と称することはおかしい。

　その証拠に、藤井はインテリアに自らデザインした椅子や照明なども置いている。客室の椅子の構造や骨格は、和装で座れる深い座面とし、帯の厚みを飲み込める形になっている。家全体の配置や人の動線全体をグローバルとすれば、ふと目をやった先にある小さな情景やそこにある什器、扉を閉じた時の閉まり具合とか窓の桟の細さとそこに刺す一本の細いピンのような鍵といった細部はローカルと言える。藤井はグローバルとローカルとが溶け合った空間を生み出したのである。決して家を個体と捉え、外観のスタイルとしてデザインをしようとはしなかった。

　住まう人の体験を写真にすることはできない。写真では説明ができない。藤井が考えた「住まう」ということは、行為の跡をテクスチャーにすることだった。だから迷路を抜けてその向こうに驚きが待っているというようなアトラクション的な驚きはそこにはない。全てが営むという機能の塊なのである。佇む、営む、ということが居るということになり、住まうということになるのである。それは飾るとか愛でる家ではない。藤井は家族で集い、住まう、ということを聴竹居の基本コンセプトにしたと聞くが、例えば子供の勉強部屋と自分の書斎を一緒にしていることにも、共に過ごすという営みの共有が現れている。それは近年の、子供がダイニングテーブルで勉強し、親もそこで仕事をするという潮流に似ている。しかもその勉強部屋・書斎が縁側側に位置しているのも、南の陽に近い側にダイニングを置く現代の自然体と似ている。

　反対に聴竹居のダイニングは山側に位置している。ほっこりとした穴のような空間は、団欒の穴である。実際に入り口はアーチ型をしている。その穴の隣にキッチンがあるがそれ以外の部屋の色とは異なり真っ白である。バウハウスのデッサウのマイスターハウスに建てられた女性を家事労働から解放する為の実験的なキッチンを想わせる。作業場であり水や火を使い行動の激しいユーティリティーが結合した場所であるから、他の部屋の落ち着きのイメージとは異なる清潔感を求めて白くしたのだろう。作業場的である。行為の導線状に全てのものが配されている。鍋を引っ掛ける位置まで決まっている。

　創作欲はアフォーダンスの発見によってもたらされる。藤井は、その場で人はどう行動し、何に目をやり、何を思うかを創意創作の源泉にしている。その細部の集合体としてのアンビエンスを結果として醸し出そうとしている。イームズの「細部は全体を決定する要素である」といったような意味の言葉を思い出す。

　美とは何を指すのだろう。スタイルだろうかコンポジションだろうか。デザインや建築でとかく捉えられがちな概念が、形や色や素材やプラン（配置）であることは言うまでもないが、行為に相即すること、それによって醸し出される場の雰囲気が、作られた全ての調和が美を成すということを聴竹居から学ぶことができる。

　とにかくここは美しく居心地のいい場なのである。

Chochikukyo
—Residence in Perfect Interfusion with Behavior

Naoto Fukasawa (Product Designer)

Affordance is a term coined by James J. Gibson, American cognitive psychologist, and its meaning relates to possible transactions between human beings and their environment. Affordance refers to the meaning people unconsciously pick up by adapting a situation and an environment. For example, a person puts his/her jacket on the chair back; a person leans against a column on the station platform; or a person hangs his/her umbrella on an armrest in the train. Affordance can be interpreted as a value identified at a place without self-consciousness, or can be a value that the environment offers. I understand affordance as a moment when the situation, the place, and people's behavior dissolve all together at once. In case a column on the station platform, an armrest in the train, or a chair back has been designed anticipating the behavior to be accrued, such design may be said as design dissolving in behavior. The aforementioned behavior is one manifested at the place, and is a self-evident value of an environment which is extended naturally.

I guess that Koji Fujii verified the self-evident value while living at the place, and repeatedly visualizing the people residing at the place and their behavior. From this study, he produced Chochikukyo. Prior to Chochikukyo, Fujii built a single-story house (the 4th house) to the north of the potential Chochikukyo site. Though he did not live in that house, he could have mapped out Chochikukyo while there. Attention to the details dissolved in the house which Fujii extended can be only realized after living in it. Such detailed attentions cannot be reached unless he lives at the place while designing the house.

Firstly, there should be the reasons why he thought of building a residence at that place. His intuitive desire to live here, namely, the perspective of the resident himself, and the analytical perspective which was triggered by an accumulation of knowledge through experience as an architect that this is the place suitable to build the residence are interlocked. View came first to motivate him to build the house in that particular place. Needless to say, he found the site after giving due consideration of a place for residence, which fits to his mode of life. Fujii must have stood still on a high point sloping down in a southern direction with a 180 degree wide open view. I wonder how many architects nowadays conceptualize the building to be built while standing still and living on the place. In comparison to these days, when the only thoughtful motive of dominant architecture is to build something unusual, Fujii must have settled down at the place, and repeatedly connected the details of behavior and actions in daily life with his physical sensitivity. How important it is to reside and think at the place in order to build something physiologically fitting. What a huge difference this is from thinking only after receiving architectural drawings. It is not to visualize a building but to feel the ambience of the location. The issue is where to stand still.

I had an experience of buying about 3,300 square meters of thickly wooded area at a gorge and there I built a cabin. In the beginning, I could not overlook the landform. I could not tell where my land ended because of overgrown weeds. First of all, I went into the grass and set up a tent in a small rather flat area at the foot of three tall trees. I slept there, looking at the stars by night, and enjoyed the morning light and twilight sunlight. I built a fire for a cup of coffee, but I could not find the flat space to put the cup. I put the coffee cup on a shallow flat space on the rumbling stone; affordance which I first found out. I sat down on a neighboring stone naturally looking southward with the land sloping down. On the left, I could hear the murmuring of the stream. I finely honed my physical senses, searched the value of the place which the environment extended and decided where to build a cabin. I discovered that I had made a rational selection of the place for the cabin after I cleared the area. I shifted my eyes from distance to close, back and forth; distant views from that place, close by trees/hedges, and window frames closer still so that balance of intimacy could be found. Deciding on the place to live, by standing still at the place, is to accumulate such behavior. The place with the front sloping down for open views, with a mountain at the back is the definition of an extremely ecological place for a place to reside.

Fujii bought 46,280 square meters land at the foot of Tennozan, Oyamazaki, as he probably read the value of the environment as affordance. From a high point on the hill top, three-river conflux, the Kizu, the Katsura, and the Uji, flowing down as the Yodo, is spread out in south. To view the conflux, and to secure the 180 degree range clear view through the windows, huge window glazings are installed up to the both corners of the house verandah without frame in the corners. The garden is made in the shape of a folding fan with a lawn and not trees. All of the aforementioned arrangement makes me feel that Chochikukyo was built, at this place, just as it was meant to be. Fujii bought this spacious land as it satisfies the conditions for the wish to build a house as an experimental venue for residential design. The wish originated from where to build before visualizing what to build. Then, I think, Chochikukyo was gradually visualized from the points where, and facing which direction, people stand and remain standing.

Fujii's Understanding of "To Live In"

Many architects care too much about the exterior form of a building and fail to stand still at the place. As the building has yet to be built, what architects can do is to picture it in his/her mind. The exterior appearance is completed as a natural course of accumulation of affordance. Fujii cherished the concept that his surroundings, namely the place, would gradually form a building. Fujii can be said to have an exceptional sensibility in sensing the value his body received from the environment. In the case of a person who cannot receive value the environment extends, an image of a building to be built, or items to be produced, comes first, which leads to error(s) accrued against the power of a place.

The resulted building/products are neither fitting nor suitable for the place, which in turn creates a sense of discomfort.

In *Kegon* doctrine (Flower Garland School of Buddhism), "perfect interfusion is mutual containment and interpenetration of all phenomena; All in one". To perfectly interfuse with a behavior to reside means to build a building. It is difficult to complete as a natural course in making objects. We tend to make a thing just as what we envision it. In other words, we miss perfect interfusion. There is common sense in making objects, and we yield to such common sense. This results in making many similar houses: for example, in the style such as Japanese or Western. We cannot avoid being influenced by the styles in the past regardless of being Japanese or Western. I assume that Fujii questioned such common sense or styles in the past. Rather he sliced the flow of behavior. He emphasized, and did not miss, the interaction between the sliced behavioral flow and resulted functions provided by the natural behavior. When he sat on the chair, what was preferable to be seen? In furling an umbrella at the entrance, how did the body move to rest it. He must have read these interactions continuously. The condition of Japanese architecture which prioritizes summer time means the harmony extended by the climate. We cannot overlook an open air intake for natural cooling, which is provided by pulling chilled air from underground plus deep overhanging eaves.

Though Chochikukyo is often appreciated as introducing Western sense in the Japanese style or as so and so style, in reality, Chochikukyo is a proposal Fujii made after pure and serious pondering how a house should be, namely it is an experimental space for and by Fujii himself. As lifestyle reflects the background of the times, Chochikukyo is indeed dissolved in the background of the times. It would be improper to label it simply Japanese style or Western style.

Proof of this is shown in the fact that Fujii placed self-designed chairs and lighting fixtures in the interior space. The structure and skeleton of the chairs in the guest room have deep seats to enable a person in Japanese attire to sit and the form is designed so that the depth of *obi* (a sash for traditional Japanese dress) is accommodated. When the total layout of the house, and the people's circulation path is referred to as global, the details such as a small scene close by, for example household utensils, a degree of convenience when a door is closed, slender window frames and fine pin-like keys put in the frames can be referred to as local. Fujii created the space dissolving something global with local. He regarded a house as an individual's personal space, and never tried to design from the exterior style.

Personal experience of a resident, who lives in a house, cannot be explained by still pictures. Still pictures cannot show images of experience. For Fujii, living in a house is to texturize the traces of behavior. Accordingly, there are no attraction-type surprises as waiting at the other side of the maize. Everything and anything is a cluster of functions of living a life. Standing still and living a life are equivalent to residing, and then to living. It is not the house to decorate or to view. I heard that Fujii's basic concept of Chochikukyo is to get together and live in a house with his family members. Sharing to live a life, for example, is revealed in his integrating of the children's reading-room with his own study. This is among recent trends where kids study on the dining table while their parents work on it, too. Furthermore, Fujii placed the study along the verandah, which also resembles the natural setup nowadays to have a dining room on the south side of the house with maximum sunshine. In contrast, Chochikukyo has the dining room on the mountain side. A relaxing and soothing cave-like space is a cave for a familyfs happy circle. The dining entry, in fact, is arch shaped. The kitchen next to the dining cave is in pure white, different from the color scheme of other rooms. This reminds me of the experimental kitchen built in Meister House in Dessau, Bauhaus, which was designed to liberalize women from household works. In the kitchen, which is the working space, water and fire are used and active utilities are combined. As a result, Fujii picked up the white color scheme for the kitchen for cleanliness, unlike the intimate image prevailing in other rooms. Everything in the kitchen is lined up along the circulation route of behavior. Even a place to hang a pan is set.

Discovery of affordance urges us to create. Fujii's ingenious devices originated from thinking how a person acts, what he/she sees, and then what he/she thinks at that place. He was trying to create ambience, aggregate of the resulted details, which reminds me of Eames' words meaning something like that "details are factors to decide the whole".

What does aesthetics refer to? Is it style or composition? It goes without saying that form, color scheme, and plan (layout) are the usual embodiment of concept in design or architecture. We can learn from Chochikukyo that perfect interfusion with people's behavior created ambiance of the place and overall total harmony, both of which consist aesthetics.

Indeed, Chochikukyo is a beautiful and intimate space.

聴竹居が伝えるもの

堀部 安嗣（建築家）

　残暑厳しい晩夏に聴竹居を再訪した。山崎駅で電車を降り、踏切を渡り、大山崎の山を登る。ふうっと息を整え、汗を拭き、そして聴竹居の入り口の石段を登ると、そこには築90年の住宅が私を迎えてくれた。
　一朝一夕では決してつくることのできない独特の気配と匂い。しかし、その気配は人に警戒を与えることなく、自然に人を受け入れてくれる寛容さを持ち合わせている。
　一通り室内を巡り、以前訪れた時と何ら変わらないありようを確認して、庭に出た。大樹の木陰の下に佇む透明感のある住宅を一人見上げていると、様々な感慨が込み上げてくる。
　昭和3年（1928年）に完成した聴竹居は、昭和〜平成という時代を生き抜いた歴史の証人のようであり、あるいは来るべき時代を見据えて建築の価値を未来に示した予言者のようでもある。太平洋戦争を挟んだこの激動の90年間に及ぶ歴史の中で、様々な出来事があり、そして様々な建築の動きや考え方、そして価値が泡のように生まれ、消えていった。聴竹居はそれらの動きを長年見守りながらも、その揺るぎない価値を静かに伝え続けてきた。そして今、人や時代が本当に建築に求めるものが、この聴竹居のもつ価値であることに巡り巡って、もう一度気づいたようにも思う。
　そんな感慨で聴竹居を眺め続ける。すると建物がまるで90歳を迎えた老師のように見えてくる。しかし、そこには説教臭さや、鈍重な威厳はない。後に続いた弟子の様々な表現を否定するわけでも、かつ認めるわけでもなく、老師が誰よりも建築を一人で存分に楽しんでおられるかのようだ。何者にも煩わされず、何にもとらわれることのない様子は90歳になっても軽やかで、若々しく、そして瑞々しい。その生き方、考え方の極意を老師に問うても"答えは君の心の中にある"とニコリと笑われそうだ。そんな老師のことをまったくの若輩者の自分が語るのは、とても難しく無謀なことである。やはり、老師を前にして自分は何一つわかっておらず、何も見えていないと思えてしまうからだ。しかし、聴竹居との思い出から少しずつ言葉を綴りはじめることで、少しでも目の前が明るくなってゆくことを試みてみよう。

出会いの想い出

　私がはじめて聴竹居の存在を知ったのは、今から30年ほど前、大学の図書館で手にした本の中だった。昭和51年（1976年）発刊の新建築臨時増刊『昭和住宅史』（新建築社）である。多くの人々に読み込まれ、いささかくたびれたその本に出会うやいなや、貸し出し手続きを済ませて下宿に持ち帰り、その誌面を食い入るように眺めたことを今でも鮮明に覚えている。本の発刊から10年ほど経った頃の話である。
　昭和の50年間の日本住宅史を振り返り、まとめることを目的としたその本の巻頭を大きく飾っていたのが、昭和のはじまりとともにできた聴竹居だった。それまで語られはしたけれども、実作を写真等で紹介されることがほとんどなかったこの住宅の発掘を、この本の目玉としていたようだ。本の編集後記で編集者の石堂威氏は1976年当時、聴竹居に対してこう記している。
　「その住宅を見たとき、50年間につくられてきた住宅の多くが一瞬に聴竹居に帰ってくるような感慨を覚えたのでした」
　まさに聴竹居からはじまり、そして聴竹居に帰るのが昭和のこの50年の日本住宅史だ、と記している。今、我々が聴竹居に感じていることはすでに40年前にも感じられていたのだ。バブルの時代を経て、時代は平成に移ってゆく中でまた聴竹居の価値はいったん忘れられ、大きく一周りして人の興味は聴竹居のもつ価値に戻ってきたのである。
　一方、まだ建築の歴史をあまり知らず、造詣のなかった当時の私はといえば、その古ぼけた聴竹居の写真からはあまり魅力を感じることはできなかった。誌面に載っていた平面図も、いくら当時の暮らしを想像しても合点のゆくものではなく、理解が難しかった。その時の私の目には昔の出来事の中での昔の住宅、としか目に映らなかったのだろう。また当時、斬新であった和洋折衷の表現が聴竹居において先駆的になされていると言われても、どっぷりと和洋折衷や洋の生活スタイルに囲まれている自分が、当時のことをいくらイメージしてもその斬新さを実感することができなかった。しかし、巻頭言を書いた横山正氏の昭和の住宅史に関する考察が大変興味深かった。
　「この50年のあいだに日本の住宅にどれだけのものが蓄積され、ゆたかな実りを上げていったかと考えると、正直なところいささか暗澹たる気持ちにおそわれずにはいられない。（中略）日本の住宅は結局これだけのものしかつくり出し得なかったのか、という想いが込みあげてくる」と。
　そして「住むというこの人間の根源的な行為についてのはっきりとした主張が、おそらく住み手の側にも建築家の側にも欠けているのである」と横山氏は書いている。
　昭和50年間の住宅を賞賛する本と思って読んだら、そこには住み手や建築家に対する苦言が呈されていたことに私は驚き、そしてその言葉に深く共感した。今まで自分が抱いていた建築家の設計する建築への疑問と重なったのだ。華々しく斬新な住宅が次々と作られるが、等身大の人の営為や風土、環境に繋がったものとは感じられなかった。それら根のない建築は、建築家が言葉を尽くして主張するには不釣り合いなほど、あっという間に賞味期限が切れると

も感じていた。ゆえに建築の技術、文化が蓄積されず、行き当たりばったりの脆弱で貧しい様相を呈していたのが、昭和の日本の建築という見方を強めてしまった。時に私が横山氏の言葉を読んだのは、バブル経済絶頂期であったこととも大きかった。

建築の何を信じるのか、建築の本当の価値はどこにあるのか、そのことがわからなくなっていた。そんな自分にとって、この昭和住宅史の貧しさをバブル以前から指摘した横山氏の言葉は"自分の感覚は間違っていなかったのだ"と肩をポンと叩いてくれたような、そんな励ましをもらったようだった。そして横山氏は、そんな貧しい50年間の中にも建築家の手による充実した素晴らしい住宅は存在すると語り、その代表として聴竹居を紹介していたのだった。聴竹居には住宅建築の本質が詰まっており、時代に適合しながらも時代を超えてゆく魅力が凝縮されているというのだ。そのことを今から40年前に書いている。

それから聴竹居は自分の中でどこか気になる存在であり続けた。今思えば、誌面の写真や平面図からは残念ながら魅力を感じられなかった自分にとって、いつかその魅力を感じられる時が来ることを、自分の一つの目標にしようとしていたのかもしれない。

実際に聴竹居を訪れることができたのは、誌面ではじめて聴竹居を見たときから20年後のことである。実際に出会った聴竹居は今まで想像してきたものとは大きく異なっていた。脳裏に焼きついていた古ぼけた写真は、意識の中で一瞬に遠くに捨て去られた。実体はあまりにも鮮明で色っぽく、軽やかだったからだ。

もちろん、聴竹居の全てを受け入れられたわけではない。空間の重心が分散されているところや過剰で濃厚なディテールなどは自分の好みと異なるところもあった。しかし、そのような個人的な経験からの好みを超えた、もっと客観的な魅力への興味と眼差しが自然と大きくなっていったと言えばいいだろうか。

同時に、時代はもう一度ここに戻ってきた、と感じさせる現代性あるいは先駆性を身体で一瞬に感じられたことが嬉しかった。はたしてその先駆性は一体どういうところにあるのだろう。

誤解を恐れずに言えば、聴竹居の魅力は日本における建築の当たり前を、当たり前に表現した魅力である。設計者の藤井厚二の思想、実践、表現はどんな時代でも変わることのない、ものづくりへの無垢な喜びであり、風土の中で建築が背負っている宿命を謙虚に表したものであり、そして等身大の日本人の心身の"居心地の感覚"を忠実に追求したものである。今はこの当たり前のことの難しさや大切さをもう一度気付ける状況にあると思うが、時にこの当たり前の価値は忘れ去られ、有象無象の表現や虚飾を身にまとった建築が世の中を席巻してゆく。

中国の書『韓非子』に次のような故事がある。王様が宮廷画家に"描きやすいものは何か？ 描きにくいものは何か？"と質問をすると画家は"鬼は描きやすく犬は描きにくい"と答える。鬼のような架空の動物はデタラメを描いても、そのデタラメを観る人が指摘することなく、むしろそのデタラメを喜んでくれる。しかし、犬のように実体のある身近な動物は筋肉や骨、そして動き、性格などを知り尽くして描かなければ観る人から変だと言われてしまう。ゆえに犬を描くにはよほどの洞察力、観察眼、そして修練が必要になるのであるが、そんな故事に例えると、藤井の実践はまるで犬を描くような行為だったと言えないだろうか。日本の風土、環境を正確に知り、日本人の動き、心理を的確に読み取り、手間を惜しまず、地味と思えることをしつこく、しつこく建築の表現に落とし込んでゆく。しかし、このような手法の先にしか、人に長きにわたって飽きられることのないものは決して生まれないことも、我々に教えてくれる。反対に、風土、環境を無視し、人の心身への洞察に欠けた建築表現はあっという間に廃れてしまうことも、我々は嫌というほど学んできたはずだ。つまり、現実的で実体的でなくては生き延びられない建築は、鬼を描く行為ではなく犬を描く行為から生まれてこなければならないのだ。

究極のパッシブデザイン

エネルギー問題、環境問題が深刻化した昨今、この時代の建築デザインの進むべき方向を示す言葉に"パッシブデザイン"がある。エコ建築、省エネ建築といった概念もこのパッシブデザインの概念に含まれるように思う。この概念と実践は現代において、ドイツなどが先駆とされているが、それよりずっと前から日本建築が大切にしてきて、実践してきたデザインそのものなのである。パッシブデザインという言葉や概念などはなくても自然と実践されていたことに日本建築のユニークさと先進性がある。このパッシブデザインの手法を狭義に簡単に説明すれば、それは冬の日射取得、夏の日射遮蔽、断熱・気密の強化ということである。

環境や自然と一体となることを主題とした日本建築は、このことを高いレベルで意匠と両立させてきた。あるいはそのためのデザインのみで、シンプルに、必然的に建築が作られていると言っても過言ではない。

夏の日差しを遮る屋根庇を出し、しかしその庇の長さを慎重に検討して冬の低い日差しは取り入れる。また、夏の庇では防ぎきれない日射は葦簾や庭の落葉樹などで防ぐ。冬の断熱のために障子や戸で挟まれた縁側という断熱・気

密層を設ける。同時に、その戸や障子を開け放てば、そこは夏においての快適な人の居場所になる。屋根にはたくさんの葦を重ねたり、瓦という性能の高い屋根材で断熱を図り、熱のロスを防ぐ。

その結果、少ないエネルギー、少ない要素で快適な環境がつくれるようになるのだが、藤井はこの日本建築がすでに持っていたパッシブデザインの手法を土台にして、建築家として、研究者として、科学的、実験的な検証を重ねてパッシブデザインを進化させていったと言えるだろう。また、その結果の表現は意匠性の高さとあいまって、実験という言葉から連想される中途半端さや質の低さは微塵もなく、科学の先にある情緒を感じさせるものになっていることに驚く。意匠と性能の両立が極めて高いレベルで実現している。このことこそ今、人々が建築に期待していることであり、私がこれから腰を据えて取り組みたい建築のアプローチとピタリと重なるのである。

90年前の先駆性が今、注目され見直されている。

一方で私は、狭義のパッシブデザインの概念を超えた広義のパッシブデザインを藤井の建築に感じていたのだが、藤井が設計に関わったとされている福山、鞆の浦の後山山荘を暑い夏に訪ねてそのことが明らかになった。

風光明媚であり、爽やかな風が海から上がってきて、かつ西日を後ろの山が防いでくれる後山山荘の土地は、パッシブデザインのためには申し分ない土地だったからである。ここでは建築はもう何もしなくてよい。ただただ環境に胸を借りるように、すでにあるものを生かすように、受け身になって素直につくればよいのだ。

また、木津川、桂川、宇治川からの水面を渡る涼しい風が上がってくる大山崎の土地を藤井が選んだことも、建築の最も大切な"はじまりのデザイン"として実に的確であったということが見えてくる。

つまり、究極のパッシブデザインは、その目的にふさわしい土地を選ぶということなのだ。藤井には、建築設計の基本中の基本にある"土地を見る眼"が、最も高いレベルで備わっていたのである。

言われてみれば当たり前のことだが、現代建築はそのことを忘れがちになり、技術によって強引にねじ伏せながらアクティブに解決させようとしているのではないだろうか。例えば、本当に地震に強い建物が欲しければ杭を打ったり、免震構造にする前に地盤のいい土地や平屋が建てられる土地を選ぶべきである。本当に夏涼しく、冬暖かい建物が欲しければ、風通しが良く日当たりのいい土地を選ぶべきである。土地選びから建築がはじまり、そのはじまりこそがすべてなのだ。現存する優れた日本の寺院建築や民家などを振り返ってみると、建物の素晴らしさ以上に建てられた場所の素晴らしさが際立っている場合がほとんどである。もちろん、様々な技術によって土地のハンディキャップを克服することも大切なことであるが、費用がかかり、エネルギーを費やし、その方法と形は複雑化してゆく。その姿は結果として、日本の風景や風土にそぐわない不自然なものになる危険性をはらんでいる。

日本の人口が急増し、住宅供給難であった時代には、ハンディキャップを抱えた土地に住むことも仕方なかったのかもしれない。しかし、これからは人口や経済は縮小し、空き家、空き地が増えてゆく時代になることは必至である。もう一度、人は少ないエネルギーで効率よく暮らすことを真剣に考えなければならず、そのためには土地、風土、環境を見る目を養わなければならないことが明白であるように思う。先端技術に安易に頼らず、環境や土地への感覚を研ぎ澄ませ、そこから建築を考えてゆけば自然とパッシブデザインが行われ、結果として日本の風土や風景が継承され、さらには自然災害による被害も抑えられてゆくように思う。

そんな現代の課題を克服してゆくためにも、藤井の眼差しと聴竹居が表現し続けてきたことに注目したい。

我々は随分遠回りをした。無駄なこともたくさんした。たくさんのお金を使って遊びに遊んだ。多くのものを手に入れ、そしてそれ以上に多くのものを失った。

しかし、もう失敗は許されないところまできている。次の失敗は千年以上にわたって脈々とつながってきた日本の建築、風土、風景の終焉を意味するように思う。今まで繋げてきたバトンを我々が生きてきた世代によって、次の世代に渡すことができないことになる。日本建築というリレーは我々が終わらせてしまうことになる。

建物という単体で建築を考える時代は、すでに終わっている。誰もがその限界と行き詰まりを感じているはずだ。

風土、風景、環境、歴史、その継承の中に建築が淀みなく溶け込んでゆくために持久力のある優れた建築と歴史をしっかりと学び、もう一度"建築とは何か""建築の役割とは何か""建築の価値とは何か"、そのことを誰もが自問しなければならない。

What Chochikukyo Conveys

Yasushi Horibe (Architect)

I visited Chochikukyo again during late summer amid the lingering summer heat. I got off the train at Yamazaki station, went over the crossing, and climbed Oyamazaki mountain. I caught my breath, mopped my brow, and went up the stone steps, then the 90 year-old residence welcomed me. Unique intimation and perfume, which cannot be created over night : such feeling embraces generosity, which casually accepts the people without cautioning them. I made one round of the residence interior, and affirmed that its state was intact since my previous visit, and went out to the garden. I was by myself, looking at the residence with a feeling of transparency, which stands under the shade of a big tree, various things stirred up inside me.

Chochikukyo, completed in 1928, is like a witness of history surviving the era Showa (1926~1989) to Heisei (1989~2019), or is like a prophet, looking at the coming years, who demonstrates the value of architecture for the future. During the past nine decades, including the Pacific War, with drastic changes, in the context of architecture, wide-ranging views, movements, and/or value have been occurred and disappeared like bubbles. Chochikukyo, long watching over such movements, has quietly conveyed its firm value. At last nowadays, people and the current times are reminded that what they are looking for in the architecture in true sense coincides with the value of Chochikukyo.

I keep viewing Chochikukyo with the afore-mentioned deep emotion. Then the residence starts appearing as a 90 year-old senior teacher. Having said that, this senior teacher's message does not sound like discourse nor does he have an oppressive dignity. He neither denies nor approves various expressions made by his followers. The senior teacher looks as if he is enjoying architecture from the bottom of his heart. He seems to be neither bothered by nor does he adhere to anything: he looks graceful, youthful, and fresh although at the age of 90. Even if he is asked about the hidden essence of his way of life and thinking, he may say that the answer lies in one's heart, with a smile on his face. It is inconsiderate and difficult for me, a novice, to talk about such a senior teacher. In front of the senior teacher, I cannot stop thinking that I neither appreciate nor see the truth. Still I would like to clarify the perspectives by composing words from my memory with Chochikukyo.

Memory of How I Encountered Chochikukyo

The first time I learned about the existence of Chochikukyo was about 30 years ago, about a decade after the book was published in 1976, I picked the book up in the university library: *Showa Jutakushi* (or History of Houses in Showa Era) *Shinkenchiku* Special Issue, *Shinkenchikusha*. It was rather battered after being studied by many people. I still vividly remember that, as soon as I saw it, I went through the check-out procedure and brought it back to the boarding house and devouring every word.

At the beginning of the book, which reviews and summarizes the history of the Japanese houses for five decades in Showa Era, Chochikukyo, as it was created at the start of Showa era, is featured. The discovery of Chochikukyo, which had been the talk of the people but had been rarely introduced with pictures of the actual work product, seems to be the special feature of this issue. The editor, Takeshi Ishido, writes about Chochikukyo in the postscript as follows: "when I saw the residence, I was overcome with emotion in less than a moment as if many houses which had been built in these five decades boiled down to Chochikukyo". Ishido explains that history of Japanese houses in these 50 years of Showa era starts with Chochikukyo and returns back to Chochikukyo. What we feel with Chochikukyo now was described some 40 years ago. In proceeding from Showa to Heisei era with the bubble economy period inbetween, the value of Chochikukyo was once forgotten, but people's interest has returned to the value of Chochikukyo after coming around a big circle.

On the other hand, when I first came to know about Chochikukyo, I was not well versed with the history of architecture, so I could not feel any charm looking at the old pictures of Chochikukyo. The floor plans, which were covered in the book, did not make sense even if I tried to guess the way of life in early Showa era; it was difficult for me to understand its virtues. To me, who was still young, Chochikukyo must have been a house in the past amid the happenings of the past. Furthermore, even if I was told that Chochikukyo was ahead of its time as it was a house that combined Western and Japanese style, I could not feel so in spite of trying to think about the times. It was because I was surrounded by the Japanese and Western style combined or Western life style. Having said that, Tadashi Yokoyama's thoughts on the history of houses in Showa era, covered in the beginning of the book, were quite interesting. He says: "I cannot help feeling gloomy when I think about, in the houses in Japan, how much has been accumulated and how productive they have been. I am seized with a thought that the house in Japan achieved so little, could have achieved much more. Yokoyama also points out that clear assertion about the human being's fundamental behavior may be absent by both the residents and the architects".

I was expecting compliments in the book about the houses of 50 years in Showa, so I was surprised to find complaints addressed both to residents and architects. At the same time, I deeply shared the same opinion. Points raised in the book were the same as the personal questions on the houses designed by the architects I have had in mind until that time. Though glorious and unconventional houses were built one after another, I could not connect them to people's realistic conduct, climate, and environment. There are quite a few examples of architecture which has no roots has become obsolete so soon, even if the architect involved exhausted his/her words to insist that his/her work product would survive forever. Accordingly, in the Japanese architecture in Showa era, architectural technologies and culture were not accumulated. As a result, I regarded such Japanese architecture as fragile and poor in nature, without prior planning. I thought so especially as I read Yokoyama's words at the peak of Japan's bubble economy.

At that time, I was at a loss as to what to believe in architecture and where the true value of architecture lay. Yokoyama, who wrote how poor the history of houses in Japan was during Showa era prior to the bubble economy, encouraged me in my thinking that my sense was not wrong. On the other hand, Yokoyama points out that, even during five decades of poor progress in architecture, there are examples of enriched and excellent houses produced by some architects. Yokoyama 40 years ago refers to Chochikukyo as the leading example of such houses. Yokoyama indicates that Chochikukyo is filled with the essence of domestic architecture. Moreover charm of such essence, which fulfills the requirements of the time yet survives over the times, is condensed in Chochikukyo.

Since then I have been conscious of Chochikukyo. When I look back, I may have set the goal that I can appreciate its charm though at that time I was not attracted by the pictures and floor plans in the book.

I visited Chochikukyo for the first time 20 years ago later I learnt about it from the book. Chochikukyo, standing in front of me, was largely differed from my perception. Aged pictures and floor plans imprinted in my mind were crossed out all at once because the actual Chochikukyo was fresh, erotic, and graceful. It goes without saying that I could not accept everything about Chochikukyo. There were points which were not to my taste, such as diffusion of gravity of space and excessively rich details. On the other hand, when I saw its charm from the objective perspectives, transcending my personal taste, my interest in Chochikukyo which has been cultivated over the years, grew.

At the same time, I was pleased to feel, in an instant, that it was contemporary and pioneering, which in turn made me feel that the times were now returning to appreciating of Chochikukyo. In which sense and part is it pioneering? At the risk of being misunderstood, I think that the charm of Chochikukyo is that something correct in Japanese architecture is expressed in the right way. Fujii's idea, practice, and expressions as an architect/designer originated from pure pleasure to make an object, which is intact regardless of the times, and it is the modest expression of the mission born by the architecture amid the climate. Moreover, his mission faithfully pursues an intimate feel as it really is, both psychologically and physically. Nowadays it is recognized again how difficult and important it is to do something correct. However, such correct value has been forgotten, and architecture in rambling expressions and ostentation has been dominant in the world.

Chinese book, *Kanpishi*, has the following anecdote: A king asked the court painter what was and wasn't easy to paint, then the painter answered that it is easy to paint a demon, but not a dog. In case of such fictitious subject as a demon, even if something ridiculous is painted, observers appreciate it, rather than criticizing it. On the other hand, in the case of a dog, when you know what a dog really is because it is a part of daily life, the observers regard the painting odd, unless the painter has a thorough knowledge of muscle, bones, and movements, as well as character. Accordingly, much insight, an observant eye and discipline are required. Referring to this anecdote, Fujii's practice may be said similar in behavior to painting a dog. Fujii studied the Japanese climate and environment accurately, read the Japanese people's actions and mentality, and reflected on those findings for the architectural expressions, making the best efforts to do something ordinary persistently. At the same time, Fujii taught us that architecture, in which the people never lose interest, can be produced only through the afore-mentioned process. In contrast, we must have realized that architectural expressions which ignore the climate and environment and which fall short of insight into the people's mind and body become obsolete before you know it. Namely, architecture, which can survive only if it is realistic and essential, must be produced from the behavior to paint not a demon but a dog.

Ultimate Passive Design

Recently, energy and the environment have been urgent problems. One of the words to indicate the direction of the architectural design in the future is passive design. Concepts such as eco architecture or energy-saving architecture are covered by the term of passive design. These days, Germany is regarded as a pioneer in its concept and practice, but Japanese architecture has nurtured such concepts and long practiced them. Japanese architecture is unique and pioneers the concept of passive design since it was naturally practiced without reference to a term or a known accepted concept of passive design.

Examples of the passive design technique, in a narrow sense, are to take in the solar radiation in winter; to cut it off during summer; to strengthen insulation and air-tightness. The theme of Japanese architecture has been to incorporate passive design in the environment and nature and it combines the technique to a high level with the interior design. Alternatively, it would be no exaggeration to say that Japanese architecture, in its simple way, as a matter of course, has only ever practiced passive design.

Sunlight in the summer is blocked by projecting roof eaves, while the low sun-light in winter is taken in by carefully calculating the depth of the eaves. Solar radiation which cannot be blocked only by the eaves is cut by reed screens or deciduous tree(s) in the garden. For heat insulation in winter, *engawa*, the insulation and airtight layer, is constructed between *shoji* and door. In summer, the door(s) and *shoji* are opened to make *engawa* a comfortable place for people to stay. On the roof, many reeds are layered or roof tiles which have good insulating performance are installed for insulation to prevent the heat loss in the winter.

The traditional passive design technique in Japanese architecture had produced a comfortable environment, which consumed little energy and used a few elements. Based on these platforms, Fujii, as an architect and as a researcher, repeated the scientific and experimental verification and made further progress. A word, experiment, is often associated with having unfinished parts or being in low quality. In contrast, I am surprised at his expressions as they are in the sophisticated interior design instead; I can feel his emotion over the science. Fujii realized the co-existence of interior design and performance at an extremely high level. This is what people expect architecture to achieve these days. These realizations completely correspond with the approach to architecture which I want to practice from now on. The pioneering efforts made 90 years ago now entertain the attention and the new merits are being found.

On the other hand, I felt the passive design in a wide sense in Fujii's architecture, which superseded the concept of passive design in a narrow sense. When I visited Ushiroyama Sansou (or mountain house), Tomonoura, Fukuyama city (Hiroshima prefecture), which is said to be designed by Fujii, during a hot summer, my impression was clarified.

The scenic site of Ushiroyama Sansou, with refreshing breezes from the sea and with the back mountain blocking the afternoon sun, then there is nothing to desire to practice the passive design. On this site, the architecture does not have any role to play. Rather architecture is built in the passive way just to leave all matters to the environment with a submissive attitude, so as to tap the most and best of what is available. It is clear that Fujii's selection of Oyamazaki with cool breezes from the Kizu, the Katsura, and the Uji for Chochikukyo was just right as the origin of the design, which is most important for architecture. In other words, an ultimate passive design is to select the site which fits the objectives. Fujii possessed excellent vision to see the site, which is the real basis of the architectural design.

It sounds as though it is a matter of course, but contemporary architecture has forgotten the afore-mentioned points and is trying to actively solve various issues by forcibly silencing them with technology. For example, when the building that is strong against an earthquake is required, prior to placing the piles or introducing base-isolated systems, the ground conditions of the site should be examined closely for a selection of a single-story house. In case you want to build the house which is cool in summer and warm in winter, you must select the well-ventilated site getting plenty of sunshine. The architecture starts in selection of the site, and its selection is everything for architecture of the building.

If you review the existing excellent Japanese temple architecture and private houses, the excellence of the sites is more remarkable than the buildings themselves. Of course it is important to overcome any handicap(s) of the site with the various technologies, which increases expense, consumes energy, and makes such measures and the forms more complex. As a result, such attitudes have the large potential risk to produce unnatural buildings that do not blend in the Japanese scenery and/or climate.

In times when houses were in short supply due to drastic population increase in Japan, there were no other options than living on the site in poor conditions. In the future, it is inevitable that the population and economy will be reduced, then vacant houses and lots will increase. We have to think seriously of how to live effectively with less energy. It is clear that we have to nurture the vision to appreciate the land, climate, and environment; instead of easily relying on advanced technologies. If we sharpen our sense to the environment and the land, based on our thoughts about the architecture, the passive design is naturally practiced. As a result, the Japanese climate and scenery will be handed over to the future generations. Furthermore, in my view, the damage caused by natural disasters will be better controlled. I would like to pay due attention to Fujii's vision, namely, what Chochikukyo has expressed to date, in order to overcome the afore-mentioned agenda that the people of today are facing.

We have come a long way round and have done many wasteful things. We have used much money, have played around a lot, and have gained much while losing more than we gained. Now, however, we are at the stage that we are not allowed to make further failures. I think the next failure will end Japanese architecture, climate, and scenery, which have been passed down from generation to generation for over 1,000 years. If we make a failure, our generation cannot pass the baton to the next generation though it has been passed down one way or another up until now. This means that we are to end the relay of Japanese architecture.

The time to think of architecture in the context of the single building is over. Everyone must feel the limit and the dead-end. In order for architecture to naturally blend in the climate, scenery, environment, history, and succession of the past architecture, we should study the excellent architecture which has been preserved for many years and the history of architecture. Any person should question him/her: what is architecture? what is the role of architecture? and what is the value of architecture?

「聴竹居」の歩み

松隈 章

聴竹居との出会い

本当に奇遇、いやご縁とは、まさにこのことを指すのだろう。

1995年に遭遇した阪神淡路大震災が端緒となり、明治を代表する建築家・武田五一が設計した「芝川邸」(1911年竣工・西宮市上甲東園、2007年に博物館・明治村に移築)が半壊し、移築のための実測調査に竹中工務店の有志の一人として参加していなければ、私はけっして藤井厚二にも、聴竹居にも、出逢うことはなかっただろう。

実測調査の結果を報告するとともに、阪神淡路大震災と文化財保護について考える機会とする趣旨で、1996年に竹中工務店大阪本店設計部主催の「芝川邸と武田五一展」(5月27日〜6月14日)が開催された。その図録と展示パネルをまとめる中で、私が主に担当したのが武田と竹中工務店との関係を紹介する部分だった。私はその時に次のことを初めて知った。

1) 武田が藤井を京都帝国大学建築学科の講師に招いたこと。武田は1920 (大正9) 年に創設された京都帝国大学建築学科を創設した一人で、自らも教授を務めたが、その講師として同じ福山の出身で東京帝国大学の後輩にあたる藤井を竹中工務店から引き抜いた。
2) 竹中工務店の黎明期に初めて東京帝国大学を卒業した学士として入社したのが藤井であったこと。藤井は当時最先端のオフィスビル「大阪朝日新聞社」(1916年竣工)などの設計を手掛け、現代に続く設計組織の礎を創った。
3) 武田と藤井は大阪朝日新聞社のプロジェクトでそれぞれ建築主側の顧問と設計担当者として知り合った。

さらに、藤井の代表作で建築関係の雑誌や書籍に紹介されている自邸「聴竹居」(1928年築)という住宅の写真を見て、現存するのであれば、ぜひ一度実物を観てみたいと思うようになっていった。

「芝川邸と武田五一展」開催の1996年頃は今とは違い、美術館でいわゆる「建築展」が開催されることはほとんど無かった時代である。たまたまその時、1920年代という10年間に限った造形美術展、「20世紀日本美術再見II 1920年代」展 (1996年9月14日〜10月20日)を企画していたのが三重県立美術館だった。同館学芸員の桑名麻理 (当時) さんが「芝川邸と武田五一展」開催の情報を得て、6月7日に視察に訪れることになり、私が応対した。

桑名さんと後に結婚することになる筑波大学 (現在教授) の花里俊廣さんの大学時代の同級生が、竹中工務店大阪本店設計部の齋藤昌英さんで、そのつながりからこの展覧会の情報を得たと言う。この視察で建築展の展示方法にヒントをつかんだ桑名さんが帰り際、「1920年代展の建築のコーナーでメインに取り扱ったらよい建物をご存じないですか?」と質問してきた。その時、「藤井厚二の聴竹居があります。1928年の建物です」と私は即答した。美術館での展示が実現すれば、現存する「聴竹居」を見学できるかもしれないという全くの下心からの提案だった。さらに、展示するのであれば、以前セゾン美術館主催の「日本の眼と空間 もうひとつのモダン・デザイン」展 (1990年) で展示された「聴竹居」の図面や写真だけでは新規性に乏しく面白くないので、新たに模型と映像にすべきだとも提案した。

桑名さんが持ち帰ったこの提案は、幸いなことに三重県立美術館の企画会議で通り、実現に至った。模型制作は、竹中工務店大阪本店設計部がいつも発注していて技術に定評のある三浦模型の三浦良雄さんに、映像制作は、広報部が竹中工務店の広報映像をしばしば発注していた麦プロダクションの高岡伸一さんにお願いすることになった。

7月6日の夏の暑い日、三重県立美術館のアポイントで、初めて大山崎の「聴竹居」を訪れた。同行者は三重県立美術館学芸員の土田眞紀さんと桑名さん、建築史家で滋賀県立大学助教授 (当時) の石田潤一郎さん、三浦模型の三浦さんとの4人。当時は80代のご婦人が一人で住み、居室 (リビングルーム) の天井からは蛍光灯がぶらさがり、床にはカーペットが敷かれ、タンスなどの家財道具が満載の状態だった。しかし、夏の本当に暑い日だったにもかかわらず、とても涼しく感じたこと、さらに、和風でもなく、と言って洋風でもない日本の住宅の近代的な新しいデザインの在り方の凛とした佇まいに驚き、感動したこと、このふたつの衝撃を昨日のことのように思い出す。私自身も建築家として、1920年代にすでに「日本の住宅」にふさわしいデザイン、環境に配慮した設計をする建築家がいたこと、しかも、その人が竹中の先輩であったことに驚かされた。こうして小さな願望が実り、1996年夏に「聴竹居」を初めて訪れることができたのである。

幻の名作住宅

出会うや「聴竹居」という建物の不思議な魅力にとりつかれた私は、その後さまざまに調べていく中で、建築家・藤井厚二の想いの奥深さにさらに引き込まれることになる。少しも大げさではなく、私は藤井の住宅建築を通して、日本、日本人、日本の建築、日本の住宅、そして、世界に誇る「日本」の存在までを教えてもらうことになった。

竹中工務店において藤井は、初めて東京帝国大学卒の設計社員として知られている。先述したように、竹中時代に同じ福山出身の先輩、武田五一と知り合い、京都帝国大

学建築学科の創設に誘われる。竹中を退社後の1919（大正8）年から1920年には欧米視察に出かけ、当時の最先端の建築スタイルのアールデコやモダニズムの萌芽に直に触れ、最新式の建築設備を目にしてきた。

その藤井に、1923（大正12）年に起こった関東大震災の惨状は大きな衝撃を与えた。地震発生から3週間後の東京に立った藤井は、「無条件で外国の建築を受けいれたものが、我国の気候風土に対して、如何なる結果を齎すかは、申迄もなく明らかなことです」と述べ、いっそう「日本」の気候風土を強く意識するところとなった。今で言う環境工学の最初期の理論書といえる『日本の住宅』（岩波書店）を著したのは1928（昭和3）年のことで、この序文には「本書の結論と称すべきもの」として第5回目住宅（後に「聴竹居」と名付けられる）を建設中であることが告げられている。

つまり「聴竹居」こそが、日本の住宅の理想として藤井が提示した到達点だと言えるだろう。しかしながら「聴竹居」は、藤井が1938（昭和13）年に49歳という若さで亡くなったことや、個人の住宅であったがゆえに、長らく知る人ぞ知る「幻の名作住宅」であった。

そうした中にあって、藤井と「聴竹居」を最初に大きく取り上げた建築評論が、小能林宏城（法政大学）の「大山崎の光悦 藤井厚二論」（新建築臨時増刊『昭和住宅史』1976年11月所収）である。小能林氏は、「数寄屋建築あるいは茶室建築のもつ自由さや住宅建築に適したスケール感を、彼なりに消化して、もうひとつ別のものに転身させているのである。そして、この"転身"あるいは"転形"は、性急に藤井のさまざまな造形産物を、"日本的"と呼ばせるのも拒むものである、と強く感じた。それらは、私には、むしろ"モダン"であると感じさせた。藤井は"転形"作業において、数寄屋建築に内在する美学や原理を選びとりはしたが、その造形パターンを選んだのではなかったのである」と記し、藤井が「聴竹居」で実現しようとした新しい「日本の住宅」への想いを見事に浮かび上がらせている。

つまり「聴竹居」には、環境工学の理論や科学を超えた新しいデザインをまとった空間が立ち現れており、そこには、藤井厚二による新しい時代に即した「日本趣味」が内蔵されていると。こうして「聴竹居」は再び注目を浴びることになる。

DOCOMOMO 20選へ

1999年、「聴竹居」は、DOCOMOMO Japanというモダン・ムーブメントにかかわる建物と環境形成の記録調査および保存のための国際組織の日本支部によって、日本を代表する近代建築として最初の「DOCOMOMO 20選」に選ばれた。当時、DOCOMOMO Japanの代表を務めていた日本の近代建築史研究の第一人者、鈴木博之（1945-2014）は、「聴竹居の世界」と題した文章（季刊「approach」2000年冬号）で次のように述べている。

英国の「レッド・ハウス」（1859）、ドイツの「ベーレンズ自邸」（1901）、アメリカにおける「プレーリー・ハウス」群、フランスの「サヴォア邸」（1931）という郊外の独立専用住居の系譜のなかに、藤井厚二の「聴竹居」（1928）を置くことは強引で、日本の立場に立ちすぎた身贔屓に過ぎるだろうか。

世界の建築史上の位置づけを公平に行うならば、たしかに「聴竹居」は無名に近い。しかし、近代を迎えた各国がそれぞれ自分たちの近代住居の模索をつづけていった歴史のなかで見る時日本における藤井厚二の試みは十分に自国の生活を見据えたオリジナルな試みなのである。

藤井が「近代」と「日本」を等価に見据え、それを単純に藤井厚二の個人的世界を結晶させた私小説的な小品と考えてはならないであろう。ここには骨太な、近代住居探求のこころざしが横溢しているのである。

藤井のこころみは西洋の住宅建築の輸入・紹介ではなく、そこに見られた近代生活の探求を自らが実践することであった。数寄屋的な表現が現れたとするならば、それは日本の住居の基本として彼が近代以前における独立専用住居のモデルをそこに置いたからにほかならない。

様式や手法の手本として西欧の建築を見るのではなく、モデル探求の方法において西欧の建築の動きを見据えた建築家は、じつはそれほど多くない。藤井の位置は、そこから判断されるべきなのである。（以上抜粋）

結論として、鈴木氏は「聴竹居」を「世界的な建築近代化の課題に取り組んだ日本の例として、極めて重要な作品」としている。

2000年には、DOCOMOMO 20選を紹介する展覧会が鎌倉、神戸などで開催され、藤井厚二と「聴竹居」の名はようやく広く一般にも知られるようになっていったのである。

後輩設計部員たちによる実測

藤井家（藤井厚二次女の小西章子さん、同孫の小西伸一さん）との繋がりを持てるようになってから約1年後の1999年12月1日、借家人として「聴竹居」を竣工当時の状態のまま、改造もせずに長年、大切に住んでおられた方がご高齢（90歳代）で亡くなり、「聴竹居」は空き家となった。伸一さん

から、「聴竹居をこれからどうしたらよいのか」と相談を受けた私は、無論その価値を重要視し、「人に貸して維持管理して遺すべき」「公開できる状態にして動態保存していくべき」と提案した。同時にこの時思いついたのが、次の3点だった。

1）この貴重な住宅を少しでも公開してもらえるような使い方を借家人にお願いできる契約とすること
2）もし、不適切な使い方をした場合、借家人に明け渡してもらえる契約とすること
3）今後修復して利活用を進めていくためのベースとなる実測図面を整備すること

1）については、竹中工務店の先輩の紹介で「聴竹居」を賃借しアトリエ（事務所）的に使用することで遺すことに貢献したいという方が現れ、そのまま、その方に借家人になってもらうこととした。2）については、ちょうど新しい法律が制定された時で、契約期限を定めるとともに、6か月前に貸主が申し出れば契約を終了できるという「定期借家契約」が適用できることがわかり、竹中工務店の法務の専門家の知恵を借りて「聴竹居　定期借家契約書」を作成することができた。私が立会人になり、2年ごとの契約期間としたこの契約書の中に「見学対応すること」の一文を入れた。そして3）については、空っぽになった「聴竹居」を実測調査し、図面化しておくことが今後の保存利活用には欠かせないと伸一さんに提案し了解を得た。

実測調査について、当初は何処かの誰かがこの作業をやってくれないかと思ったが、すぐに「武田五一・芝川邸と同じように竹中工務店設計部の有志に声がけしてみよう」「実測調査の成果は芝川邸と同じように、設計部長に一定の費用負担をお願いし、図録にまとめて展覧会を開催しよう」と思い直した。そこで、設計部長（当時）に進言するとともに、「芝川邸」の実測調査を行ったメンバーを中心に有志を募った。結果、竹中工務店大阪本店設計部の有志による「聴竹居実測調査団」を結成することができた。1995年、96年の「芝川邸実測調査団」による活動と成果発表からあまり時を隔てることなく、同じくこうした自主的な活動に気概を持ったメンバーが集まってくれたことは本当に幸運だった。

こうして空き家の状態となった中で、藤井の後輩（竹中工務店設計部有志）が、「聴竹居」の実物に手を触れながらその精神と技を学び取ることができる絶好の機会を得ることになったのである。監修者として滋賀県立大学の石田助教授（当時）を迎え、実測調査は2000年3月にスタートした。まだまだ寒く、手がかじかんでいた3月から暑さや蚊に悩まされる7月までの休日を利用し、延べ18日間、朝から夕方まで、メジャー片手に「聴竹居」とじっくりと向き合ったのである。

実測は、精神修養にも似た単調で黙々とした作業の連続だったが、普段設計を実務としているメンバーにとって、それは藤井の設計意図を探り、つじつまの合わない部分の謎解きをしながら設計プロセスを追体験する貴重な機会となった。「聴竹居」を構成する「本屋」「閑室」「茶室（実測当時は「下閑室」と呼ばれていた）」の3棟には、優れたデザインやディテールが数多くあり、実測スケッチの総枚数は優に200枚を超えた。

その実測調査の意義について、新聞の取材を受けた石田氏は、「現代建築の設計者にとって文化財が無縁なものでなく、自らが歴史の方へ踏み込むことで、設計の中でかかわっていけるという一つの見識を示した」と評価している（日刊建設工業新聞　2000年4月25日）。

地域で守る生きた文化遺産

私が立会人となり、竹中工務店の法務の専門家に相談しながら作成した「定期借家契約書」に基づき、2000年5月から8年の間、「聴竹居」はオフィスとして活用された。しかし、契約書に盛り込んだ「見学対応すること」の条文に対し、見学やたびたび申し込まれた雑誌や新聞の取材に対しても十分な対応がなされなかった時期もあり、さらに地元の大山崎町役場や地域住民ともあまり関係を築けていない状態が続いた結果、所有者（貸主）の意向もあり、借家人には2008年4月をもって退去してもらうことになった。

その決定後の2007年12月14日、もともと繋がりをもっていた大山崎町役場の文化財担当の林亨さん、大学の歴史研の後輩で京都府教育委員会文化財技師の吉田理（さとし）さんと今後について相談をした。その時、私は大山崎町の地元の方々によるボランティア組織をつくり、一般公開することを提案した。林さんからは「適任の人が居るので紹介します」との心強い一言をもらうことができた。そして、2008年の2月1日夕刻に長岡京市駅前で林さんに紹介されて初めてお会いしたのが、のちに任意団体の聴竹居倶楽部の事務局長になる荻野和雄さんだった。荻野さんは、大山崎町のボランティア団体のふるさとガイドの会で既に活動・活躍されており、「人物的に信頼できる地元のボランティア数人を集めることができる」との有難い返答ももらえた。この瞬間私は、内心喜んだ。これで大山崎町の誰かが、藤井家から「聴竹居」を定期借家契約でお借りし、地元のボランティアメンバーで公開することが実現できると思ったのである。ところが、林さんと荻野さんから思いもかけない言葉が発せられた。「地元のボランティアメンバーで公開することは引き受けるが、藤井家から定期借家契約をするのは、小西章子さん（藤井厚二の次女）、伸一さん（同孫）

の信頼を得ているあなたしかいない」と。こうして、図らずも自らが作成した「定期借家契約書」の「立会人」から「借家人」に移行して定期借家契約を締結することになった。

私は伸一さんから鍵を受け取り、2008年5月4日から借家人（持主は小西章子さん）となった。6月1日には地元・大山崎町の皆さんと任意団体・聴竹居倶楽部を結成し代表に就任、より積極的に公開活用すべく行動を始めた。

建築専門家の中でも、そう多くの方がその存在を知っているわけではない「聴竹居」。ましてや、個人邸であるがゆえに一般の方々には、まだまだ知られていなかった。2008年5月17日、荻野さんの呼びかけで集まっていただいた「聴竹居」の徒歩圏に住む地元の有志数人は、「どこが良いのか」「どこが凄いのか」理解できず、その価値がわからずに一様にきょとんとされていた。

一般公開のしくみや入場料等の設定、管理体制を整えたうえで、多くの方々への情報発信手段としてまずホームページを作ろうということになった。ホームページを作って歴史的建造物の認知度アップと集客をスムーズに行う実例として先行していたのが、実は私の自宅のある神戸・塩屋の「旧グッゲンハイム邸」だった。それは、なかなかシンプルですっきりとした画面ながら、機能的には十分なものだった。そこで、同じようなホームページにすべく、「旧グッゲンハイム邸」のホームページを制作した塩屋在住の浜崎良嗣さんに「聴竹居」のホームページの制作をお願いした。

7月25日、初めてアップしたホームページによる事前予約制での一般公開を恐るおそる始めた。まずは建築関係者の間で噂が広がりを見せはじめ、初年度こそ数百人だったものの、その後、全国各地から多くの見学者が来られるようになり、その数は年々増加した。

建物の保存活用は、建物を生きた形で使うことが大切だ。「聴竹居」は住宅として建てられた建物である。しかし、「其の国の建築を代表するものは住宅建築」として生涯、日本の気候風土に適合し、日本人の理想となる住まいを追求した藤井厚二の思想と空間を、より多くの方々に体感してもらうために、敢えて、ある個人や企業が専有する住まいとして独占するのではなく、週3日の予約制の見学や各種イベントを通じて、誰でもが時空間を体感できる、開かれ、生きた「住まい」（リビング・ヘリテージ＝生きた文化遺産）としてきた。

2008年春に任意団体聴竹居倶楽部を発足させ、一般公開を開始した当初は、口コミで情報を得た建築関係者の建物見学会が続いていた。しかし、2009年春には、庭での新緑コンサート、同年秋には室内での紅葉コンサートも開催することができた。この年の晩秋には、今では恒例となったイベント「紅葉をめでる会」の第1回目を開催している。

春の「新緑をめでる会」と秋の「紅葉をめでる会」は、「新緑」や「紅葉」に包まれた「聴竹居」を気軽に見ていただこうとの主旨から始めたイベントで、新緑や紅葉が一番美しい時の土曜日の10時から15時まで事前予約なしで庭までを開放、さらに希望者は室内の見学も順次可能として、初めての方やリピーターの方々など、なんとわずか1日で約500人もの方々が訪れる恒例行事としてすっかり定着している。2009年春には、聴竹居の空間をアーティストの展覧会の場にした漆作家の展覧会「聴竹居との出会い　栗本夏樹展」を、2013年春には、現代アーティストの「聴竹居との出会い　河口龍夫展」を開催し、「聴竹居」の空間と現代アートとの対話を愉しんで頂ける展覧会、イベントになった。

こうして2016年、見学者は年間約4500人に達するようになった。

「聴竹居倶楽部」の発展

前述したように2008年春から私が個人的に藤井家から「聴竹居」を定期借家として借りて、地元のスタッフが日常維持管理、保存公開活動を始めた。2013年の正月に放映されたNHK教育テレビの番組「美の壺」をご覧になられたことがきっかけで、同年6月24日、天皇皇后両陛下が行幸啓された。「聴竹居」はさらに脚光を浴びることになったと同時に、行幸啓された建物として存続のための持続可能な体制への転換を迫られるようになった。「聴竹居」の存続に関しては次の3つの問題点があった。

1）相続や固定資産税など個人財産のまま永続的に所有・維持管理していくことには限界があること
2）任意団体の聴竹居倶楽部ではボランティア的で脆弱な組織であるがゆえに、世代交代とモチベーションの維持には限界があること
3）文化財的に無指定なままではいつ何時更地売却されてしまうかもしれないと危惧されること

そして、2016年、「聴竹居」の存続に対しての問題点を解消すべく、竹中工務店が「聴竹居」を藤井家の意向を受ける形で譲り受け、次の4つの観点から企業の社会貢献（CSR）活動の一環として取得することを決定した。

1）竹中工務店にとって、黎明期に設計組織の礎を築いた藤井厚二の存在は重要であること
2）個人財産のまま永続的に維持管理していくことには限界があり、藤井家が竹中工務店であれば譲ることを希望し了承していること
3）2018年は藤井厚二生誕130年・没後80年、「聴竹居」

竣工90年の節目を迎えること
　4）2019年は竹中工務店の創立120周年の年にあたり、「聴竹居」の取得と保存公開を社会文化的な記念事業として位置付けること

　同時に「聴竹居」取得後の日常管理運営を今まで通り、地元住民中心の組織「聴竹居倶楽部」で継続していくことも決定した。こうして「聴竹居」の土地・建物の所有は株式会社竹中工務店、日常維持管理と公開活動は「聴竹居倶楽部」とする大きな方針のもと、2016年12月に「聴竹居」の土地・建物の所有権移転を終えた。

　「聴竹居倶楽部」については、組織的には脆弱な「任意団体」から、より公益性の高い「一般社団法人」に移行させることになった。法人設立の目的を「昭和初期を代表とするモダニズム建築である『聴竹居』を維持保全するとともに施設公開、文化展示、イベント、知名度向上に関する事業を行い、建築文化・教育普及、地域振興に寄与する」とした「定款」をつくり、2016年12月に京都法務局に法人登記した。

　株式会社竹中工務店が主体的に創った一般社団法人ではあるが、特にこだわった点が、その役員構成だった。法人の設立時の役員は最小限の人数とした上で、3人の理事の一人を大山崎町役場の役職者に、さらに2人の監事のうちの一人を藤井家とすることだった。そして理事には大山崎町の現在の副町長の杉山英樹さんに、監事を前所有者の小西章子さんにお願いし了解を得ることができた。趣旨としては、地域の大切な文化資源である「聴竹居」の日常の維持管理・利活用を、所有者である企業の竹中工務店という閉じた組織だけでなく、地元の大山崎町役場、さらに、藤井厚二の遺族とともに行っていくことが望ましい姿であると考えたからである。こうして、竹中工務店＋大山崎町＋藤井家共同の役員構成とした「一般社団法人聴竹居倶楽部」が誕生した。

　一方、今まで任意団体として推進してきたガイド付き見学対応等の実務を実際に担う体制については、大山崎町の住民有志、聴竹居の近隣住民の見学対応スタッフを拡充しながら継続していくことにした。事務局長は、2008年春に任意団体を立ち上げるときからずっとお世話になった荻野和雄さんから、見学対応スタッフとしてここ数年、実績を上げてきた田邊さんに代えてお願いすることとした。田邊さんの自宅は「聴竹居」のすぐ近くで、生まれも育ちも大山崎。さらに「藤井厚二の遺族から土地を分けてもらって両親が建てた家で生まれ育った。聴竹居を遺していくことに関わることができて嬉しい」とおしゃってくれた。専従の事務局としては、大山崎出身の石山佳永子さんに加わっていただくことにした。見学対応スタッフは、初期のメンバーの荻野和雄さん、谷口久敏さん、森本素生さん、林亨さんに、近年は近所のメンバーである富永健司さん、美濃部幸治さん、坂爪寛人さんが加わり、2017年からは鍛治覚さん、塩田洋一さん、林良次さん、安田演之さん、宮本貴子さん、藤原真名美さんが加わり、田邊均さんを含めて総勢14名になった。さらに、以前から献身的に手伝ってくれていた土井洋子さん（土井さんは藤井が住宅普及のプロトタイプとして建てた小住宅で生まれ育った）をはじめとする近隣の方々も数多く参加、地元中心の体制を創ることができた。

　聴竹居倶楽部と竹中工務店の役割分担については、さまざまな関係者との検討・調整を経て、土地・建物の維持管理については所有者である竹中工務店が、見学者対応・見学料（大人1000円、学生500円等。2018年4月現在）の徴収・定期清掃・日常管理業務については、竹中工務店から業務委託契約により聴竹居倶楽部が行うこととした。さらに、両者が単に業務委託関係であることを越えて、「相互に協力して聴竹居の文化的価値向上に努めること」を趣旨とした覚書も締結した。こうした体制を構築することも、竹中工務店としては初めてのことであり、本社の様々な部署、さらには関連会社を含め、オール竹中として総力を生かして取り組んでいくことになった。

国の重要文化財指定へ

　昭和初期の木造モダニズム建築を代表するものとして「聴竹居」は、1999年にDOCOMOMO 20選に選ばれたが、その頃から文化庁や京都府教育庁文化財など関係者の間では、昭和の住宅として初となる「重要文化財指定」の話がささやかれ始めていた。

　なかなか重要文化財指定の話が具体化していかない中、2005年7月21日に「聴竹居」の所有者代行の小西伸一さんと京都府教育庁文化財保護課の平井信行係長（当時）と私の3人で文化庁に堀勇良参事官付主任調査官（当時）を訪ね、「聴竹居」の重要文化財指定について相談した。その時は、個人財産として「聴竹居」を国の重要文化財に指定しても、固定資産税や相続税の減免措置、保存修理工事費の補助に留まるのであれば、個人所有者としては「重要文化財指定」に同意することはできないとの話だった。「重要文化財」に指定されると、通常は売却が困難になることもあり、不動産価値が下がるとともに、指定後に行われる保存修理工事費の個人負担（国・府・町が最大8割5分補助するものの、残りは個人負担）が発生するからだ。「聴竹居」は文化庁をはじめとする文化財行政、建築史家などの有識者からは、国の「重要文化財」の価値があると評価されつつも、経済的な負担が大きい個人所有の限界により無指定のまま

推移していた。

　それからかなりの時が経ち、2016年に「聴竹居」を竹中工務店が藤井家から譲り受けて保存公開することの意向が固まりつつあった頃、たまたま私事で文化庁の熊本達哉参事官（当時）に初めて会う機会があったので、そのことを内々にお伝えした。かねてより「聴竹居」の価値に鑑みた文化財としての保存を考えていた熊本参事官は、「個人所有から企業所有になることは望ましい方向ですね」とおっしゃった。それを受けて、2017年4月に行われる「重要文化財指定」の諮問を目途に動き出すことになり、京都府教育庁文化財保護課、さらに大山崎町教育委員会文化財課とともに、指定のための準備作業を開始した。

　指定のためには当然のことながら、指定範囲を決定する土地測量図、指定建物の図面、建物の写真が必要不可欠だった。土地測量図については、既に所有権移転の手続きの中で測量と図面化が進んでいた。一方で、指定を受ける3つの建物（本屋・閑室・茶室）の図面については、所有者となる竹中工務店が独自に用意する必要があった。すぐさま図面作成業務の担当に指名された竹中工務店大阪本店設計部の有田博さん、中村圭祐さんと連絡を取った。2000年に大阪本店設計部の有志（リーダー・松隈章ほか28名）が実測した時の図面データ（CADデータ）は私が大事に保管していたが、コンピューターソフトの更新はここ十数年で激しく、その当時の図面データを現在のソフトで読み込み、修正ができるかどうかは怪しかった。しかし、幸運にも実測したときに作成したすべての図面データは使うことができたのである。

　こうして2000年に大阪本店設計部の有志で行った実測調査が十数年を経て、今回の重要文化財指定のための大事な基本資料として活用されることになった。実は、有田さん、中村さんも私とともに当時、実測調査団に参加した有志のメンバーだった。休日を返上して、実測調査に献身的に参加してくれたメンバーの想いが、今回の取り組みにも繋がるという嬉しい出来事となった。建物の写真についても、2015年3月に刊行された平凡社コロナ・ブックス『聴竹居　藤井厚二の木造モダニズム建築』のために約1年をかけて新撮にあたった大阪本店総務部所属社員でカメラマンの古川泰造さんの写真（クレジットは竹中工務店）を使うことができたことも幸運だった。

　2016年12月末に竹中工務店が「聴竹居」を取得してからは準備作業も本格化する。文化庁の西岡聡参事官付主任調査官、京都府教育庁文化財保護課の竹下弘展さん、大山崎町教育委員会文化財課の寺嶋千春さん、そして大阪本店設計部の中村圭祐さんが共同で準備作業を進めていった。そして「聴竹居」は、2017年5月19日に行われた文化審議会文化財分科会で無事、松野文部科学大臣に答申され、7月31日付の官報で正式に国の重要文化財に指定となったのである。

理想の住宅を未来へ繋ぐ

　京都帝国大学教授・建築家の藤井厚二は、明治維新以来の欧化政策により欧米の模倣と日本の伝統とがただ雑然と混交している生活様式の状況を憂い、環境工学の理論書『日本の住宅』を執筆・発行している（概略は150頁～152頁に掲載）。

　この著書の中で藤井は、和風・洋風の2つの様式について、「生活様式」「構造および意匠装飾」「間取り」「壁」「軒および庇」「夏の設備」など10項目について比較・考察し、それぞれの長所に拠った様式を追求した。そして、住宅において自ら興した環境工学を基礎とした設計方法論を展開している。欧米諸国・都市と日本の気候データとの比較を行って、主に温熱環境について人間が快適である状態を明らかにした上で、それを獲得するための日本の住宅における基本的な考え方を提示し、科学的に裏付けているのである。

　教鞭をとった京都帝国大学でも藤井はこの設計方法論を展開した。環境との共生が叫ばれる現代では当たり前にも思えるが、約90年も前に第5回自邸「聴竹居」でそれを実践した。日本の住宅の理想形＝「聴竹居」で実現されている藤井の先進性を示す主なものは、大きくは次の4つに集約できるだろう。

1）科学的アプローチを駆使したパッシブな（自然エネルギーを生かす）工夫

　藤井は、日本の住まいで伝統的に取り入れられてきた気候風土に合わせる建築方法を、科学的な観点から見直した。科学的な目で捉えなおすスタートとして、人体が快適だと感じる標準的な温湿度を欧米の研究者の研究成果と比較考察し、おそらく日本人として初めて体感温度を設計の際の根拠とした。藤井の取り組みは兼好法師の言う「家の作りやうは、夏をむねとすべし。冬はいかなる所にも住まる。暑き比わろき住居は、堪へがたき事なり」を科学的に追求し、日本の気候風土にあった建築理論の構築に繋がった。特に夏の対策が重要だとして、聴竹居では次のようなことを実現している。

・室内の風通しを良くするために一屋一室（ひとつの建物はひとつの部屋とする）とする

・屋根裏（天井裏）を換気に利用して夏の暑さを避ける

・夏の日差しを避け、冬の日差しを取り入れるため庇の出を決める

・床下や地中から外気を導入し、室内へ導く

・床下と天井裏をつなぐ通気筒を設け、床下で冷やされた空気を屋根裏に通して、温度を下げるとともに換気を盛んにする

2）洋風と和風そしてモダンを統合したデザイン
「聴竹居」は外観、内観ともに何処か懐かしい雰囲気を持ったモダンなデザインになっている。一見すると普通の和風住宅に見えてしまうものの、細部を観ていくと洋風住宅の要素も巧みに取り入れているのが分かる。それは、「洋風」と「和風」の住まいを理論的に比較する中から生み出された、時代の流行に押し流されることのない真摯な取組み「洋と和の幸せな統合」の結果であり、日本人が昔から築いてきた「日本の住宅」を近代化しようとしたオリジナルな試みの結果とも言える。例えば、下記のようなことが上げられる。
・椅子に座った人と畳に座った人の目線を合わせるために畳の床を約30cm高く設定
・数寄屋建築に伝統的に用いられてきた木、和紙、竹、土壁など自然系材料の採用
・黎明期にあった欧米のアールデコやモダニズムと、日本の数寄屋のデザイン融合

3）住まいの"原型"としての居間中心、家族中心のプランニング
大正期から昭和初期の一般的な住まいの多くは、玄関を入ると中廊下があり、手前に洋間の応接室、その隣に床の間のある接客用の畳敷きの座敷、その奥に家族が集う茶の間などが追いやられ、接客空間を第一にしたプランニングになっていた。そのことに疑問を感じた建築家の一人が藤井だった。「聴竹居」では、玄関に入ると右手には客用のトイレが、左手には客室（椅子式の応接室）が設えられていて、その奥には広い居室（リビング）が続いている。つまり「聴竹居」のリビング・インの平面は、現代でも通用するプランニングになっている。居室を中心に貫入・連続された縁側、読書室、食事室を含んだ空間全体で人が集う場としての「居間」をつくり、家族それぞれが居場所を確保しながら繋がりあえる豊かな家族のための空間が生まれている。

4）新しい「日本の住宅」のライフスタイル全体をデザイン
大山崎に約1万2千坪とも言われる広大な敷地（山林）を購入した藤井は、単体の住宅はもちろん理想とする住宅地を創造していこうとしていた。藤井はその広大な敷地に、「藤焼（ふじやき）」窯（藤井自らが「藤焼」と名づけ、茶碗や湯飲みといった日用雑器や花瓶に絵付けをした上で清水焼の陶工・川島松次郎に作陶させた）、山崎の豊かな地下水を汲み上げて飲料用の水源にするとともに、長さ25m、幅6mの鉄筋コンクリート製のプールを造り、さらにフルサイズのテニスコートを設けている。「聴竹居」周辺では小川や池、滝がある傾斜を生かしたランドスケープも実現している。さらに茶道、華道を嗜み、建築だけではなく、家具、照明、絨毯、日用雑器、自著の本の装丁など生活していく上で必要なあらゆるものをデザインした。

この日本の住宅の理想形に、私は偶然出会った。1996年以来「聴竹居」に関わってきて今想うことは、一つの建物の持つ可能性の大きさだ。一つの建物が、人と人、人と自然、さらに人と地域、そして過去・現在・未来を「繋ぐ」大事な存在だということである。グローバル社会、経済至上主義など、全てがフラットに効率やカネを優先した現代では見えにくくなってしまったものにふと気を付かせてくれる存在だともいえる。

私自身も経験したことだが、1995年阪神淡路大震災、2011年東日本大震災など一瞬にして日常が不可逆的なものだと気が付かされる災害に見舞われた時、建物や地域の風景の大切さや愛おしさを自覚することになる。ふだん何気なく暮らし、見ている建物や地域の風景の環境から実は大きな影響を受けているし、それらは人生にとっての大切な記憶装置になっている。私も「聴竹居」に出会わなければ、大山崎町を訪れることもなかっただろうし、地域の方々との交流も生まれえなかっただろう。さらに「聴竹居」を通じて、藤井厚二の「日本の住宅」という思想に触れることができた。日本の住まいの歴史、日本における建築の在り方、日本人の自然との付き合い方などにも想いを馳せることにも繋がった。大山崎町の方々も、きっと同じようなことを感じただろうし、何よりも「聴竹居」の存在によって大山崎を誇らしく思う地域愛（シビックプライド）醸成の一助になったのではないかと思う。地域とともに存在し続ける生きた建物には、「愛着の連鎖、継承」を支える「たてものがかり」の存在が不可欠だが、聴竹居倶楽部はまさに「聴竹居」の「たてものがかり」となっている。

一方、国の重要文化財「聴竹居」を所有することになったのが竹中工務店だ。今後、建物の所有者として文化庁、京都府教育庁文化財保護課、大山崎町文化財課のご指導のもと、逐次実施に移されていく保存修理工事の当事者の立場で深く関わっていくことになる。こうした地道で息の長い活動を通じて歴史的建築物を使い続ける工夫のノウハウを蓄積し社会へ還元するとともに、建築文化発信に取り組

んでいく。それは、経営理念「最良の作品を世に遺し、社会に貢献する」を掲げ、建物づくりを専業とし脈々と続けてきた竹中工務店の、企業としての社会的責任であり矜持と言えるだろう。

「聴竹居」と出会ってから22年、ようやく「聴竹居」を国の重要文化財としてきちんと次代に遺していく社会的な機運や体制づくりが整った。さらに、その次の大きな動きもある。2017年12月8日、日本イコモス国内委員会第14小委員会（20世紀建築遺産）とISC 20 c（イコモス20世紀遺産に関する国際学術委員会）が、「聴竹居」を含む「日本の20世紀遺産20選の選定」を発表したのだ。

6つの世界文化遺産選定のための評価基準（顕著で普遍的価値）のうち、「聴竹居」は、以下の2つに該当するとされた。
　1）人類の創造的才能を表す傑作であること
　2）建築や技術、記念碑的芸術、都市計画、景観設計の発展に関連し、ある期間にわたる、又は世界のある文化圏における人類の価値観の重要な交流を示していること

こうして「伝統を生かし、近代の環境工学の思想を取り入れた傑作」として「聴竹居」は、「日本の20世紀遺産20選」の一つに選ばれたのである。この20選の中でいわゆる個人邸、戸建て住宅は「聴竹居」が唯一であり、いかに重要な「日本の住宅」であるかが示されることとなった。

藤井厚二の遺した名言に「其の国の建築を代表するものは住宅建築である」がある。

藤井は1930（昭和5）年に英文の著書『THE JAPANESE DWELLING-HOUSE』を発刊した。自ら確立した環境工学の視点から日本の気候風土の特長を概説し、図面と絵や写真で完成形としての「聴竹居」を実例として掲載し、志向した日本の気候風土と日本人のライフスタイルや趣味に適合した「日本の住宅」の思想を世界に向け発表した。それから88年。藤井のこの想いをのせて、これからも「聴竹居」は、20世紀の日本を代表する世界的な住宅遺産として、さらに世界文化遺産として、この思想を世界へ発信し続けるだろう。

The Course of Chochikukyo

Akira Matsukuma

My Encounter with Chochikukyo

How I encountered Chochikukyo was indeed by pure chance or, may be said, as my destiny. The Shibakawa Residence (built in 1911 in Kotoen, Nishinomiya and then rebuilt in Museum Meiji-mura in 2007) was designed by Goichi Takeda, leading architect during the Meiji period (1868 - 1912). Due to the 1995 Great Hanshin Awaji Earthquake the Shibakawa Residence half collapsed. If the Residence not been so badly damaged and had I not been one of the member of the volunteers group sent by Takenaka Corporation to conduct the field survey for relocation, I would never have come to know of either Koji Fujii or Chochikukyo. In 1996 from May 27 to June 14, Building Design Department of Takenaka Corporation Osaka Headquarter presented The Shibakawa Residence and Goichi Takeda Exhibition as an opportunity to report the result of the field survey of the Shibakawa Residence and to give thought to the preservation of cultural assets. In the preparation of pictorial record and exhibit panels, I was mainly in charge of the portion that introduced how Takeda was related to Takenaka & Co. I learned the following facts:

1) Takeda invited Fujii to join the Department of Architecture, Kyoto Imperial Universitas a lecturer. Takeda was among the founding members of the Department in 1920. He was also serving as a professor. Takeda headhunted Fuji, who was from same home town, Fukuyama, and Takeda's junior in Tokyo Imperial University, from Takenaka & Co.
2) Fujii was the first employee of Takenaka & Co., who graduated from Tokyo Imperial University and received Bachelor degree. Fujii was involved in the design work of Osaka Asahi Shinbun (newspaper) Corporate Office built in 1916, the most modern office at that time, and many other buildings. Fujii established the foundation of current building design organization of Takenaka.
3) Takeda and Fujii met while working on the Osaka Asahi Shinbun Project. Takeda served as advisor to the client, while Fujii was the design architect in charge of the Project.

Furthermore, once I saw photographs of Fujii's residence Chochikukyo (built in 1928) that were introduced in architectural magazines and publications, I thought that if the opportunity arose, I would like to see Chochikukyo for myself. Around 1996, at a time when museums hardly ever hosted exhibitions featuring architecture, The Shibakawa Residence and Goichi Takeda Exhibition was held. From September 14 to October 20, 1996 Mie Prefectural Art Museum held an exhibition entitled Rediscovery of 20 Century Japanese Art II - Featuring 1920s. This exhibition focused only on formative art during the 1920's. Ms. Mari Kuwana was the curator and she learned of The Shibakawa Residence and Goichi Takeda Exhibition which she visited on June 7, 1996, when I had the pleasure of escorting her through the exhibition. Later on Ms. Kuwana married Toshihiro Hanazato of Tsukuba University (currently serving as a professor). Hanazato was a former classmate of Masahide Saito, Department of Building Design, Takenaka Corporation Osaka Headquarter. Ms. Kuwana, through this personal networking, learned about the exhibition at Takenaka and through her visit, gained some insight on how to exhibit architecture at the art museum. When she was leaving the exhibition, she asked me, 'do you know of any suitable building that could be a key feature in the exhibition corner featuring 1920's?' Without hesitation I answered, 'Chochikukyo by Koji Fujii is the best candidate. It was built in 1928.' I answered in this way as I had a secret desire to see the existing Chochikukyo if it would be exhibited in the museum. Chochikukyo was covered in the exhibition in 1990 by Saison Art Museum on Japanese Eyes & Space - Another Modern Design with drawings and photos. Accordingly, I proposed that new exhibition format for the corner should feature a miniature model and video of Chochikukyo, as drawings and photographs alone, which were previously exhibited at Saison Art Museum, would be less interesting.

Kuwana took my proposal back to Mie Prefectural Art Museum where it was approved in the planning meeting and preparations commenced. The experts who had worked for Takenaka Corporation were involved. Miniature model of Chochikukyo was commissioned to Yoshio Miura of Miura Mokei, as he was acknowledge, in Building Design Department of Takenaka Corporation Osaka Headquarter, as having excellent reputation as a skilled craftsman in making miniature models. Shinichi Takaoka of Mugi Production had frequently been requested to work on PR videos for Department of Public Relations of Takenaka Corporation and now accepted to work on the video of Chochikukyo.

On July 6, 1996, a hot summer day, I visited Chochikukyo in Oyamazaki for the first time. Mie Prefectural Art Museum staff had made the appointment for a group of 5 of us to visit, so I attended together with Ms. Maki Tsuchida & Mari Kuwana of Mie Art Prefectural Museum, Junichiro Ishida, historian of architecture & assistant professor (then) of Shiga Prefectural University, and Yoshio Miura of Miura Mokei. At that time, a lady in her 80's, was living by herself. Fluorescent lamps were hanging from the ceiling of the living-room; the floor was carpeted; the house was packed with furniture and household goods. However the two-fold impact I got on that day remains as fresh in my memory as though it happened yesterday: I felt very cool though it was a very hot day in summer, and I was surprised and moved by the dignified form displaying a new modern design of house, which was neither Japanese nor Western in style. As a design architect, I was surprised by the fact that as early as 1920's there was an architect who could render a design suitable for houses in Japan, which also took local environmental conditions into consideration and that the architect used to work for Takenaka & Co.

The small desire I cherished came true. I was able to visit Chochikukyo for the first time in the summer of 1996.

A Masterpiece Residence – Not Yet Well Known to the World –

As I was fascinated by the amazing charm of Chochikukyo as soon as I saw it, I kept looking into Chochikukyo and Fujii. I was further charmed by the profoundness of Fujii's way of thinking as an architect. It is not an exaggeration to say that Fujii, through his residential architecture, taught me about Japan, the Japanese, architecture in Japan, houses in Japan and I realized how Japan could be proud of its architecture internationally.
In Takenaka Corporation, Fujii is known to have been the first full-time architect who graduated from Tokyo Imperial University. As previously mentioned, Fujii met Goichi Takeda while he was with Takenaka & Co., and both from Fukuyama. Takeda invited Fujii to help founding Department of Architecture at Kyoto Imperial University. After leaving Takenaka, Fujii visited America and Europe in 1919 and 1920, experienced the emerging advanced architectural styles such as Art Deco and Modernism and observed the newest facility/equipments of architecture.

After returning from his trip to the West, Fujii was shocked to see the aftermath of the 1923 Great Kanto Earthquake. Fujii saw Tokyo three weeks after the quake and mentioned: In the Japanese climate, the result of applying architecture of foreign countries without conditions is clear cut. This made him even more conscious of climatic and environmental conditions of Japan. In 1928, Fujii published *Nihon-no-Jutaku* (Dwelling-Houses in Japan) from *Iwanami Shoten*, which can be referred to as the first theoretical/scientific book on environmental engineering. In the preface, Fujii stated that "the 5th experimental house (, which would be named as Chochikukyo later on,) was under construction and therefore would be positioned as the conclusion of the book". Chochikukyo can be referred to as a culmination of Fujii's ideal house in Japan. However Fujii died young at the age of 49 in 1938, and Chochikukyo, having been built for the personal living, Chochikukyo was not widely known to the public, but only to a small group of concerned people.

The first architectural review that covered Fujii and Chochikukyo was *Oyamazaki-no-Koetsu* (Sophisticated Delight in Oyamazaki); Essay on Koji Fujii by Hiroki Onobayashi (then lecturer at Hosei University) in 1976 November Special Issue of *Shinkenchiku* on *Showa-Jutaku-shi* (History of Houses in Japan during Showa Era). Onobayashi mentioned as follows: "Fujii absorbed the freedom and proportion of *Sukiya* or Tea Room architectural style in Japan and "transformed" it in the different form/profile. I strongly felt that this process of "transformation or transfigure" refused to label various forms/shapes which Fujii created as architecture of "Japan-ness" without conditions. I felt Fujii's creations were "Modern". Fujii, in "transfiguring" process, picked up aesthetics and principles that are inherent in architecture in *Sukiya* style, not the pattern of forms". Onobayashi clearly described Fujii's approach to new houses in Japan, which Fujii tried to realize in Chochikukyo. In summary, Chochikukyo realizes the space in new design, which supersedes theory/science of environmental engineering. Furthermore, Chochikukyo has Japanese taste by Fujii, which corresponds to the new era. As a result, Chochikukyo entertained the renewed attention.

Chochikukyo - DOCOMOMO Japan Selection 20

In 1999, DOCOMOMO Japan, national chapter of an international organization for documentation and conservation of buildings, sites and neighborhoods of the modern movement, included Chochikukyo in their DOCOMOMO Selection 20, as a representation of modern architecture in Japan. Hiroyuki Suzuki (1945-2014), then head of DOCOMOMO Japan, was the leading researcher on the history of Japanese modern architecture. He wrote an essay entitled *Chochikukyo-no-Sekai* (World of Chochikukyo) that was published in the 2000 winter issue of Takenaka Corporation Quarterly Magazine, Approach in which he states:

"Is it too aggressive or too pro-Japanese to position Chochikukyo (1928) by Koji Fujii in the lineage of free-standing private houses in the suburbs, covering "Red House" in 1859, England, "Behrens Personal Residence" in 1901, Germany, "Prairie Houses", America, and "Villa Savoye" in 1931, France? To be fair in positioning Chochikukyo in the international history of architecture, Chochikukyo was unknown. On the other side of the coin, from the perspective of the history trying to find its own modern houses in each country/region in modern days, Fujii's trial in Japan was indeed an original endeavor with the in-depth observation of the lifestyle in Japan. Chochikukyo should not be regarded as Fujii's fruit of his personal work based on his approach to Japan in modern times. Rather Chochikukyo is filled with Fujii's search for modern houses supported by solid backbone. Fujii did not try to import/introduce domestic architecture from the West. Instead he searched the modern way of life, which was found in the Western architecture. If Chochikukyo has expression(s) of *sukiya* style of architecture, Fujii regarded *Sukiya* style as a model of free-standing private residence during the period prior to modern times, which serves as the base of Japanese houses. There are not many architects who observe Western architecture not as model for forms/techniques. Fujii appreciated the movement of Western architecture as a way to know the ways to search the model. The positioning of Fujii should be judged from the approach that Fujii took".

As a result, Suzuki regarded "Chochikukyo to be an extremely important work as an example to address international movement to modernize architecture in Japan". In 2000, Selection 20 by DOCOMOMO exhibition made a circuit of Kamakura and Kobe among other cities in Japan. At last, Koji Fujii and Chochikukyo were widely known to the Japanese general public.

Field Survey by Members of Department of Building Design, who joined Takenaka Corporation long after Fujii

About a year after I became acquainted with the Fujii family (Ms. Akiko Konishi, Koji Fujii's second daughter, and Mr. Shinichi Konishi, his grandson), a lady, who had lived in Chochikukyo with care as a tenant for a long time without reforming it from the time of its completion died on December 1, 1999 at the age of the 90's. Chochikukyo was unoccupied. Shinichi consulted me, "What shall we do with Chochikukyo from now on?" Needless to say, I appreciated its value and proposed, "Chochikukyo should be preserved and maintained by leasing to a tenant. 'Chochikukyo should be preserved in a dynamic state, namely to be kept in the conditions to allow the visitors to take a look." At the same time, I came up with the following three points:

1) The lease agreement should ask the tenant to use Chochikukyo on the understanding that this valuable residence be opened for viewing on limited occasions.
2) The lease agreement should include a provision that the owner can ask a tenant to vacate the house in case the tenant uses Chochikukyo inappropriately.
3) Field surveyed drawings should be prepared as a base to proceed with necessary repair/maintenance works and good use/utilization of Chochikukyo.

As for the first point, senior staff at Takenaka Corporation referred a perspective tenant to me, who wanted to play a role in the preservation of Chochikukyo by using it as a studio (office). On the second point concerning possible inappropriate use, the new law had just been enacted and it turned out that a fixed-term house lease contract was relevant. The period of lease could be fixed and the owner can ask a tenant to vacate the premises, provided 6 months notice was given. A Fixed-term House Lease Agreement for Chochikukyo was prepared with the cooperation of paralegal staff of Takenaka Corporation. I served as a witness to the signing of this two-year contract, where the lease was to be reviewed every two years. The provision to accept visitors was included in the contract. As for the third point concerning good utilization of the residence, I proposed to Shinichi that the field surveyed drawings of Chochikukyo would be indispensable to preservation work and maintenance in the years to come. Shinichi accepted my proposal.

In the beginning, I was thinking of recruiting someone to work on the field survey. However I soon changed my mind, and followed the style of the Shibakawa Residence (by Goichi Takeda), namely to call for volunteers among members of the Department of Building Design, Takenaka Corporation. I also thought that, as in the case of the Shibakawa Residence, a pictorial record could be organized in an exhibition, and the general manager of the Takenaka's Building Design Department could be approached to bear certain expenses. I proposed my idea to the general manager, as well as calling for volunteers among those who worked on the Shibakawa Residence, and from the Building Design Department. As a result, volunteers among the members of Building Design Department organized "Field Survey Group on Chochikukyo". It was fortunate that members who had completed the field survey on the Shibakawa Residence and exhibited the results in 1995 and 1996 were well versed in this type of voluntary work and totally dedicated, got together. While Chochikukyo was unoccupied, volunteers who joined Takenaka's Building Design Department long after Fujii were given a perfect opportunity to learn Fujii's mindset and techniques while touching Chochikukyo. Assistant Professor Junichiro Ishida of Shiga Prefectural University (at that time) was invited as a supervisor. Field survey started in March 2000, when our fingertips were stiff with cold, and continued through July, when we suffered from the heat and mosquitoes. We volunteers spent 18 days at Chochikukyo working from morning to evening with our tape measures, using our personal time, i.e., by using weekend or holiday time. We observed and surveyed Chochikukyo thoroughly.

The field survey work was a continuation of simple work in silence, something like mental discipline. For volunteers who were practicing design work, the field survey was a valuable opportunity to follow Fujii's design process by searching for Fujii's design intent and solving inconsistencies. Three buildings - house proper, room of quiet, and tea room (labeled as lower room of quiet at the time of field survey) – make up Chochikukyo. These three buildings have many of excellent designs and details. The survey resulted in well over 200 sketches. When the newspaper journalist asked Dr. Junichiro Ishida about the significance of this field survey, he appreciated the work as follows in April 25, 2000 issue of Daily Industry News: "Cultural assets are not irrelevant to architects/designers involved in contemporary architecture. The field survey of Chochikukyo demonstrates one such perspective where architects/designers can be involved of the cultural assets in the design work by surveying the historical building(s)."

Living Cultural Asset Protected by the Local Community

Based on Fixed-term House Lease Agreement for Chochikukyo, which I prepared in consultation with paralegal experts of Takenaka Corporation, and to which I served as a witness of signing of it, Chochikukyo was used as an office for 8 years from May 2000. However, with regard to the provision to accept visitor(s), there was the period that the tenant did not make satisfactory response to the request for visit and/or repeated approach by the media such as magazines and newspapers. Furthermore, the tenant failed to have contact with Oyamazaki Town House or local residents. As a result, reflecting the will of the landlord (owner), it was decided that the tenant would vacate Chochikukyo in April 2008. Right after it was decided to ask the tenant to vacate Chochikukyo, on December 14, 2007, I met my acquaintances, Mr. Toru Hayashi, in charge of cultural assets at Oyamazaki Town House, and Satoshi Yoshida, who was junior to me at the history research group at the university I graduated and a technical expert on cultural assets of Kyoto Prefectural Board of Education, to talk what to do with Chochikukyo. During the meeting, I proposed to set up a volunteer organization by the local people of Oyamazaki-cho (town), and open Chochikukyo to the general public. In turn, Toru Hayashi made an encouraging comment that he could suggest a suitable candidate to me to lead of such a volunteer organization. In the evening of February 1, 2008, at a shop in front of Hankyu Nagaokakyoshi station, Hayashi introduced me Kazuo Ogino. Ogino assumed a position of secretary general of Chochikukyo Club, a voluntary organization, when it was established later. Ogino was already very active as a member of Local Guide Group, a volunteer organization in Oyamazaki-cho. He promised me that he could bring together several local volunteers, all of whom were quite reliable. At this moment, I was relieved. I thought that some person in Oyamazaki-cho would borrow Chochikukyo from the Fujii family, based on Fixed-term House Lease Agreement for Chochikukyo, and that the local volunteers could host the open house of Chochikukyo. In turn, Hayashi and Ogino made an unexpected comment, "We are happy to accept your proposal that the local volunteers would work on opening Chochikukyo to the general public. However there is no one besides you, whom Akiko and Shinichi Konishi rely on, to rent Chochikukyo on the fixed-term lease from the Fujii family." As a result, unexpectedly, I switched my position from the witness to the tenant of Fixed-term House Lease Agreement for Chochikukyo, which I was involved in preparing.

Shinichi Konishi gave me the keys of Chochikukyo. As of May 4, 2008, I was a tenant of Chochikukyo; the owner was Akiko Konishi, Fujii's second daughter. On June 1, 2008, together with the local people of Oyamazaki-cho, Chochikukyo Club, a voluntary organization, was established and I became a representative. We started to take necessary action to use and show Chochikukyo more actively. At that time, Chochikukyo was not widely known even among professionals/experts of architecture. Thus it was not known to the general public as it was a personal residence. On May 17, 2008, Ogino organized a meeting of several local volunteers. They lived within walking distance from Chochikukyo, but at a loss what to do, as they failed to understand why or how Chochikukyo is great, exceptionally excellent in certain ways, or appreciate its value.

Firstly, the scheme of the open house, admission fee, and management system were set. Then we decided to open a web site in order to share the relevant information to the lager public. A prior case, which set up a web page to raise the degree of recognition and to facilitate visitors for open house, was the former Guggenheim House in Shioya, Kobe. By the way my house is also in Shioya. Their web page was quite simple and straightforward yet all the necessary information was covered. In order to follow their web page, we asked Yoshisuke Hamazaki, a resident of Shioya, who worked on the web page of the former Guggenheim House to work on Chochikukyo. On July 25, we started, without confidence, to entertain visitors for open house on prior booking on the web page of Chochikukyo which had just been launched. Chochikukyo was first often talked about among the people involved in architecture. In the first year, several hundred people visited Chochikukyo. In the following years, the number of visitors increased year by year with more people throughout the whole of Japan visiting Chochikukyo.

In order to preserve and use buildings, it is important to use buildings in a living form. Chochikukyo is a building which was built as a house. On the other side of the coin, Fujii regarded "domestic architecture as representative of architecture in Japan". Throughout his career he pursued the ideal house for the Japanese, which fit to the Japanese climate and environment. In order to allow access for more people to experience Koji Fujii's ideas and space, we intentionally decided that Chochikukyo would not be occupied by an individual or company as a residence. Rather Chochikukyo would be preserved as a living house, or living heritage, to enable any and every person to experience the time and space in Chochikukyo by the open house (three days a week on prior booking) and/or various events. In the beginning of the open house, after we established Chochikukyo Club, a volunteer organization, in spring 2008, architects/designers toured Chochikukyo as they learnt about it by word of mouth. In spring 2009, we held a concert amid fresh greenery in the garden of Chochikukyo. In autumn 2009, the first event to enjoy the colored leaves, which is now an annual event, was held. A spring event to enjoy fresh greenery and an autumn event to enjoy colored leaves were launched to enjoy Chochikukyo. On a Saturday with the best fresh greenery or colored leaves, from 10:00 to 15:00, the garden of Chochikukyo was opened without prior booking. We also accepted small groups for the tour of house one after another for those who wanted to look the interior of Chochikukyo. These annual events are now well established to welcome about 500 visitors a day (including first-time visitors and repeaters). In spring 2009, Chochikukyo was used as an exhibition space for a lacquer ware artist: "Meet Chochikukyo: Natsuki Kurimoto Exhibit". In spring 2013, an exhibition by contemporary artist, "Meet Chochikukyo: Tatsuo Kawaguchi Exhibit" was held. Visitors could enjoy the dialogue between space of Chochikukyo and contemporary art works. In 2016, annual visitors to Chochikukyo reached about 4,500 people.

Development of Chochikukyo Club

As mentioned previously, in spring 2008, I personally became a fixed-term tenant of Chochikukyo and rented the residence of the Fujii family. In parallel, the local volunteer started to be involved in daily maintenance and management and in the preservation/open house activities. It was a great privilege and honor to welcome His Majesty the Emperor and Her Majesty the Empress to Chochikukyo on June 24, 2013. Their Majesties became interested in Chochikukyo when they watched NHK E-tele (educational channel) TV program, *Bi-no-Tsubo* (Featuring Beauty), which was broadcast during the New Year holidays in 2013. As a result, Chochikukyo was brought into the brighter spotlight. At the same time, we were to come up with a sustainable system to preserve Chochikukyo, which His and Her Majesty visited. There were three issues to be addressed for the preservation of Chochikukyo:

1) It is not feasible to own, maintain, and manage Chochikukyo forever as a personal asset due to the tax burden such as property and inheritance taxes.

2) Chochikukyo Club is quite a fragile organization as it is supported only by volunteers: there is a limit on resources both financial and human, when it comes to passing over to generation by generation or to maintain motivation of volunteers.

3) There is a potential risk that Chochikukyo could be demolished and the lot be disposed of, as far as Chochikukyo has not received any protective designation as a cultural asset.

In 2016, in order to clear the issues raised to preserve Chochikukyo, and also in response to the intent of the Fujii family, Takenaka Corporation decided to acquire Chochikukyo. Takenaka made this decision as a part of its Corporate Social Responsibility (CSR) activities with the consideration of the following four points:

1) For Takenaka Corporation, Koji Fujii, who paved the way for the building design team/organization in an early stage of the company, is important.
2) There are limitations to maintenance and management of Chochikukyo as a personal asset. The Fujii family hopes and accepts to transfer Chochikukyo to Takenaka Corporation.
3) Year 2018 is an epoch-making year for Fujii and Chochikukyo: 130th anniversary of Koji Fujii's birth, 80th anniversary of his death, and 90 years since Chochikukyo was built
4) In 2019, Takenaka Corporation will celebrate 120th anniversary of the founding. To acquire, to preserve, and open Chochikukyo to public is to be a social and cultural commemorative project of the anniversary.

At the same time, we decided that Chochikukyo Club by the local people would continue to be involved in the daily maintenance, operation, and management of Chochikukyo after Takenaka's acquisition. Based on the general division of responsibility, Takenaka Corporation owns the lot and buildings of Chochikukyo while Chochikukyo Club is in charge of its daily maintenance, operation, and management. In December 2016, the right of ownership of Chochikukyo (including the lot and the buildings) was transferred from the Fujii family to Takenaka Corporation. It was also decided to transfer Chochikukyo Club from voluntary organization to a general incorporated association, which better serves public benefits.

The Articles of Association provide an objective of incorporation as follows: "To maintain/preserve Chochikukyo, Modernism architecture which represents early Showa, as well as to open it to the public, to host cultural exhibits, events, and other programs so that Chochikukyo will be further well known. Through these activities, we contribute to the architectural culture, enrichment/enlargement of educational footprint, and promotion of local community." In December 2016, Chochikukyo Club was registered as an incorporated association at Kyoto Regional Legal Affairs Bureau.

Chochikukyo Club as a general incorporated association was organized under the initiative taken by Takenaka Corporation, giving great consideration to the mix of the inaugurating board members. Number of officers from Takenaka Corporation is to be limited to the minimum, while one out of three trustees is an executive of Oyamazaki Town House, and one of two auditors is from the Fujii family. We asked Hideki Sugiyama, Vice Mayor of Oyamazaki Town House, to be a trustee and Akiko Konishi, the previous owner, to be an auditor, and both of them accepted our request. We came up with this board-member mix as we think it preferable for Takenaka Corporation to work closely with the local Oyamazaki Town House, plus Koji Fujii's family, in the daily maintenance/management and good use of Chochikukyo, as an important local cultural resource. It is important for Takenaka not to form the closed corporate community as an owner of Chochikukyo. Chochikukyo Club as a general incorporated association was launched with the joint board members representing Takenaka Corporation, Oyamazaki Town House, and the Fujii family.

As for the volunteer group to be involved in the daily practice, such as guides to tour Chochikukyo, facilitated under Chochikukyo Club as a voluntary organization, we decided to continue the group. At the same time more volunteers were sought among the residents of Oyamazaki-cho, and volunteer guides among the neighbors of Chochikukyo. Secretary General was transferred from Kazuo Ogino, who supported since launching Chochikukyo Club in spring 2008, to Hitoshi Tanabe, who was an experienced guide for the open house for several years. Tanabe lives near Chochikukyo. He was born and brought up in Oyamazaki. He said, "I was born and brought up in the house which my parents built on the lot which the family of Koji Fujii shared with my parents. I am pleased to be involved in passing Chochikukyo to future generations." Ms. Kaeko Ishiyama, who is from Oayamazaki, joined as a full-time secretariat staff. With regard to guide staff, besides Hitoshi Tanabe, those among the initial volunteers, Kazuo Ogino, Hisatoshi Taniguchi, Motoki Morimoto, and Toru Hayashi remained. On top of these guides, from the neighborhood, Kenji Tominaga, Koji Minobe, and Hiroto Sakazume newly joined. In 2017, Satoru Kaji, Yoichi Shioda, Ryoji Hayashi, Nobuyuki Yasuda, Takako Miyamoto(Ms), and Mayumi Fujiwara(Ms) also joined. Including Tanabe, total 14 guides are touring the visitors. Yoko Doi (Ms.), who had devoted herself to support the activities for a long time, and the more people living in the neighborhood participated in the local support team. (Doi was born and brought up in a small house which Fujii built as a prototype to wide spread free-standing houses.) The supporting and responding scheme which is led by the local people could be established.

The specific division of responsibilities between Chochikukyo Club and Takenaka Corporation, through the repeated study/consultation with all the concerned parties, was decided as follows: Takenaka Corporation as an owner is in charge of maintenance and management of the lot and the buildings. Takenaka Corporation has an outsourcing contract with Chochikukyo Club to conduct services such as accepting visitors, collecting admission fees (1,000 yen for an adult, 500 yen for a student, etc.), conducting regular cleaning and daily management. Furthermore, Takenaka Corporation and Chochikukyo Club concluded a Memorandum of Understanding and provided that both parties are not only the parties to the outsourcing contract but to make the best efforts to improve cultural value of Chochikukyo through the mutual cooperation. It was the first time for Takenaka Corporation to be involved in this type of cooperating scheme, so they are committed to invite various departments in the head offices and the affiliated companies to maximize the use of competence of "ALL Takenaka".

Heading for Designation of Chochikukyo as National Important Cultural Asset

In 1999, Chochikukyo, which represents early Showa era wooden Modernism architecture, was included in DOCOMOMO Japan Selection 20. Around that time, concerned members at the Agency for Cultural Affairs and Cultural Properties Division, Kyoto Prefectural Board of Education started to think about the possibility of designating Chochikukyo as an important cultural asset. This was the first case scenario for a residence in Showa era. However the specific steps for designation were not taken in a timely fashion. Not until July 21, 2005, did three of us including Shinichi Konishi, on behalf of the owner of Chochikukyo, Nobuyuki Hirai, a chief clerk of Cultural Properties Division, Kyoto Prefectural Board of Education and myself meet Takeyoshi Hori, then Senior Specialist to Director, National Agency of Cultural Affairs to talk about possible designation of Chochikukyo as a national important cultural asset. At that time, Hori explained a range of benefits rendered to the personal owner of the building(s)once designated as a national important cultural asset: reduction in property and inheritance taxes, plus a small subsidy payable to support expenses of preservation/restoration works. The owner of Chochikukyo at that time could not agree to the designation of Chochikukyo as an important cultural asset as the pubic support would be limited. It was understandable that, once designated as an important cultural asset, the real estate value would be reduced as it would be difficult to sell the property. However, the subsidy for expenses, from the national, prefectural, and/or town government, related to preservation/restoration work after the designation would, at best, be no more than 85%, the remainder to be born by the owner of the property. Though experts in National Agency of Cultural Affairs and other related authorities, plus historians of architecture appreciated the value of Chochikukyo as perspective national important cultural asset, there is a limit for the individual owner to assume the tremendous financial burden. Therefore no further action was taken as time passed.

In July 2016, when Takenaka Corporation was finalizing its intention to accept the transfer of Chochikukyo from the Fujii family, I happened to have an opportunity to meet Tatsuya Kumamoto, then Director of National Agency of Cultural Affairs. I took that opportunity to communicate the status of Chochikukyo to him. As Director Kumamoto had been thinking to preserve Chochikukyo as a cultural asset in consideration of its value, he commented that it would be in preferable direction that the ownership of Chochikukyo would be transferred from the individual ownership to the corporate ownership. Preparation work began in the hope that it would be ready to report Chochikukyo for perspective designation to the Minister of Education, Culture, Sports, Science, and Technology, scheduled in April 2017. The preparation work began in collaboration with Cultural Properties Division of Kyoto Prefectural Board of Education and also with Cultural Properties Group of Oyamazaki Town Board of Education. To complete the designation process, it was necessary to provide survey maps that showed the scope of the designation, drawings of building(s) to be included in the designation, plus photos of such buildings. Survey maps were in the process of preparation, including the field survey and documentation, for the procedure of transfer of ownership. As a future owner, Takenaka Corporation needed to prepare drawings of the three buildings to be designated; the house proper, room of quiet, and tea room. Two members of the Building Design Department of Takenaka Corporation Osaka Headquarter were named to be in charge of documentation, namely Hiroshi Arita and Keisuke Nakamura. When the field survey conducted in 2000, under my leadership, by 28 volunteers of Takenaka Corporation, drawing data in CAD data formation had been prepared and I still treasured this data. However 10 years had passed, during which time computer software had been repeatedly updated so it was with great relief that all the documentation data prepared upon the field survey could be retrieved and used. Document based on field survey of 2000 were fully utilized as an important base document for the designation. Both Arita and Nakamura, who were in charge of documentation for the designation, were among the volunteers for the 2000 survey. It was most pleasing to realize that the time and effort put in by volunteers was now leading to preparation for the designation. As for the buildings, it was fortunate that Takenaka Corporation had kept the copyright/ credit of all the photographs, despite the fact that Heibonsha Corona Book published many photographs in Chochikukyo – *Fujii Koji-no-Mokuzo Modernism Kenchiku* (Wooden Modernism Architecture by Koji Fujii). All photographs were taken by Taizo Furukawa, full-time camera person of Takenaka, who spent nearly a year.

By the end of December 2016, when Takenaka Corporation became the rightful owner of Chochikukyo, further work on the documentation for designation was facilitated in a full-fledge manner. Satoshi Nishioka, Senior Specialist to Director, National Agency of Cultural Affairs, Hironobu Takeshita, Cultural Property Division of Kyoto Prefectural Board of Education, Chiharu Terashima (Ms.), in charge of cultural property, Oyamazaki Town Board of Education, and Keisuke Nakamura, Building Design Department of Takenaka Osaka, all assisted, in collaboration, with the preparation of the documents for designation. Finally, as planned, on May 19, 2017, Cultural Property Session of Cultural Council reported Chochikukyo to be among the newly designated national important cultural assets to Hirokazu Matsuno, Minister of Education, Culture, Sports, Science, and Technology, at that time. An official gazette dated July 31, 2017 released news of Chochikukyo's official designation as an important cultural asset of Japan.

Passing on the Ideal Residence to the Future

Professor of Kyoto Imperial University and architect, Koji Fujii, was concerned with the Japanese mode of living, particularly that where Western and Japanese traditions were mixed in an ad hoc manner. This had become prevalent in Japan since the Meiji Restoration and was a result of the national policy to westernize the country. Concern for such issues resulted in Fujii publishing a book on environmental engineering theory: *Nihon no Jutaku* (Japanese Dwelling Houses), Iwanami Shoten in 1928. A summary outline of Fujii's book can be found in pages 153 ~ 156. In *Nihon no Jutaku*, Fujii analyzes and compares ten main items of Japanese and Western architectural styles including modes of living, structure and interior decoration, arrangement of rooms, wall, pentice/ eaves, and facilitiy/equipments for summer time. Fujii compared climate data between Western and Japanese cities so as to understand differences in climatic conditions. He then presented the basic way of thinking in the design of Japanese dwelling-house in order to clarify the thermal environment in which human beings feel most comfortable in a Japanese climate. Through this extensive research of the advantages of Japanese and Western styles he developed his own residential design and methodology based on his sound study of environmental engineering. It is surprising to note that Fujii shared the design methodology theory based on the environmental engineering, which he initiated, at Kyoto Imperial University, where he was teaching. If it were these days, then it is nothing special when environmental concerns are addressed. However, Fujii did this about 90 years ago when he designed his 5th house, Chochikukyo. The major pioneering views that Fujii realized in Chochikukyo, his ideal house design in Japan, are summarized in the following four points:

1) Passive design (use of natural energy) by Scientific Method
Fujii revisited the Japanese traditionally-applied building methods that seemed to respond to the climate and natural features of Japan. As a starting point he conducted a scientific review, by comparing and analyzing research results of studies conducted by Western researchers on standard temperature and humidity levels in which human beings felt comfortable. It is assumed that Fujii was the first architect/designer in Japan to base the design on a desirable temperature for the comfort of human beings. Fujii scientifically pursued the idea which Kenko-houshi stated: "A house should be so built to address the living during summer time as a priority. We can live in any place in winter. We cannot stand the simmering heat

in the house." This led Fujii to establish a theory of architecture which conforms to the Japanese climate and natural features. Fujii prioritized the measures to address the heat in summer and realized the following in Chochikukyo:

• In order to enable the good ventilation in rooms, a concept of "one room under one roof" is applied.

• Loft (or ceiling space) is used for ventilation to let summer heat escape.

• Length of eave projection decided to avoid summer sunlight as well as to allow intake of winter sunlight.

• Fresh air is led into rooms from under-the-floor and under-the-ground.

• Air tubes connect under-the-floor and the loft, which carry air which was naturally cool under the floor to the loft. Then temperature is lowered and air vent is activated.

2) Design which integrates Western style, Japanese style, and Modernism

Both the interior and exterior of Chochikukyo are in modern design. At the same time it allows us to feel somewhat nostalgic. At a glance, Chochikukyo appears to be an ordinary Japanese house, but the details tell us how the elements of Western houses are ingeniously reflected. It was the result of Fujii's sincere approach of the scientific method that led to this integration of Western and Japanese styles in the design of the residence. He first scientifically compared Western and Japanese style of houses and then came up with design details, which are not influenced at all by the trend of the times. Chochikukyo can be referred to as the result of original trial, as listed in the following, by Fujii to modernize Japanese houses, which the Japanese people had built from the ancient time:

• Tatami-mat floor is raised by 30 cm from the wooden floor: people either sitting on chairs or mats in the same room can sit face to face without looking up or down.

• Use natural material such as wood, Japanese *Washi* craft paper, and earthen walls, which were traditionally used in the *Sukiya* style of architecture.

• Design of the *Sukiya* style of architecture in Japan and emerging Art Deco and Modernism in the West are applied in harmony.

3) Model of Japanese Houses – Planning which Emphasizes Living Room and Life of Family

In most of ordinary houses in Japan around Taisho era (1912 – 1926) and early Showa era (around 1927 – 1940), a middle corridor was arranged following the vestibule. The middle corridor was aligned with a parlor containing a table and sofas, and then a tatami-mat drawing-room with an alcove to receive guests. The end of the corridor was a *cho-no-ma*, family living room. Floor planning prioritized the space for guests while the family space was pushed to the back of the house. Fujii was one of the architects/designers, who questioned this conventional planning. In Chochikukyo, next to the vestibule on the right is a restroom for guest while the drawing room (with table and chairs) is on the left, followed by the living-room. The floor plan of Chochikukyo is based on "living-room in" approach (the remaining rooms for the family are arranged after walking through the living-room), which is applicable these days. Space for family, including verandah, family reading-room, and dining-room are located through the living-room one next to the other, and this forms space for daily activities. This realizes the enriched space for the family in which each family member secures his/her own place to stay while every family member is mutually connected.

4) Design of Overall Lifestyle for New Dwelling-house in Japan

Fujii, who bought a spacious lot (or mountain), which is said to be have been 46,280 square meters in area, in Oyamazaki, was to create an ideal residential community besides individual houses. In this spacious lot, Fujii built a kiln to bake Fuji-yaki, which is his original pottery. He painted miscellaneous pottery for daily use such as bowls and tea cups or flower vases, and asked Matsujiro Kawashima, a potter of *Kiyomizu-yaki*, to finish them. Fujii pumped up rich ground water in Yamazaki for drinking water, and a source/for a 25m-long and 6m-wide swimming pool in reinforced concrete. Full-sized tennis court was also constructed. Around Chochikukyo, Fujii created an exterior landscape with a stream, a pond, and a waterfall, which effectively used the natural slope. Fujii enjoyed The Way of Tea and the art of flower arrangement. He designed not only architecture but also everything necessary in the daily life such as furniture, lighting fixtures, carpet, and miscellaneous pottery for daily use, and design/binding of books he wrote.

By chance I came across this ideal form of house in Japan. What I can say, based on my experience that I have been involved in Chochikukyo since 1996, is the large potential one building can have. One building plays a very important role in making connection. For example, people need to be connected each other, to their communities, regions and nature, and through past, present and future generations. Chochikukyo reminds us of what is difficult to perceive these days in the so called global society or economy supremacy doctrine when effectiveness or money is prioritized without conditions.

As I experienced, when devastated by a natural disaster such as the 1995 Great Hanshin Awaji Earthquake or the 2011 Great East Japan Earthquake and Tsunami, we are reminded that daily life is irreversible; we realize how the buildings and scenery are important and precious. We are largely influenced by an environment which we unintentionally live and see in daily life, including buildings and regional/local landscape. The environment is an important driver of memory for our life. If I had not encountered Chochikukyo, I would have neither visited Oyamazaki nor enjoyed close ties with the local people. Moreover Chochikukyo led me to Koji Fujii's ideas on Japanese dwelling house, which, in turn, made me think about the history of houses in Japan, the approach to architecture in Japan, and how Japanese people are involved in nature. I am sure that people in Oyamazaki have also thought of something similar. I assume that Chochikukyo has been and is of help for the local people to nurture civic pride, to be proud of Oyamazaki. A building which survives with the local community requires management of the building to support it and a chain/succession of passion. In case of Chochikukyo, Chochikukyo Club is, indeed, the management in charge of the building. In addition, Takenaka Corporation now owns Chochikukyo, national important cultural asset. In the future, under the navigation rendered by National Agency of Cultural Affairs, Cultural Property Division of Kyoto Prefectural Board of Education, and Cultural Property Team, Oyamazaki Town Board of Education, Takenaka Corporation, as the owner of Chochikukyo, will be deeply involved in preservation and repair works to be continuously conducted. Takenaka is to build up ways/means and know how to continue to use historical buildings through long-lasting and steady activities. Takenaka is to share the knowledge it acquired with the society and to contribute to the enhancement of architectural culture. Takenaka Corporation has been continuously devoting itself to create architectural works under the corporate motto to contribute to society by passing on the best works to future generations. For Takenaka Corporation, the aforementioned activities are a part of its corporate social responsibilities and they can be proud of this.

It is 22 years since I came to know Chochikukyo. At last, social sentiment and system are now well organized to pass Chochikukyo as the national important cultural asset to coming generations. Furthermore, there is another big movement. On December 8, 2017, JAPAN ICOMOS National Committee 14th Sub-committee on Architectural Legacy of 20th Century and ISC20s (International Scientific Committee on 20th Century Heritage) released Selection 20, 20th century cultural legacy in Japan. Chochikukyo is among Selection 20. Out of six selection criteria of World Cultural Heritage (of outstanding universal value), Chochikukyo met the following two criteria:

•*to represent a masterpiece of human creative genius*
•*to exhibit an important interchange of human values, over a span of time or within a cultural area of the world, on developments in architecture or technology, monumental arts, town-planning or landscape design*

As a masterpiece which best used the tradition as well as applied the idea of environmental engineering, Chochikukyo was selected among Selection 20, 20th century cultural legacy in Japan. Chochikukyo is the only personal residence/free-standing house among Selection 20, which demonstrates the importance of Chochikukyo as a Japanese dwelling-house.

One of the famous sayings by Koji Fujii is that domestic architecture represents architecture of the country/region. In 1930, Fujii wrote THE JAPANESE DWELLING-HOUSE in English. He outlined the climate and natural features of Japan from the view point of environmental engineering, for which he is noted, and posted plans, sketches, and pictures of Chochikukyo as an ideal house. It is 88 years since Fujii announced to the world the idea of Japanese dwelling-house, which conforms to the Japanese climate/natural features and reflects lifestyle and taste of the Japanese people. Chochikukyo, which represents Fujii's ideas, will continue to send out Fujii's approach to housing. Chochikukyo, in the years to come, will continue to tell Fujii's ideas as internationally-famous heritage of Japanese residence and as a world cultural heritage site once it is designated, representing the 20th century Japan.

参考―『日本の住宅』各論概説

藤井厚二の著書『日本の住宅』『THE JAPANESE DWELLING-HOUSE』の内容を概説する。

第1章　和風住宅と洋風住宅

1　和と洋が雑然としていた昭和初期の日本人の生活環境
「我国の住宅建築として確立すべき一定の様式はいかなるものであるかを考察する」ために、まず和風住宅と洋風住宅の比較を行っている。当時の事物は、非常なる激変の結果、単にそのまま模倣したもの、日本化されないもの、猶も旧態を脱しないものなどがあり、「極めて雑然たる状態」だった。

2　和風住宅と洋風住宅の比較
両者の相違を明らかにするために「生活様式」「構造および意匠装飾」「間取り」「壁」「屋根」「床」「天井」「軒および庇」「窓」「戸」の10項目について特長を挙げて比較している。

3　滑稽な「諸外国の住宅の見本を陳列」状態
人情・風俗・習慣・気候・風土の同じ日本に和と洋が混在しているのは不可解であるとし、諸外国の住宅の見本を陳列したような状況も批判している。

4　気候風土が建築に及ぼす影響
日本の多雨と道路の汚泥を考えると住宅の内外において同一の履物を持ちうる可能性は極めて低く、「腰掛式」と「座式」が併用できるのが望ましいとしている。気候・風土は、時代の移り変わりに左右されず国によって特有のものであり、夫々の国で発達してきた事物がその影響を受けた実例として、平地が多く雑草が少ないために発達したイギリスのゴルフ、夏の日射が強く中庭に面した窓から光を取り入れるイタリアの建物、そして雨量に応じて屋根勾配をとるが、降雨量が同じでも風の強い地方だと勾配はさらにきつくなる日本などをあげている。

5　真の文化住宅の創成を
住宅は、その構造は堅牢で、風雨火震災及び腐朽に対して安全、かつ衛生的で換気暖房及び採光等は完全でよく快感を与え、装飾において我々の性情に適応して気持ちのよいものでなければならないとしている。さらに機械的発明をできる限り応用して便利にして生活能率の増進を図るべきだとしている。そして、「日本特有の建築様式」が住宅において表現されるべき時代を迎えていて、1日も早く「我国固有の環境に調和し、吾人の生活に適応すべき真の文化住宅の創成せられんことを熱望」と記している。

第2章　気候

1　建築学上重要な家屋気候を形成するために必要な諸般の設備
家屋を「恒温動物である人類の寒暑乾湿を適当に調節し、換気・気流を適度にし、外界の状態がいかに変化しても、我々の環境に特種の気候を形成するものである」と定義。現代の科学が一層進歩しても、機械的装置によってこれを自由に調節しえるようになるのは遠い将来であり、外界の気候ならびに変化の状況が地球上到る処で相違し千差万別なので、それに対応する建築設備についても相違があるのは当然であるとしている。

2　人間にとって快適な気候（温度、湿度、気流）
世界の科学者8人の諸説をあげた中からレオナルド・ヒル及びルブネルの言を標準としている。「無風状態（室内を意味す）で、気温華氏80度（摂氏26度67）以上の時には裸体で居るがよく、華氏90度（摂氏32度22）以上において裸体となるのみにては不十分にして風にあたることが必要である。標準の表し方は湿球温度を以て為すべきもので、無風時湿球温度華氏五六度（摂氏13度33）を常態における好適標準とする」。

3　我国の気候の代表は北緯38度以南の3府37県

4　夏季が著しく不適当な日本の気候
日本各地の気候データを整理し分析を行ったうえで、「我国にては春秋二季における外気の常態は其の標準に近き場合も多々ありますが、夏季は高温多湿、冬季は低温少湿にして欲求する気候とは甚だしき懸隔が起こります。而して更に夏冬二季の何れかが一層甚だしき不良の状態にあるかを比較すれば、夏季に著しく不適当であり、且つ屋内にては気流減少し人体其の他より発散する熱及び水分が加わるので、やや不快の感を増します」としている。

5　日本と英、独、仏、北米合衆国の気候の比較
建築的に範となっている欧米諸国と日本の気候を比較して、以下の結論を導き出している。
「其の住宅の設備は冬季に対する研究も極めて重大ですが、夏季における設備の研究を一層緊要とし、これを主眼として考究せねばなりません。即ち外気の高温多湿の影響を防

ぎ、日光の直射によって建築物の外面及び其の周囲の高熱となるも之を屋内に伝達せず、且つ屋内にあっては人体其の他より発散する熱及び水分を除くが為に、各室の通風を能う限り盛にせねばなりません」とした。

6　夏季に死亡率が増加

京都帝国大学の戸田博士による死亡率調査の結果から、「住宅において夏季の高温多湿を調節なすの設備を怠る時には死亡率は著しく増加し、国民の幸福を甚だしく阻害する事が明らかです」としている。別の資料から夏季には妊娠率や作業能率が低下することや木材が腐りやすいことも指摘している。

第3章　設備

1　住宅の設備と意匠装飾は面白い研究対象

気候風土を対象としてそれに適応させることが住宅の最大の必要条件であり、そのためには二大様式である和風住宅と洋風住宅の主要部分の長短を比較し明らかにすることが重要としている。

2　日本の気候風土と日本人のライフスタイルに適応した設計の要点

●　間取り
日射を受けるためには南北に2列にしたものを東西に長く配列する間取りが適当。

●　換気・通風
夏季の室内の環境を良くするためには、すべての部屋に欄間を設けて「一屋一室」として気積を大にして通風を確保する必要がある。さらに夏季の通風を良くするためには風向きの大きさによって間取りを決定すべきとしている。例えば、東京では南北、大阪・神戸では西風が多い。

●　設備の目的
従来は接客に重点を置いていたが、ホテルなどが発達したので家族の居住に重点を置けばよい。従来はひとつの部屋を様々な用途に用いていたが不便・不経済なので、居間と寝室を基本に、各室の用途を分けてそれに適した設備を整えるのがよい。

●　各室の大きさ及び配置
世の変遷は激しくなり自己及び家族の将来も変わりやすいが、約10年から15年先を想像して計画すれば充分である。

●　腰掛式と座式
別々の部屋を設けずに一室内に設けるべき（あるいは襖で仕切る）。座式の部分は腰掛式の部分より、30〜36cm高くして目線の高さを同一にする。

●　室の配置
平屋建てが原則。地震にも強く、生活の能率が上がり外観を自然と融和させることができる。2階建ての場合には、居間を1階にする。階段が重要で、汚れた空気が上昇するのを防ぐため階段室を別に設け換気を完全に行い、踊り場のある上がりやすいものとすること。空間が狭い場合には食堂を居間の一部に設ける。玄関や階段室を省略するのは良くない。食堂と台所は接することが大事。縁側は西、西南にまとめて設ければ、夏冬共に室内の気候は良好になる。

3　日本における断熱の第一の目的は外壁面に受ける高熱を屋内に対して絶縁すること

木舞壁、土蔵壁、木摺壁、煉瓦壁、中空煉瓦壁、鉄筋コンクリート壁を同じ大きさで作り、夏季の太陽光線を直射させて内部温度を比較した。結果は、木舞壁○、土蔵壁○、木摺壁△、煉瓦壁○、中空煉瓦壁△、鉄筋コンクリート壁×。第3回住宅は木舞壁、第4回住宅は土蔵壁としたが、実験成績の良さから第5回住宅は土蔵壁とした。

4　屋根も壁と同様に外界気候の動揺に対して家屋気候の調節には重要

断熱性を高めるためには屋根面と天井との間の屋根裏を利用することが大事。

●　日本の気候には深い庇が有効
高温多湿の気候では深い軒や庇が有効。夏季の太陽高度をロンドンと比較。軒及び庇は深いほうが良いので、屋内にかかる屋根と区別して銅板葺のような軽いものを使うのが良いとした。

5　引き違い窓が日本の住宅には最適

窓の主要な目的は採光と通風であるが、日本では地勢の変化に富み風光明媚で築庭も普及しているので、屋外の眺望を図ることも重要とした。日本の気候風土には、洋風住宅に用いられている開き窓や上下窓は眺望や通風・換気の面で不完全で、不向きであり、日本の住宅には引き違い窓が最適とした。引き違い窓の改善策として、換気窓を上部に設ける、雨水の浸入を防ぐために窓枠を外に出す、隙間風を防ぐ工夫、防犯対策を示している。硝子障子の内側に紙障子を使うことで、冬季暖房の保温、夏季日光の直射防止、快感を与える散光による適度な光、硝子に対して温柔の感、換気調節などの効果があるとした。

6　耐震耐火耐久の研究にかたよった鉄筋混凝土造（コンクリート）

断熱性、遮音性、調湿性、換気、模様替え、施工性等が劣っている鉄筋混凝土造については、現時点では住宅には不向きであり、耐震耐火耐久が優れていても誤用濫用すべきではないと慎重な態度を記している。

第4章　夏の設備

1　経済負担の大きい冷房装置を使わない夏季の家屋気候改善案を提示

可能な限り標準気候の状態に近づけることと不良な状態にある時間を可能な限り短縮するために、建物の内外周囲における空気の理学的状態について考察し、家屋気候改善策を提示している。

2　日光の直射の有無によって甚だしく温度差の生じる各室や屋根裏と変化の少ない床下

建物の周囲は日光の直射の有無つまり方位により甚だしく温度差が生じる。内部において各室の温度差が著しいのは、午後0時から1時頃までと5～6時ごろの2回。階上、屋根裏は日没後も高温であり、その状態が長時間持続するとした。

3　建物各所における空気の状態の差異を利用して改善するのが重要

午後4時以後は外気を可能な限り迅速且つ大量に導いて、室内温度の下降を計るのが得策であり、日没後より日の出までの夜間に室内の各部を可能な限り冷却しておけば、日の出後の温度上昇を遅らせることができるとした。
夏季好状態にある空気を自由に室内に取り入れて、可能な限り気流を盛んにすることはすこぶる有利とした。

4　夏季高温になる屋根裏を通風によって低温にすることが重要

通風窓を構造上容易にかつ有効に設けることができる切妻造の屋根が日本の住宅建築においては最も適当。床下と屋根裏との間を通気筒で垂直につなぎ上下に気流を起こせば比較的容易にかつ完全に換気できる。さらに床下の気温は安定しているので、夏季は屋根裏が高温になるのを緩和し、冬季は屋根裏が急激に冷却されるのを防ぐ助けにもなる。

5　日本の住宅における夏の設備の4つの注意点

①建物の周囲において比較的良好な状態にある空気を室内に流入させること。
②室内の汚れた空気は天井に設けた排気口を通じて屋根裏に排出させて、屋根裏の通風窓より屋外に流出させること。
③屋根裏が高温となるのを防ぐため、通風の容易に行える窓を設けて換気に努めること。
④床下の多湿を防ぐために通風を盛んにし、かつその比較的低温な空気を利用して屋根裏を冷却すること。

第5章　趣味

1　気持ちよく住み得る家は落ち着きのある趣味の深い住宅

住宅は単に構造が堅牢、震火風雨・腐朽に対して安全、生存に必要な衛生的な諸種の条件を満たすだけでは不充分であり、精神上も慰安を与え、各人の性情に適応した愉快なものであることが必要。約言すれば気持ちよく住み得る家でなければならない。今の世は物質文明が偏重されて実利や能率が強調される時代なので、科学の進歩に応じて直ちにそれを適当に利用することが必要であり、ゆったりとした落ち着きのある高雅な気分に浸ることの出来得る趣味の深い住宅を造ることが極めて肝要。現今は西洋の建築趣味の中でも下手な「いろは」の手本を学んだごとき、一寸も面白みのない不愉快な住宅の多いことは遺憾。そのように建築上に西洋趣味を模して俗悪なるものに陥りやすい理由は、現今の人々の趣味を求める範囲が建築に限らずすべてにおいて極めて広くも浅薄であることから起こるのではないかと指摘している。

2　強烈な刺激を要求する濃厚な西洋趣味と清楚にして淡白なる日本趣味

建築を楽しみ趣味の豊かなる住宅を造って、高雅なる気分に浸る人々を、多く輩出させることを切に希望している。また、我国の現状は欧米の先進諸国の事物の賛美が常に行われているが、模倣は趣味の上から見てもまことに不愉快であり、西洋趣味と日本趣味を混和することは困難、いずれかを選ぶべきと主張する。

3　住宅は自然に同化してこれに包容され周囲に反抗しないもの

住宅において刺激が少なく閑雅を欲する場合には日本趣味を選ぶのが適当。変化に富む地勢で風景絶佳の我国においては、緑と類似の色を使用して同色の調和を求め、環境との調和を破らないことに留意することが必要としている。

4　住宅における日本趣味、3つの特長

①木材のほか土、紙など使用するいずれの材料も素材そのものの美しさを生かし、表面の仕上げにペンキを用いない。そうすれば、極めて清楚で、自然に調和させることができる。
②複雑な曲線を殆ど用いず、すべてが直線のみで、単調を破るために平面にて区割した種々の凸凹を設けることが有効。床の間を置くことによって多くの小なる凸凹のある空間が作られ、種々の面白い変化と多くの余裕を与えることができる。
③和風住宅における室内の光線は洋風住宅のそれに比較すれば、著しく軟らかさをもち、すこぶる快感を与えることができる。

5　種々の方向にある散光によることが我国住宅の一大特長

「主要なる室の外側には縁側があり、其の外には深い軒が出て、室内と外界との境は何処にあるか極めて不明瞭で、従って内外の変化は複雑。室内は極めて軟らかき光線によって照明され高雅なる落ち着いた感を与え、そこに無限の情緒が湧く」と指摘している。

6　高雅な趣味を備えている我国の住宅建築

「欧米の風を模する風潮が盛んで、衣食住における形式上の問題のみならず、精神上その他すべての点において欧米を謳歌するものも現れ、それは自国の美点に気がつかず盲目的に心酔しているのだと思いますが、建築上に関しては我国土に同化できない異国風の直喩を介てることは洵に憐むべき無知であり失策であると信じる」と、当時の風潮に警鐘を鳴らしている。

住宅建築文献集成第3巻　藤井厚二『日本の住宅』（柏書房・2009年発行　内田青蔵／編　松隈章／解説）所収
「藤井厚二『日本の住宅』が問いかけるもの」より抜粋、一部手を加え転載

Reference: Brief of *Nippon no Jutaku*

The followings are the outlines of Fujii's publications: *Nihon no Jutaku* (in Japanese) in 1928 and THE JAPANESE DWELLING-HOUSE (in English) in 1930.

Chapter 1
Japanese Dwelling-Houses and Western Dwelling-Houses

1 The Japanese Living Environment Early Showa Era(late 1920's/early 1930's), in a Mess with the Japanese and the Western Style Mixed-up

Fujii, in the beginning, compares the Japanese and the Western style in order to study "the perfect style of domestic architecture peculiar to Japan". As a result of the extraordinary violent changes, things at that time were just copied, yet to be Japanized, or still in the old state, namely in an extremely messy state.

2 Comparison of Japanese and Western Dwelling-Houses

In order to clarify the differences between the two, Fujii lists features by 10 items and makes the comparisons: "modes of living", "structure and interior decoration", "arrangement of rooms", "wall", "roof", "floor", "ceiling", "pentice/eaves", "windows" and "doors".

3 Ridiculous State of "Displaying Foreign Dwelling-House Samples"

Fujii points out that it is incomprehensible that the Japanese and Western styles are mixed in Japan, where sentiments, customs, habits, climate, and natural features of the place are same. He also criticizes the state as if samples of foreign dwelling-house are displayed.

4 Influences of the Climate over Architecture

Considering large precipitation and sludge on the roads, *the prospect of the same foot-gear being used both indoors and outdoors in Japan is very remote*. Fujii's preference is to use table/chairs and tatami mats conjointly in the house. Climate and natural features are unique to the country, which have little to do with the transition of the times. Fujii lists the examples of the things susceptible to these factors developed in different countries: Golf has been popular in England with abundant flatland with few weeds; Italian architecture allowing the light from windows facing courtyards due to the strong radiation during summer; and in Japan sloped roofs corresponding to the level of precipitation, whose pitch is steeper in the regions with stronger winds even though the precipitation level is same.

5 For the Creation of True Japanese Dwelling-houses Incorporating Western Elements

Fujii claims that dwelling-houses should be solid in structure, safe against wind, rain, fire, earthquake & rot/decay and clean. Ventilation, heating and lighting intake should be perfect for comfort. Decoration should be cozy, suitable for the Japanese character. Furthermore; mechanical inventions should be utilized as much as possible for application for further convenience and living efficiency. It is high time, according to Fujii, to express the architecture style unique to Japan. Thus he is impatient for Japanese dwelling-houses incorporating Western elements, suitable for the environment peculiar to Japan and fitting to the Japanese' mode of living.

Chapter 2
Climate

1 Various Mechanical Means in the Architectural Study to Create Indoor Climate

Fujii defines the house is, for human beings, homeothermic animal, to *properly modify the effects of weather and atmospheric temperature and regulate ventilation and draughts so that we can always create around us a suitable climate, which is a proof against changes in the outside world*. He thinks without doubt that time is still very far off when we shall be able to regulate the indoor environment even if science is remarkably progressed. Fujii takes it for granted that mechanical means in architecture differ among the countries as the open air climate and its variations are different.

2 Climate (Temperature, Humidity and Draughts) Most Suited for Mankind

In listing views of 8 scholars around the world, Fujii refers to the views of Dr. Leonard Hill and Dr. Rubner as the standard climate: *when there is still air (indoors) with a temperature of 80°F (26.67°C), it is well for us to be nude, but when the temperature is above 90°F (32.22°C), it is not enough for one to be naked, one must have some active currents of air. The standard ought to be indicated by a wet bulb temperature and in the normal state the wet bulb temperature of 56°F (13.33°C) is the most desirable condition in still air.*

3 Representative Climate in Japan: 38 degrees N. lat. and further south, covering 40 prefectures

4 Japanese Climate with Summertime Being Extremely Inappropriate

Fujii compiles and analyzes climatic data around Japan and summarizes as follows: *the open air climate in spring and autumn of Japan is often approximate to the standard climate required for our comfortable existence, but in summer and in winter it falls very short of the standard climate, for in the former season we have high temperature and abundant humidity, while in the latter season low temperature and little humidity.* He further compares summer and winter to identify which season is extremely unfavorable. *Of these two seasons, summer is the worse. Moreover, within doors the air currents are poor, and the heat and the moisture emanating from the body and other objects increase, to make life all the more uncomfortable.*

5 Comparison of Climate in Japan vs. Climate in England, Germany, France, and North America

Fujii compares the climate in Japan and that in the Western countries, the architecture of which serves as model for Japanese architecture and reaches the following conclusion: *the equipment of the house must be attended to with the needs of the winter season chiefly in view the needs of summer season must be primarily studied in Japanese house-building. Care must be taken to prevent the indoor climate from being influenced by the high temperature and abundant humidity outdoors…Despite the intense heat of the outside surface of the building and surroundings caused by direct sunbeams, all rooms must be ventilated as effectually as possible in order to preclude the bad effects of the heat and moisture issuing from the body.*

6 Increased Death Rate in Summer Season

Dr. Toda of Kyoto Imperial University conducted a survey on death rates. Based on survey's result, Fujii comments that it is clear that, in case the dwelling-house failed to be furnished with equipment to control high temperatures and abundant humidity, the death rate remarkably increases and the well being of the people is largely impaired. He also points out, in an other paper, that the rate of pregnancy and business efficiency are lowered. In addition, timbers rot easily.

Chapter 3
Equipment

1 Equipment and Interior Decoration of Dwelling-House Interesting Subjects of Research

The necessary conditions of dwelling-house are to be suitable for the climate. To that end, Fujii pointed out that it is important to compare and clarify the strength and weakness of key features of the two leading styles, the Japanese and the Western.

2 Key Design Points Suitable for Japanese Climate

•Space configuration
The appropriate arrangement to let in sunlight is that *two of the rooms almost always run north and south, connecting with each other……. is repeated east or west in parallel.*
•Ventilation & Draft
To improve the indoor environment in summer, it is necessary to secure draft with maximum air mass, by arranging all the rooms under one roof, and each room be provided with transom windows. Furthermore, for the better draft in summe space configuration should be decided depending on the dominant direction of wind. For example, south to north wind and west bound wind is predominant in Tokyo and Osaka/Kobe, respectively.
•Objects of Equipment
In the past, the reception of guests was the priority, but as hotels have been developed life of family has become the priority. Until now, one room has been used for multi-purpose, which is inconvenient and wasteful. Instead, a living room and a bedroom are the core, furnished with the equipment fitting to the use of the room.
Size and Layout of Rooms
The future of self and the family is changeable as a result of drastic changes in the world. Fujii thinks it is enough to picture 10 to 15 years to come.
Table/chairs and Tatami Mats
Instead of providing separate rooms for table/chairs and tatami mats, Fujii's view is to equip a room with both chairs and mats (or division of the space with *fusuma*). The part with mats has a floor 30 to 36 cm higher than the rest, so that all those sitting in the room share the same eye height.
•Arrangement and Size of Rooms
In principle, a single-story house is preferable as it is strong against earthquakes, it enhances efficiency of living, and its exterior appearance can harmonize with nature. In case of two-story house, a living room is on the 1st floor. Stairs are important: separate staircase should be provided for perfect ventilation and stairs should be easy to walk up with a landing. In case of the limited space, a dining area is included in a living room. It is not good to drop a vestibule or stairwell. It is important to layout dining next to kitchen. The indoor climate is favorable both in summer and winter by providing the verandah in the west and/or southwest.

3 In Japan the first care of insulation is to insulate the heat on outside wall surfaces from that inside.

To compare the interior temperatures of the different types of wall structure, Fujii built the following mock-ups in the same size and exposed them to the direct sunlight wood lath earth wall, soil wall, wood lath plaster wall, brick wall, hollow brick wall and reinforced concrete wall. The results were as follows: wood lath earth wall ○, soil wall ○, wood lath plaster wall △, brick wall ○, hollow brick wall △, and reinforced concrete wall ×. The 3rd house was in wood lath earth wall, the 4th house was in soil wall, while the 5th house was in soil earthen wall as its result of the experiment was favorable.

4 Like the Wall, the Roof Very Important to Regulate Indoor Climate in response to the Variations of the Open-air Climate

In order to enhance the insulation effectiveness, it is important to use the loft between the roof surface and the ceiling surface.
•Deep eave being Effective in the Japanese Climate
In the climate with high temperatures and abundant humidity, far-projecting eaves are effective. Fujii compares solar altitudes in summer in the cities in Japan with that in London. As it is better to have far-projecting eaves, Fujii proposes to use light roofing material such as sheet copper, separate from roof structure extending indoors.

5 Horizontal Sliding Windows Being Most Suitable for Japanese Dwelling-Houses

The main object of windows is to let in light and to facilitate ventilation. In a country like Japan, where physical features are so diversified that scenic views abound and also where gardening is very popular, however, it is often the case that a window's chief object is that of enabling the inmates to look out on the surrounding scenery. Casement windows and sash windows used in Western houses are not suitable for the dwelling-houses in Japan as view and draft/ventilation are imperfect amid the Japanese climate. Fujii points out that the horizontal sliding windows are fitted, instead. He explains ways to improve these windows: ventilation windows above, window frames to be located outside to stop rain driven in, measures to prevent draft, and ways to enhance security. He points out that "double grooves with glazed *shoji* on the outer side and paper *shoji* on the inner side are effective in facilitating the warming of a room in winter; in preventing the exposure of the room to the direct sunlight in summer; in maintaining appropriate light level for the better comfort by scattered light; in extending a warm and soft feeling by the glazing, and in controlling ventilation.

6 Reinforced Concrete (RC) Structure Emphasizing too much on Research on Earthquake-, Fire-proof and Durability

Fujii comments that reinforced concrete structures are, at the moment, unsuitable for dwelling-houses because they are less favorable in insulation, sound-proofing, humidity control, ventilation, refurbishment, and workability. He is cautious about misapplication and improper use of RC structures even if they are good in earthquakes-, fire-proof, and durable.

Chapter 4
Equipment in Summer

1 Proposal of Ways to Improve Indoor Climate during Summer Season without Cooling Apparatus Causing Heavy Economic Burden

In order to come close to the standard climate as much as possible and to minimize the hours with an unfavorable climate state, Fujii studies the scientific conditions of air indoor, open-air, and at peripheral and proposes the ways to improve indoor climate.

2 Rooms and Loft with Wide Variation in Temperatures & Basement with Less Variation

The temperatures at the building peripheral largely fluctuate depending on whether there is direct sunlight or not, namely with on direction. Indoor room temperatures largely fluctuate twice a day: between around 12:00 p.m. and 1:00 p.m., and 5:00 p.m. and 6:00 p.m. Upper floors and loft retain high temperatures even after sunset for long hours according to Fujii.

3 Importance of Improving Conditions of Indoor Air Tapping Temperature Differences among Points/Places in Dwelling-House

In Fujii's view, at 4:00 p.m. or later, it is good to drop the indoor temperature by taking in outdoor air as fast as possible and as much as possible. Furthermore, temperature rise after sunrise can be delayed by cooling every point inside the house as much as possible during nighttime, between sun set and sun rise. He points out that, in summer, it is advantageous to take in favorable air freely to activate air flow as much as possible.

4 Importance of Lowering Temperature of Loft, which gets High in Summer, by Draft

Fujii recommends gable roof as most suitable in the Japanese domestic architecture, the structure of which easily and effectively enables installation of a draft window. Perfect ventilation can be provided comparably easily by connecting under-floor and loft with vertical air pipe, which moves air up and down. Moreover, temperature under the floor is stable, which mitigates high temperature rise in loft in summer, and prevents sudden cooling in winter.

5 Four Points of Attention about Equipment in Summer in case of Japanese Dwelling-House

① Let comparable favorable air at the building peripheral, flow into the building interior.
② Dirty indoor air is exhausted to the loft through vent(s) on the ceiling, and then flows outside through the draft window in the loft.
③ In order to prevent high temperature rise in the loft, window(s) which easily enable draft is/are provided for ventilation.
④ In order to prevent high humidity under the floor, active draft is provided, and also comparably low temperature under the floor is tapped to cool the loft.

Chapter 5
Taste and Interest

1 Calm House in Rich Taste – Comfortable House to Live -

It is not enough for the dwelling-house to be in solid structure, safe against earthquakes, fire, wind, precipitation, and rot/decay and to satisfy various hygienic conditions for people's survival. Fujii comments that the dwelling-house should provide psychological rest, relaxation and feel pleasant, fitting to each person's nature. In short, a dwelling-house should be a comfortable place to live. In Fujii's view, these days, material culture is overemphasized and material interests and efficiency are underlined. In response to the progress in science, such progress should be used promptly. At the same time, it is of vital importance to build the dwelling-house in good taste, which enables residents to feel comfortable, intimate, and elegant. These days, if poor basics among the Western architectural tastes are modeled, Fujii regrets that there will be many unpleasant dwelling-houses without any bit of artistic interest. As for the reasons why it is easy to get down to vulgar architecture, imitating the Western architectural taste, he points out the range of tastes people of the time was sought extremely wide but superficial in general, not only limited to architectural tastes.

2 Heavy Western Taste Seeking Strong Stimuli in Contrast to

Neat and Subdued Japanese Taste

Fujii earnestly hopes that by enjoying architecture and building dwelling-houses in good taste, more people filled with a sense of elegance would be produced. At that time, though the objects of Western advanced countries were always admired, Fujii regards imitations to be extremely unpleasant. He claims that it is difficult to mix Western taste with Japanese taste and that one of the two tastes should be selected.

3   Dwelling-house to be Assimilated to Nature, to be Embraced by Nature, not Resisting against Nature

According to Fujii, in a dwelling-house, it is appropriate to select the Japanese taste with intention of refined ambience and less stimuli. In Japan, a country of scenic beauty, with wide-ranging topography, it is necessary to use a color similar to green for the harmony with green color. Attention should be made not to break the harmony with the environment.

4   Three Features of the Japanese Taste in case of Dwelling-house

① Besides timber, any other material used including earth or paper, should reflect its own material, without using painted surface finish. The result is a dwelling-house that is neat and harmonizes with nature.
② Complex curved lines are minimized, and making nearly all lines straight lines. To break the monotony, Fujii points out that it is effective to provide a variety of irregularities dividing with the planes. Alcoves can create many small irregular spaces, which offer diverse interesting variations and much comfort.
③ Indoor rays of light in the Japanese dwelling-house, in comparison with that in the Western counterpart, is extremely soft and offers an excellent feeling of pleasure.

5   Leading Feature of the Japanese Dwelling-House: Scattered Light in Various Directions

Fujii points out that a verandah is provided at the outside of main rooms with far-projecting eaves, which in turn blurs the boundary between indoor and outdoor. As a result, changes in light vary in complex ways. Indoor is lit up with extremely soft light for the calm and elegant ambiance, which inspires infinite emotion.

6   Japanese Domestic Architecture with Elegant Taste

Fujii alerts us to the fact that it was current trend of the time to imitate the Western customs, not only imitating the styles of housing, food, and clothing but also glorifying the West in psychological views and many other points. Such people devote themselves blindly, without noticing the virtue of their own country. In the case of architecture, Fujii advised us to refrain from referring to foreign styles, which cannot be assimilated to the Japanese climate as it is ignorant and mistaken.

Notes:

Abstract with partial re-wordings of *Fujii Koji Nihon-no-Jutaku ga toikakeru mono*
(What does "Japanese Dwelling-house" by Koji Fujii address?) in *Nippon-no-Jutaku* in the 3rd collection of Residential Architecture References 2009, edited by Seizo Uchida with Akira Matsukuma's commentary, published by Kashiwa-shobo in 2009

.

実測図

この実測図は、平成12（2000）年の実測データに基づき、竹中工務店大阪本店設計部で作成した。
後に設計時の姿に戻された部分は、現状とは異なる。

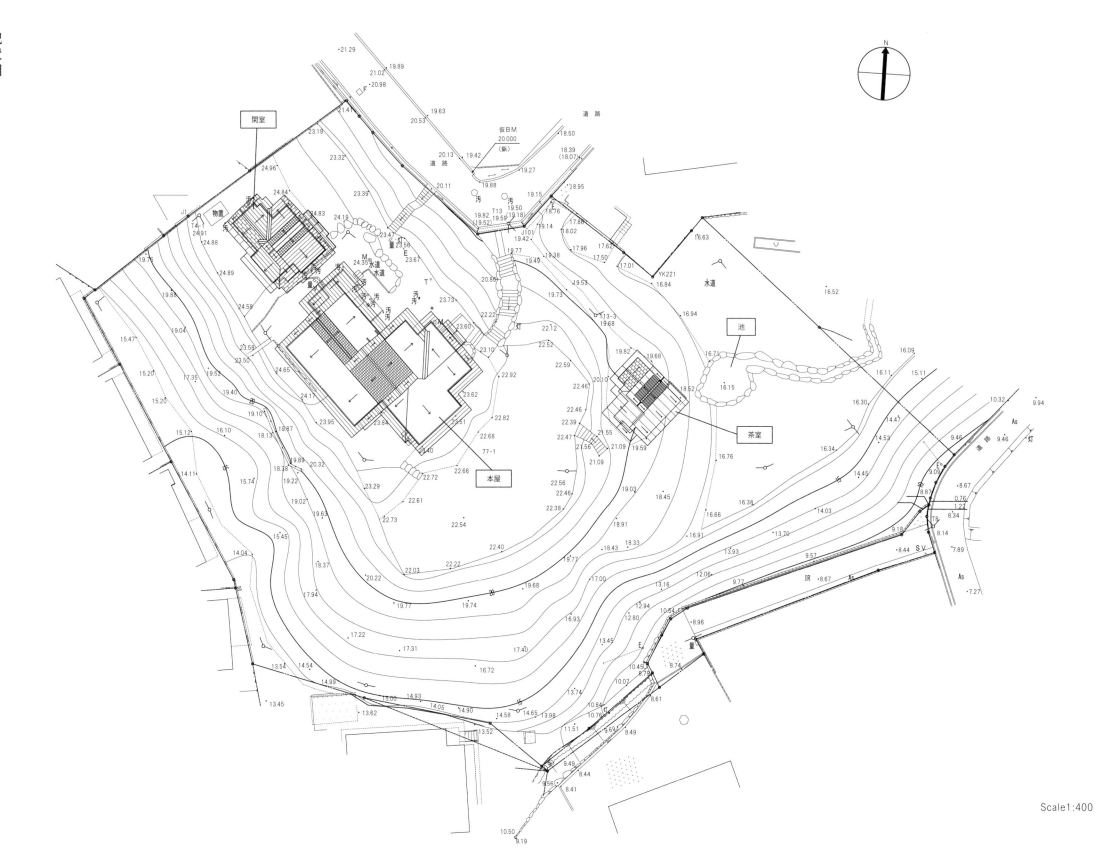

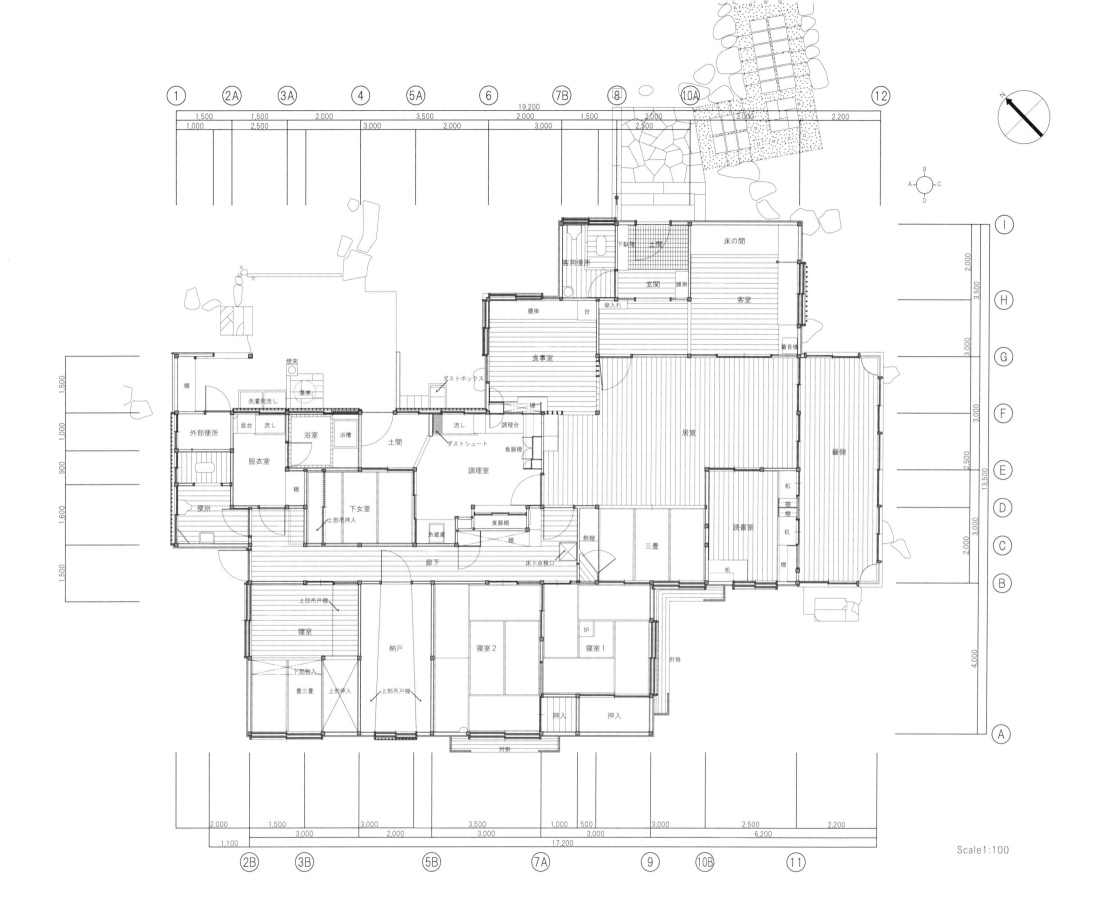

天井伏図（本屋）

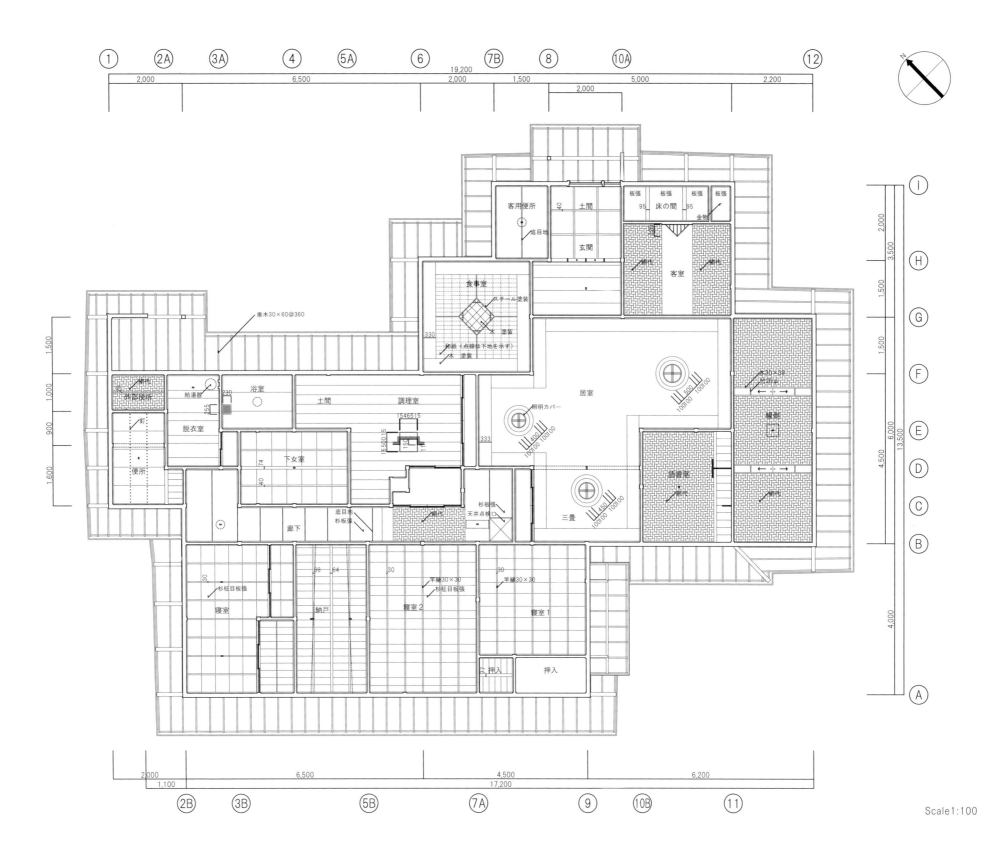

Scale 1:100

屋根伏図（本屋）

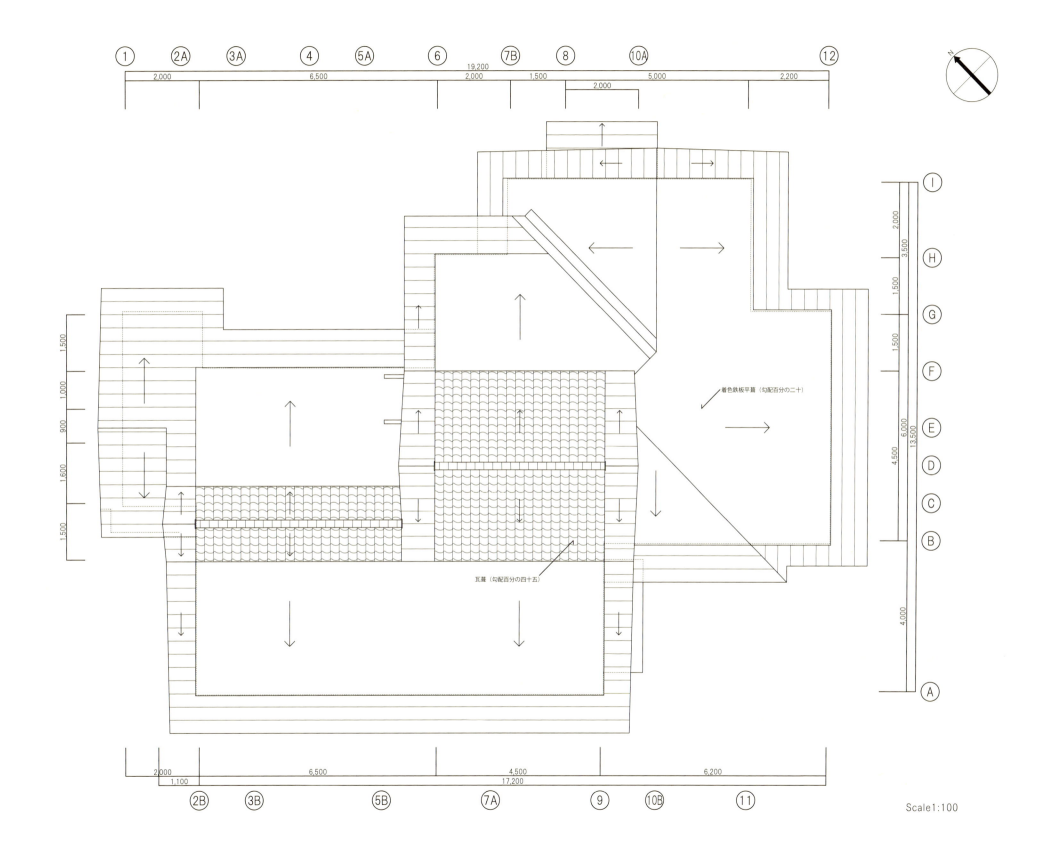

Scale 1:100

立面図（本屋）

東立面図

南立面図

Scale1:100

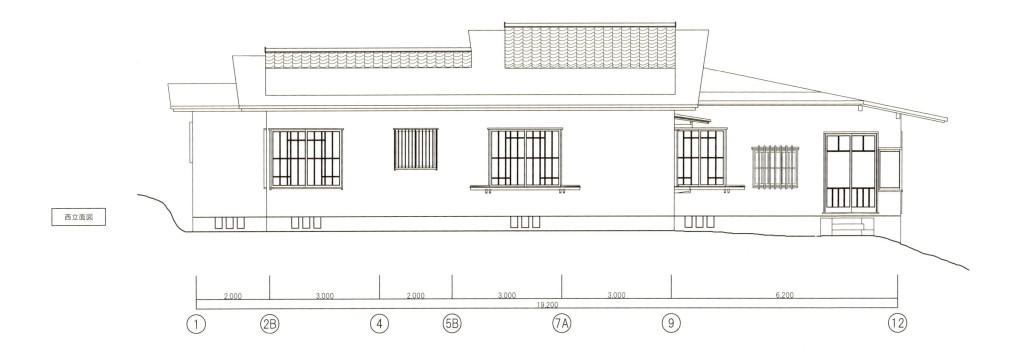
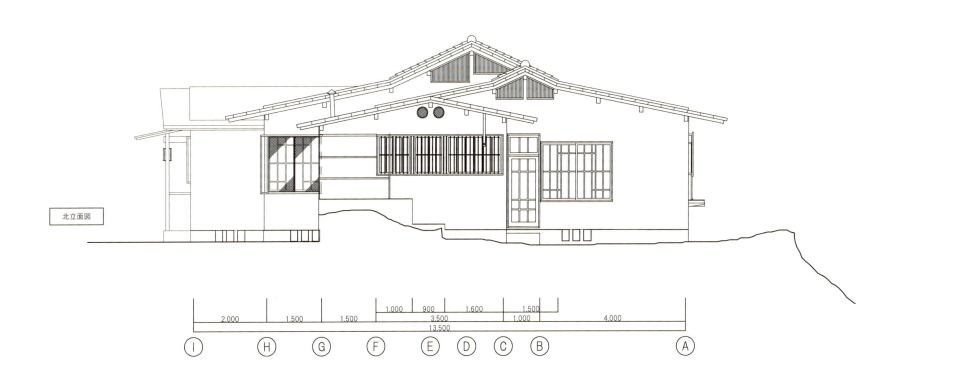

断面図（本屋）

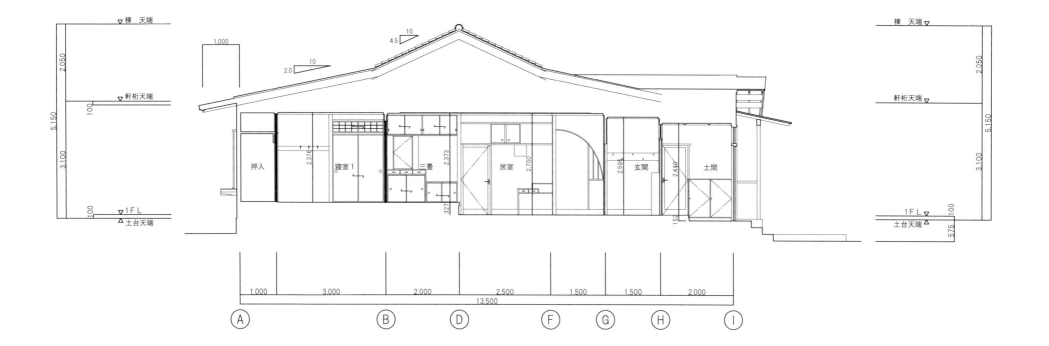

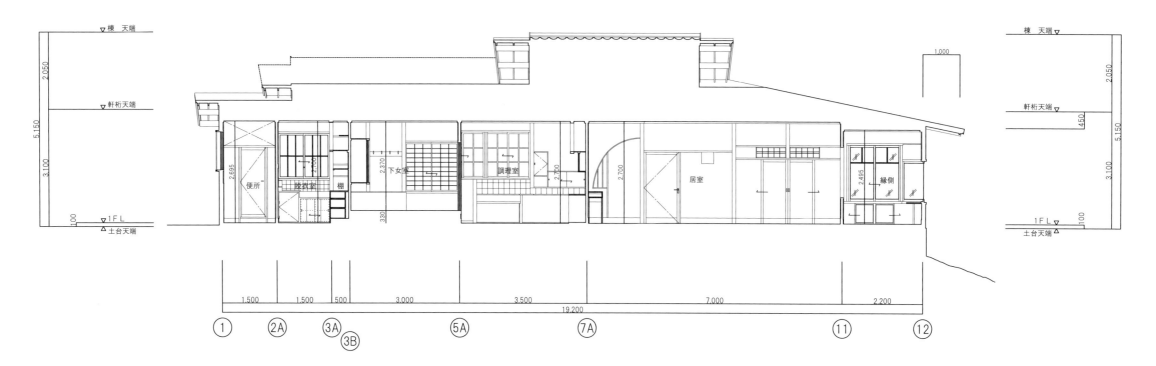

Scale 1:100

立面詳細図（本屋東面／玄関・食事室ほか）

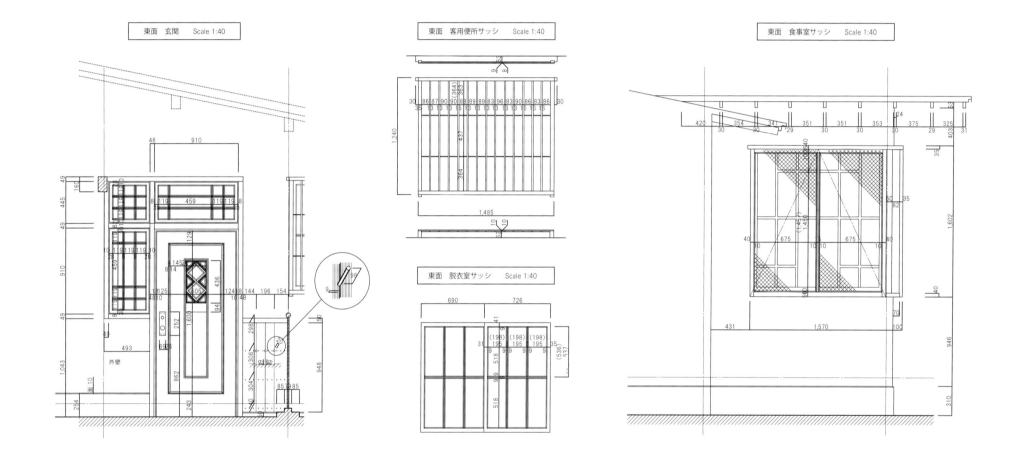

立面詳細図（本屋南面／縁側）

Scale 1:40

立面詳細図（本屋南面／寝室・客室ほか）

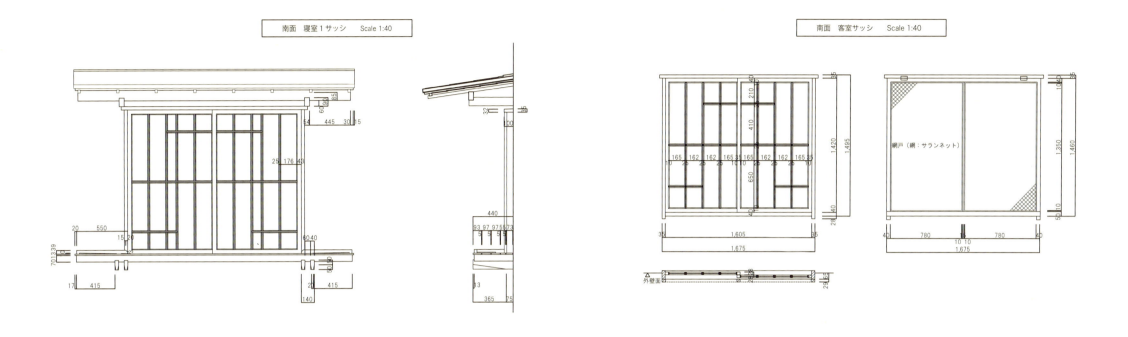

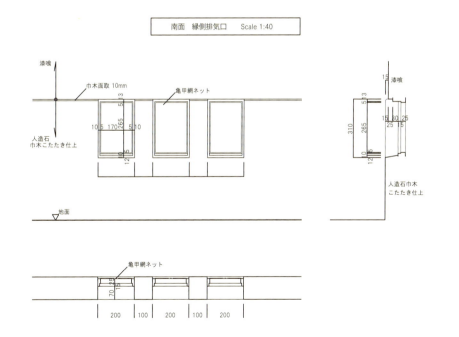

立面詳細図（本屋西面／縁側・読書室・小上がり）

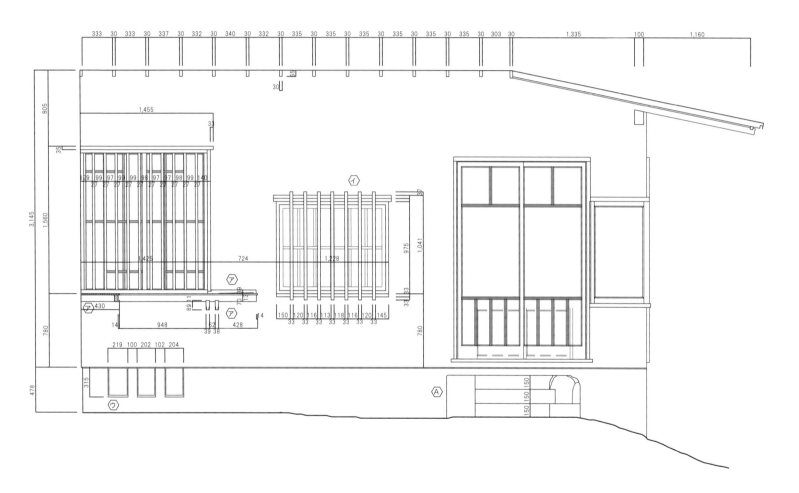

Scale 1:40

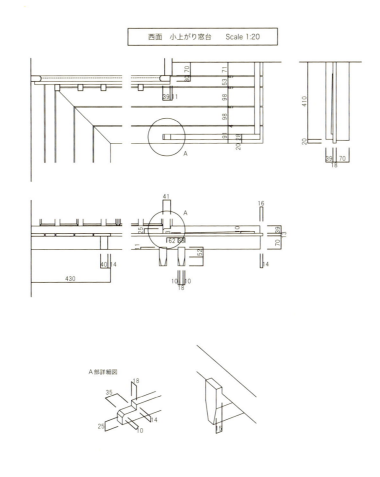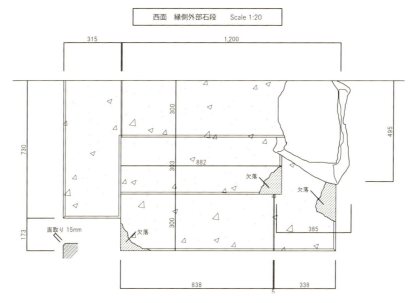

立面詳細図（本屋北面／廊下・便所）

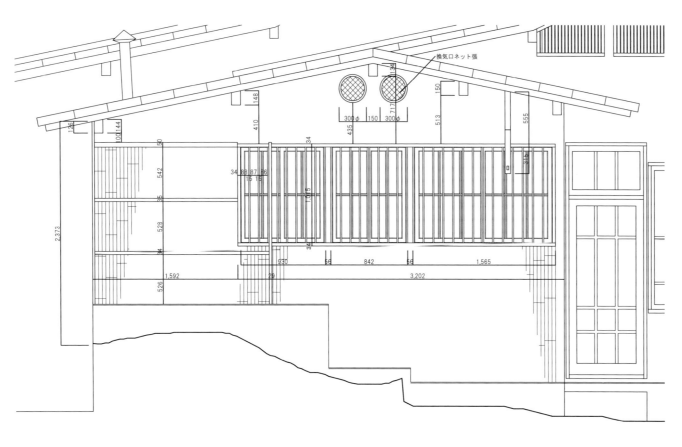
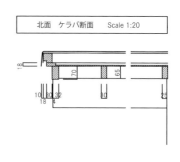

立面詳細図（本屋東面／調理室・浴室・脱衣室・外部便所）

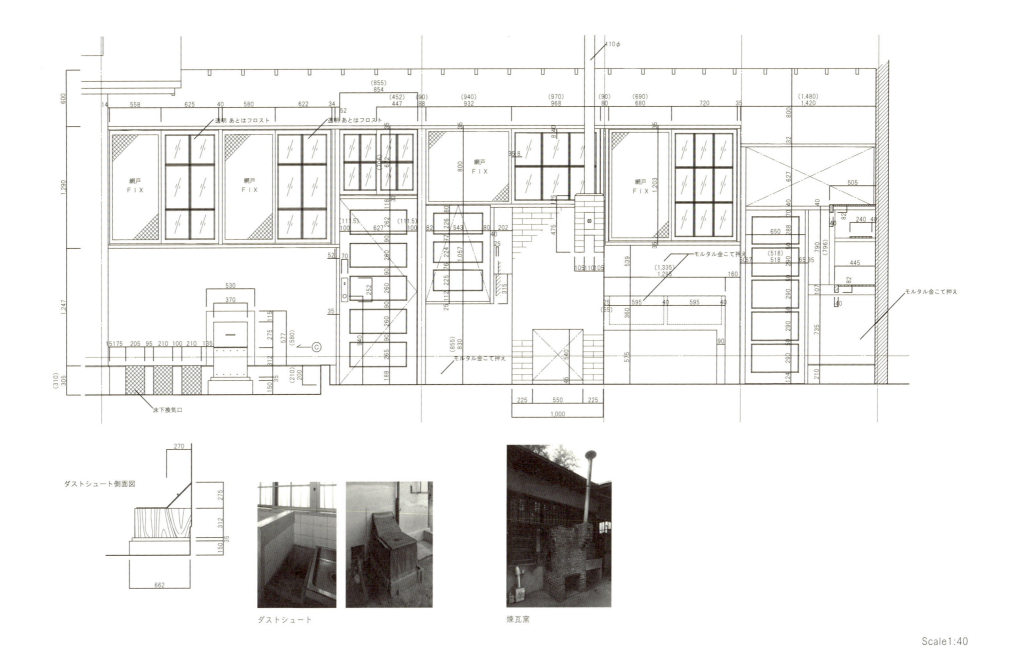

ダストシュート側面図

ダストシュート　　煉瓦窯

Scale 1:40

立面詳細図（本屋東面／脱衣室・外部便所入り口目隠し壁）

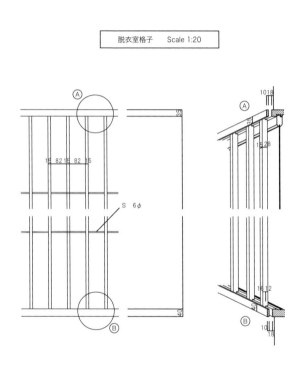

脱衣室格子　Scale 1:20

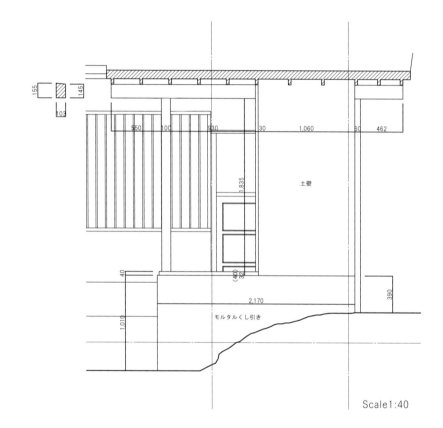

Scale 1:40

立面詳細図（本屋北面／食事室）

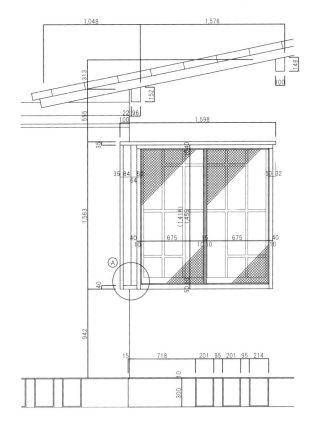

A部詳細図　Scale 1:20

網戸を閉じた状態　　　　　網戸を跳ね上げた状態

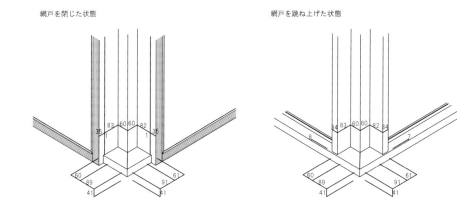

展開図（本屋／玄関・客用便所）

Scale 1:60

部分詳細図（本屋／玄関・扉）

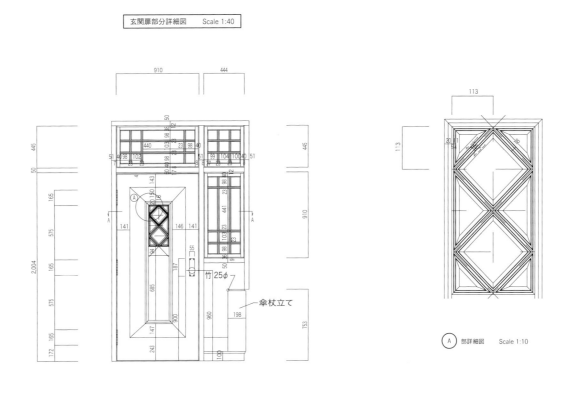

玄関扉部分詳細図　Scale 1:40

A　部詳細図　Scale 1:10

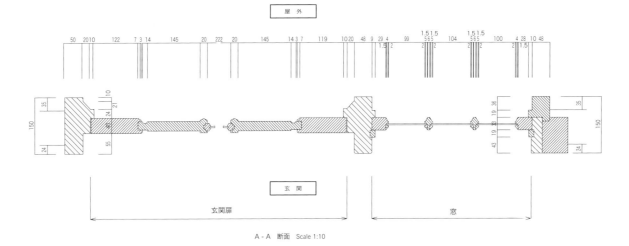

A - A　断面　Scale 1:10

展開図（本屋／居室）

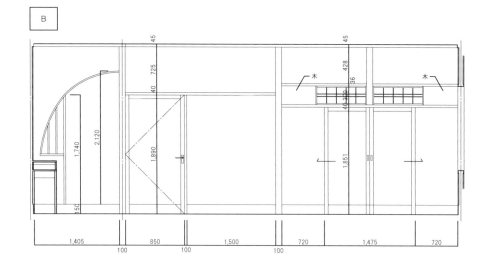
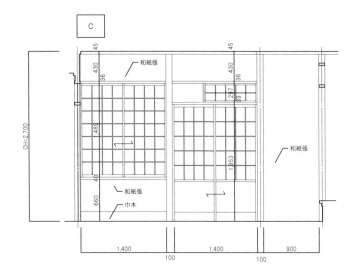
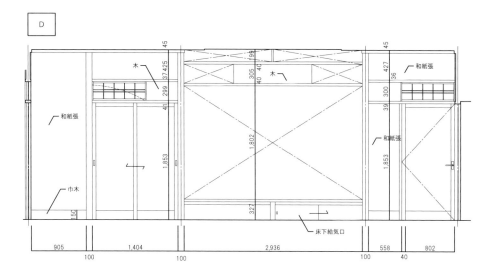

Scale 1:60

部分詳細図（本屋／居室）

建具廻り部分（居室展開図C）

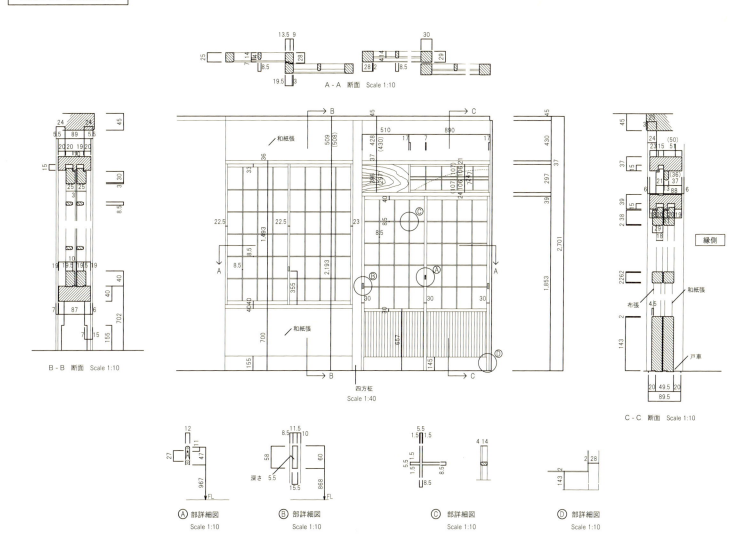

部分詳細図（本屋／居室）

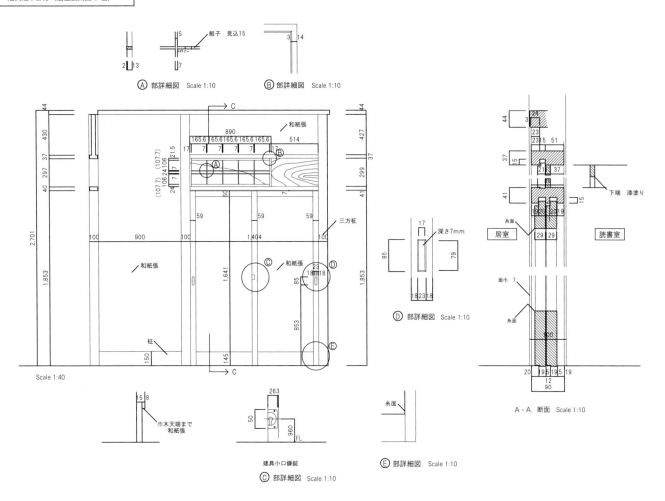

建具廻り部分（居室展開図Ｄ右）

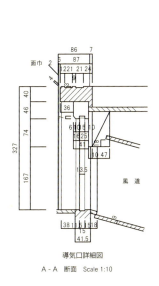

導気口詳細図
A-A 断面 Scale 1:10

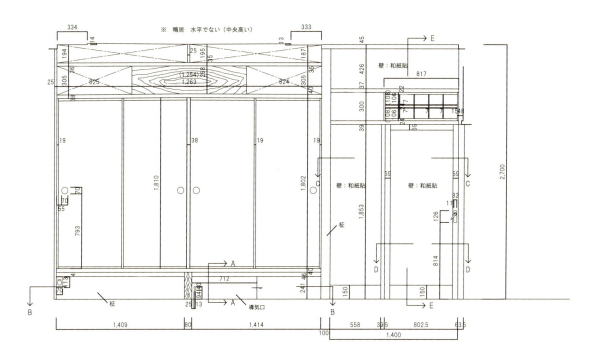

＊後に取り付けられた欄間と襖は撤去されている。

Scale 1:40

部分詳細図（本屋／居室）

建具廻り部分詳細（居室展開図D右）

B-B 断面 Scale 1:10

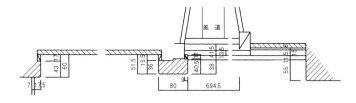

C-C 断面 Scale 1:10

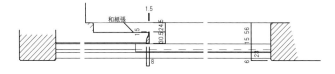

D-D 断面 Scale 1:10

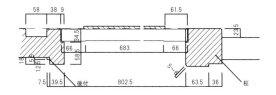

E-E 断面 Scale 1:10

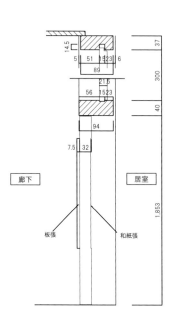

部分詳細図（本屋／居室）

壁時計（展開図 B） Scale 1:4

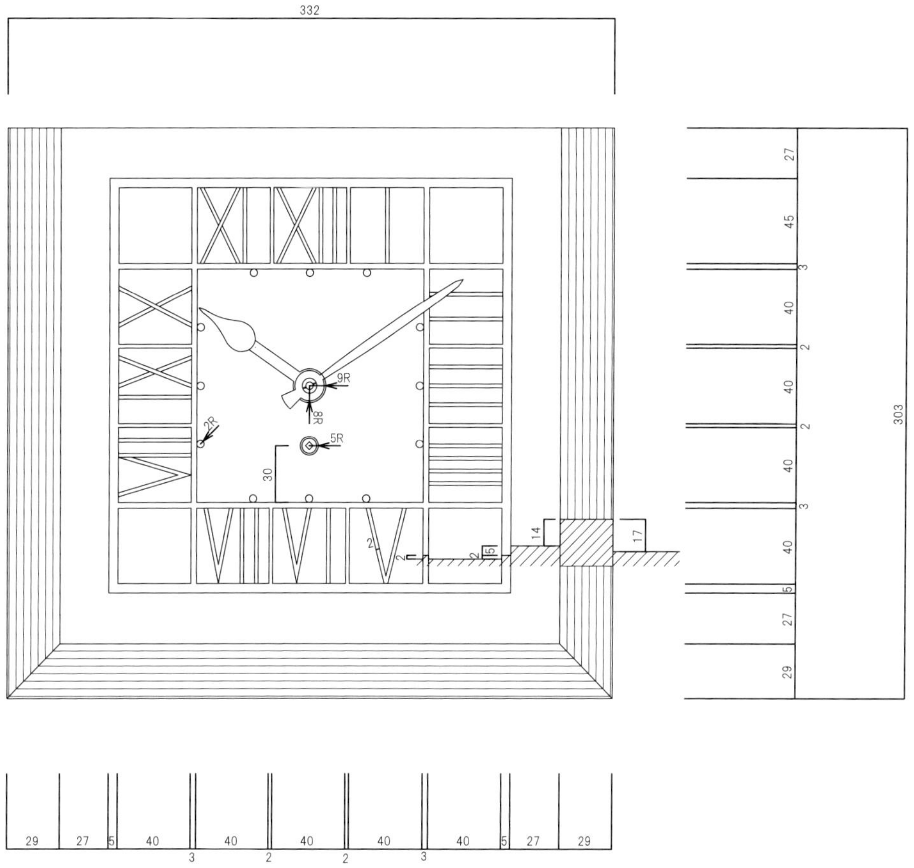

部分詳細図（本屋／居室）

造付け棚（展開図B） Scale 1:10

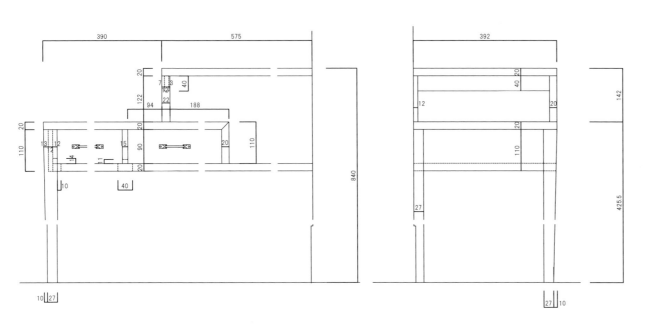
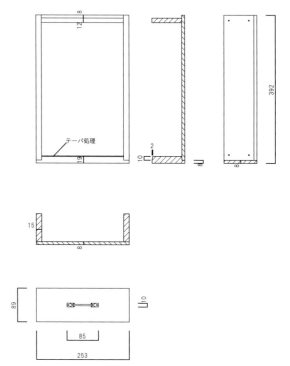

正面　　　　　　　　　　　　断面　　　　　　　　　　　　引出詳細図

神棚（展開図 B） Scale 1:10

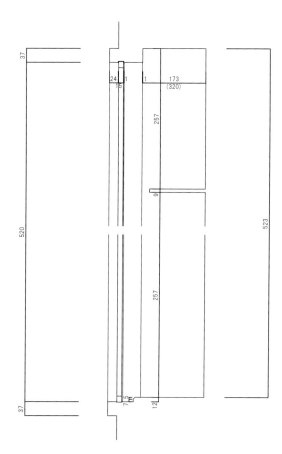

展開図（本屋／食事室）

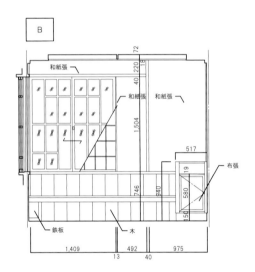
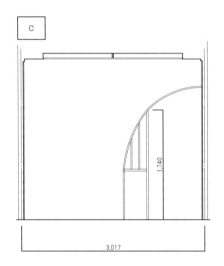
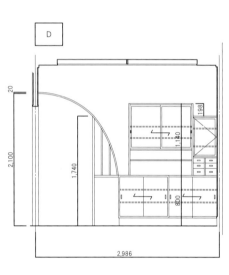

Scale1:60

部分詳細図（本屋／食事室）

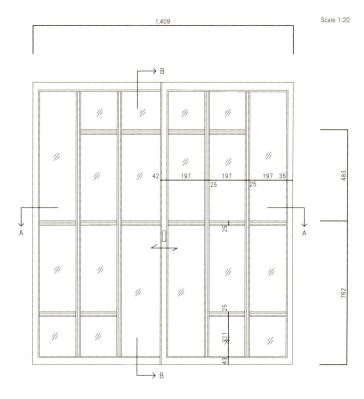

東面（展開図A）建具部分

A-A 断面 Scale 1:20

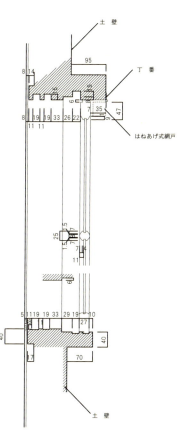

B-B 断面 Scale 1:10

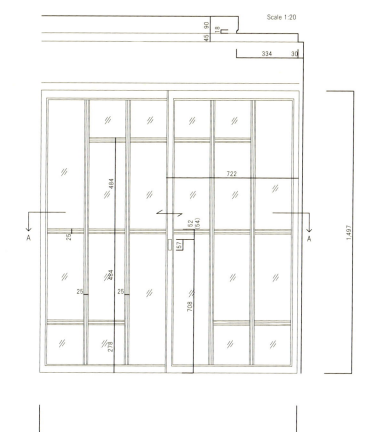

北面（展開図B）建具部分

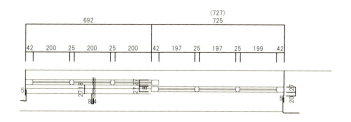

A-A 断面 Scale 1:20

部分詳細図（本屋／食事室・造付け棚）

西面（展開図D）造付け棚立面

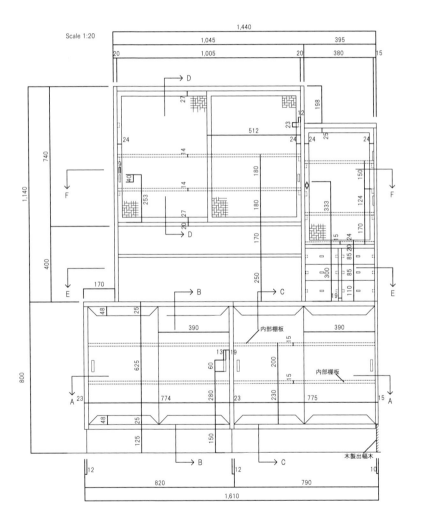

A-A 断面 Scale 1:20

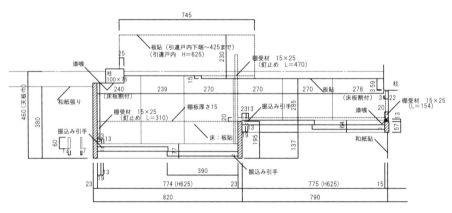

F-F 断面 Scale 1:20

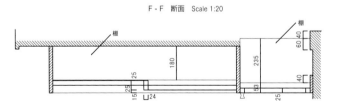

引手詳細図 Scale 1:10

B - B 断面 Scale 1:4

C - C 断面 Scale 1:4

D - D 断面 Scale 1:4

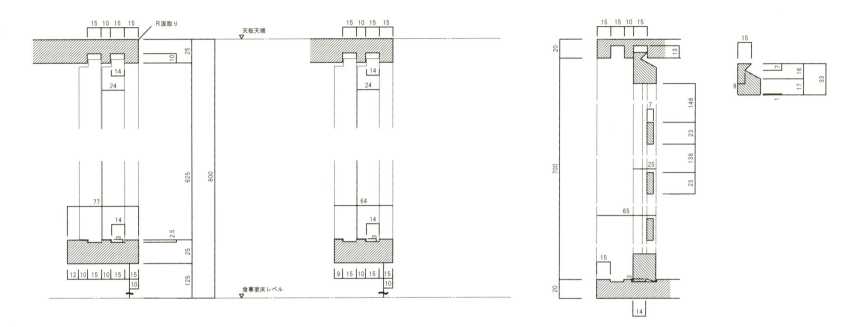

E - E 断面 Scale 1:20

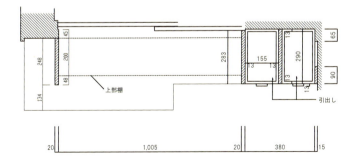

展開図（本屋／読書室）

読書室

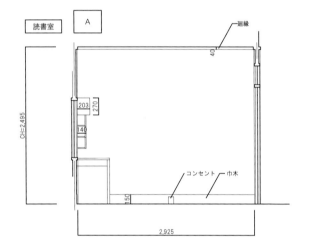
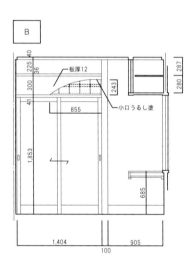
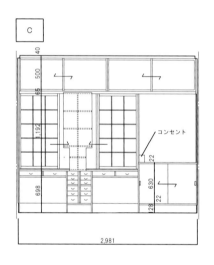
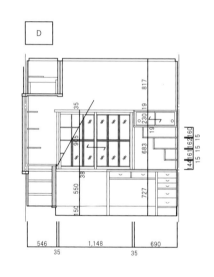

Scale 1:60

部分詳細図（本屋／読書室）

建具廻り（展開図A）

建具廻り（展開図B）

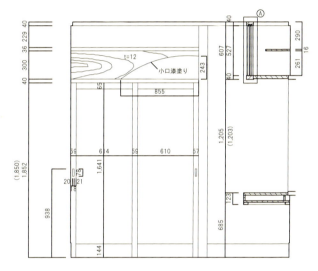
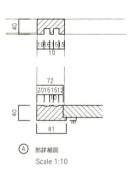

Ⓐ 部詳細図 Scale 1:10

Ⓑ 部詳細図 Scale 1:10

t=12
小口漆塗り

Ⓐ 部詳細図 Scale 1:10

Scale 1:40

Scale 1:40

部分詳細図（本屋／読書室）

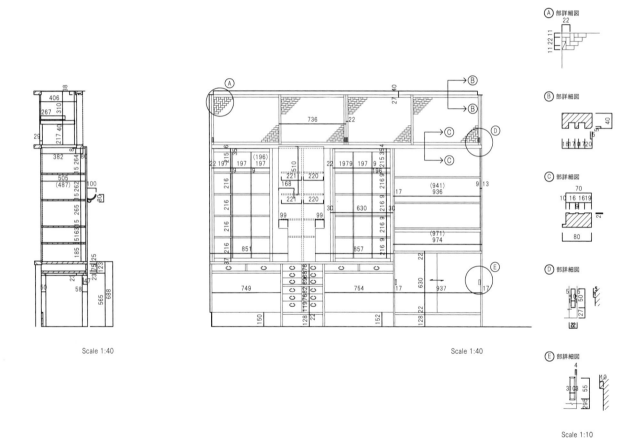

建具廻り（展開図D）

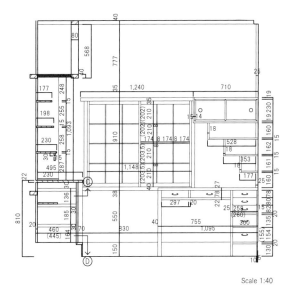

Scale 1:40

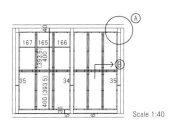

Scale 1:40

Ⓐ 部詳細図　　Ⓑ 部詳細図

Ⓒ 部詳細図　　Ⓓ 部詳細図

Scale 1:10

部分詳細図（本屋／縁側）

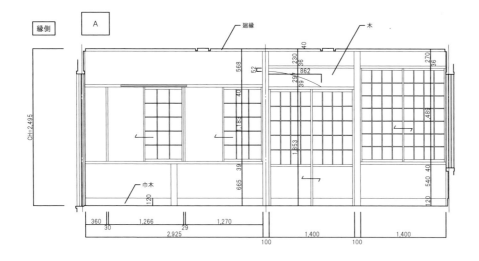

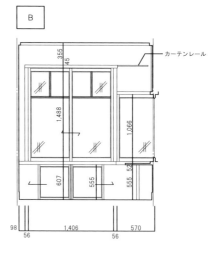

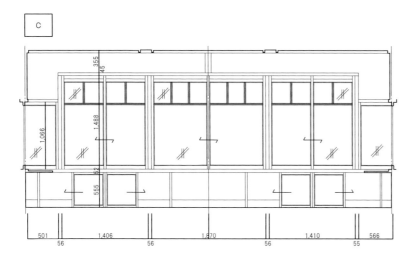

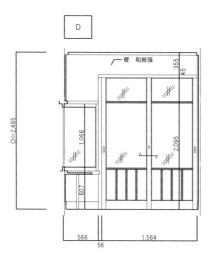

Scale 1:60

部分詳細図（本屋／縁側）

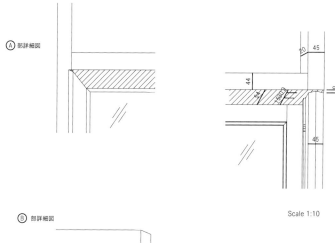

部分詳細図（本屋／縁側）

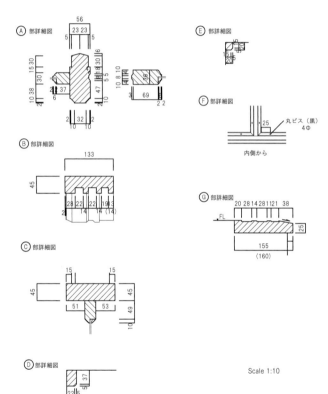

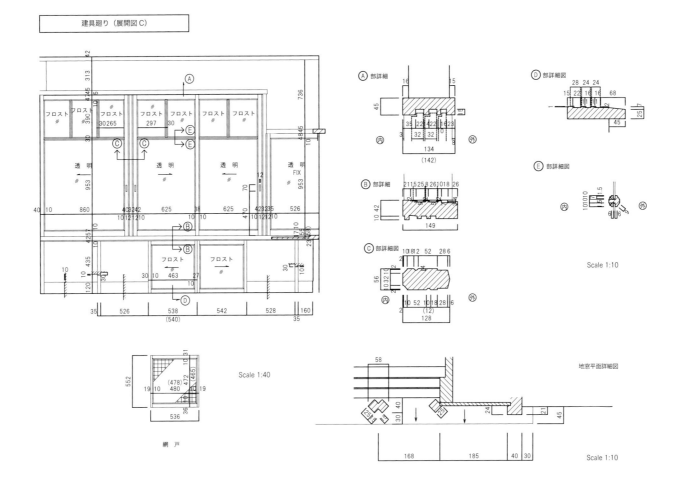

部分詳細図（本屋／縁側）

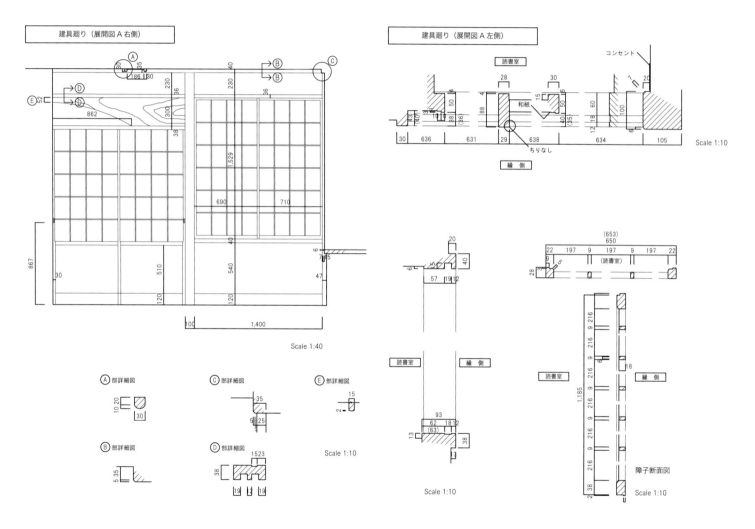

展開図（本屋／客室）

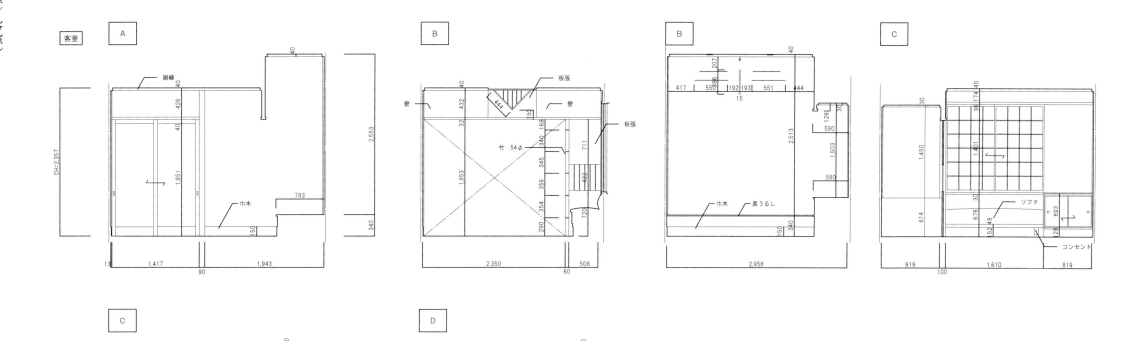

Scale1:60

部分詳細図（本屋／客室）

建具廻り（展開図C）

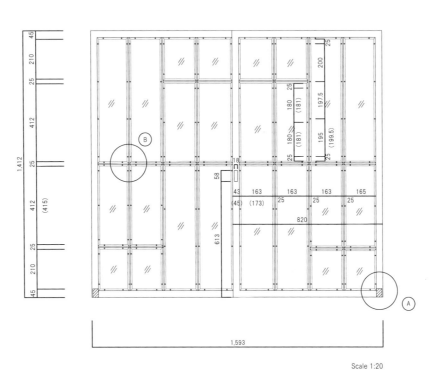

Scale 1:20

Ⓐ 部詳細図　Scale 1:10

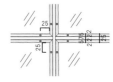

Ⓑ 部詳細図　Scale 1:10

展開図（本屋／小上がり）

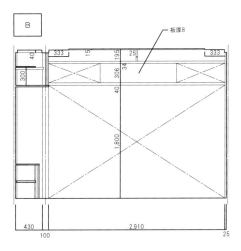
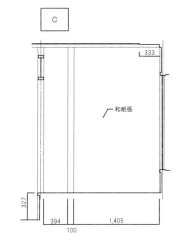
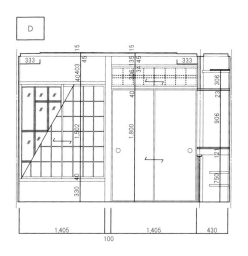

＊後に取り付けられた欄間と襖は撤去されている。

Scale1:60

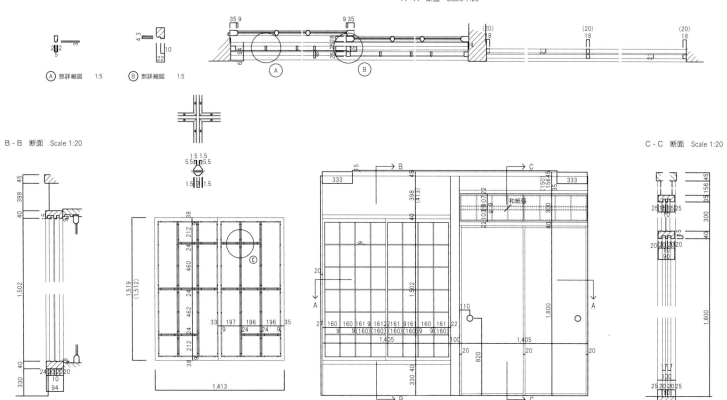

建具廻り（展開図 A） 建具廻り（展開図 B）

Scale 1:40　　　　　A - A 断面 Scale 1:20　　　　　A - A 断面 Scale 1:20　　　　　Scale 1:40

中央部

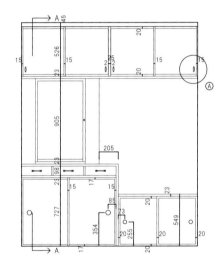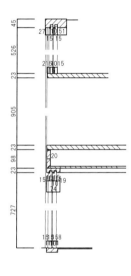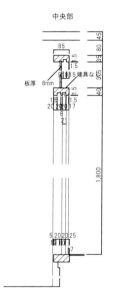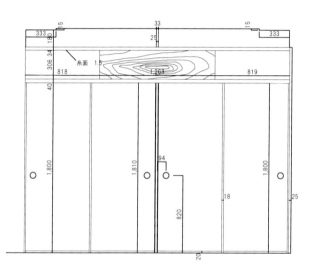

201

Ⓐ 部詳細図　Scale 1:10

＊後に取り付けられた欄間と襖は撤去されている。

部分詳細図（本屋／小上がり）

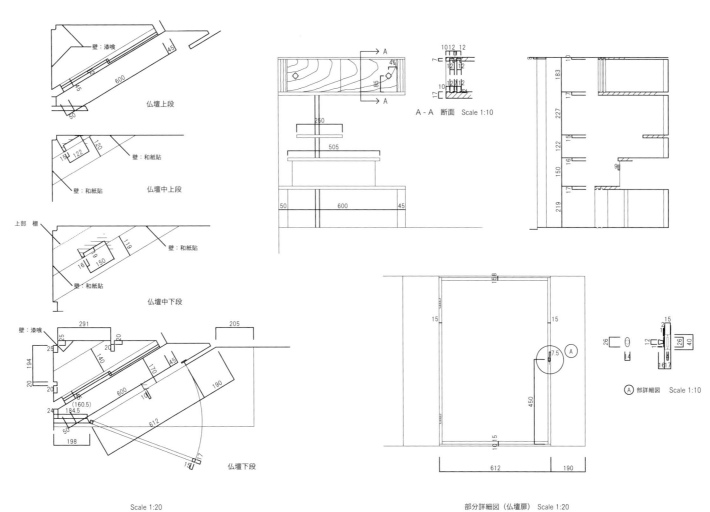

Scale 1:20

部分詳細図（仏壇扉） Scale 1:20

展開図（本屋／調理室・下女室）

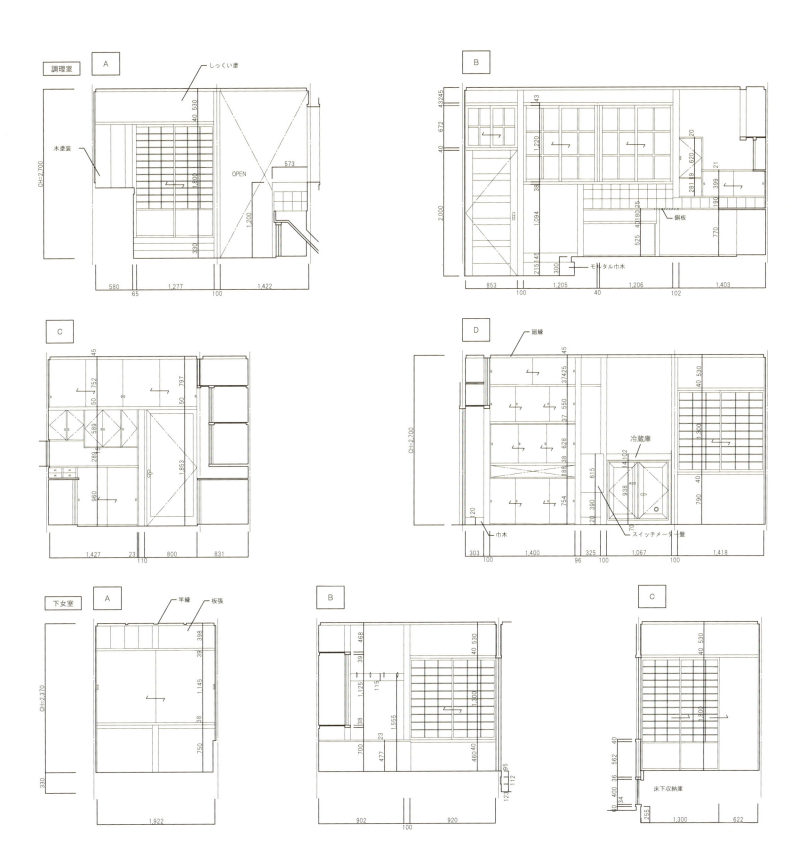
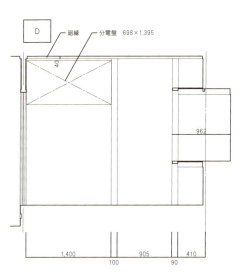

下女室

部分詳細図（本屋／廊下）

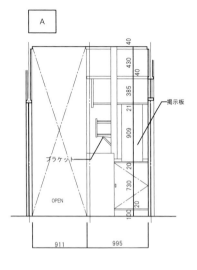
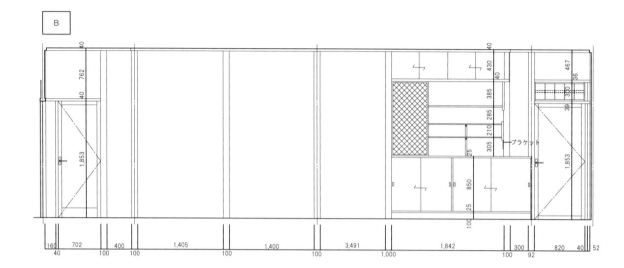
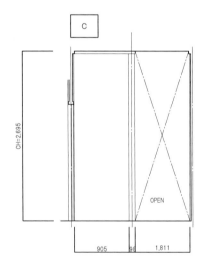
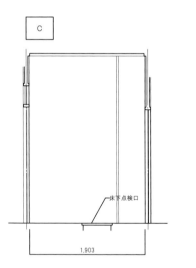
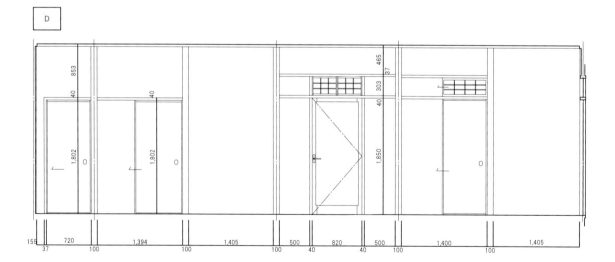

Scale 1:60

部分詳細図（本屋／廊下）

廊下棚（展開図B）

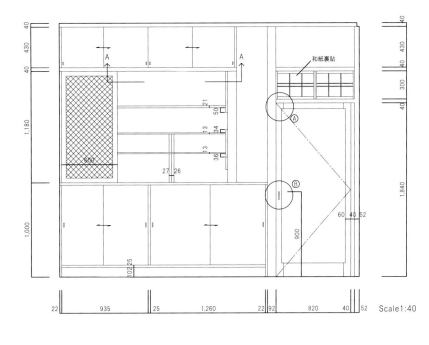

Scale1:40

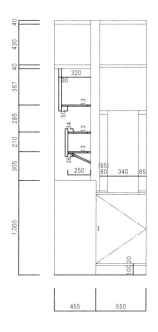

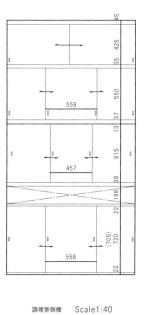

調理室側棚　Scale1:40

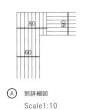

Ⓐ　部詳細図
Scale1:10

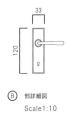

Ⓑ　部詳細図
Scale1:10

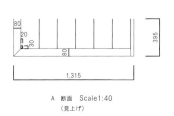

A　断面　Scale1:40
（見上げ）

Scale1:60

廊下棚

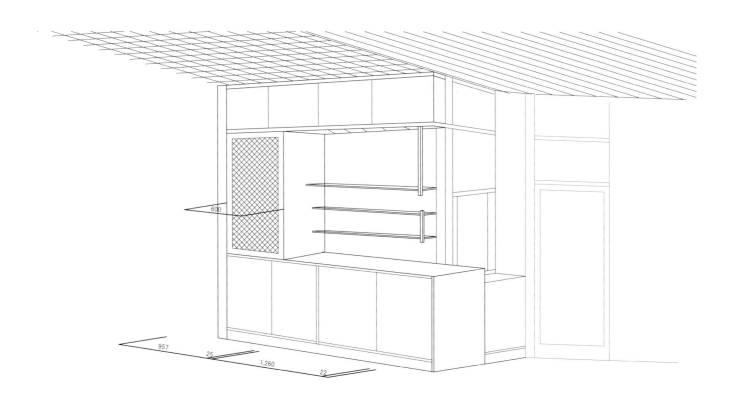

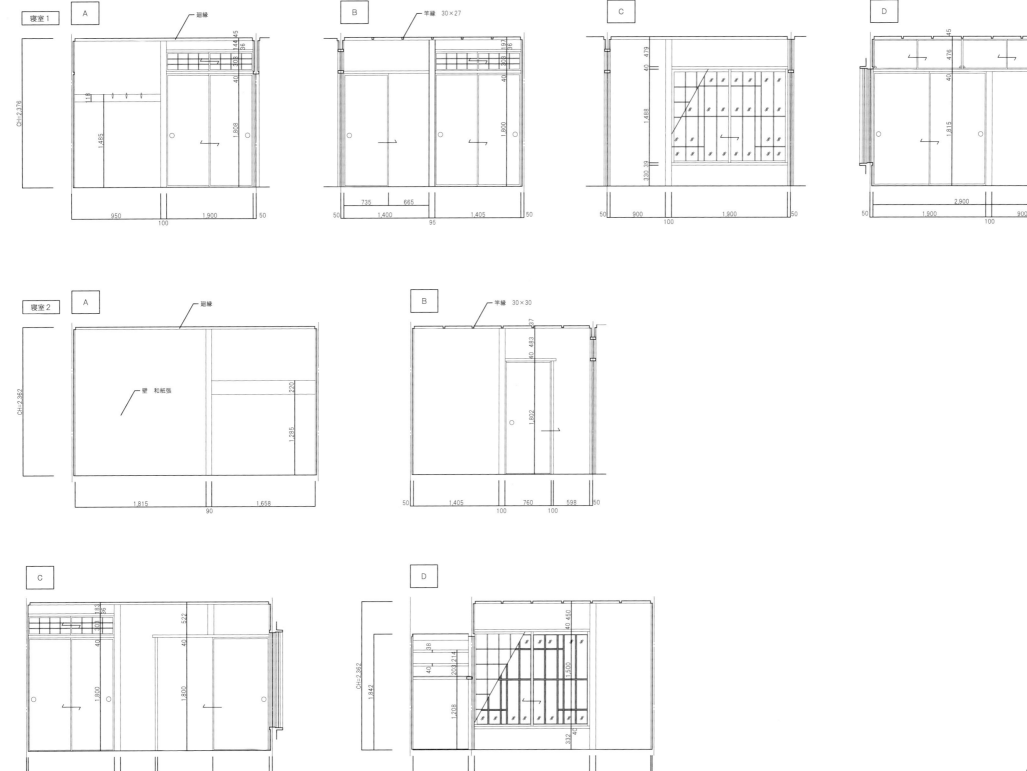

部分詳細図（本屋／寝室）

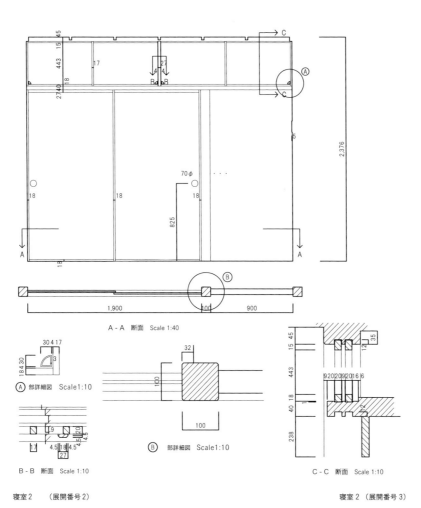
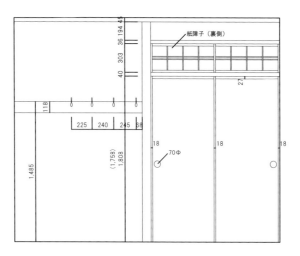

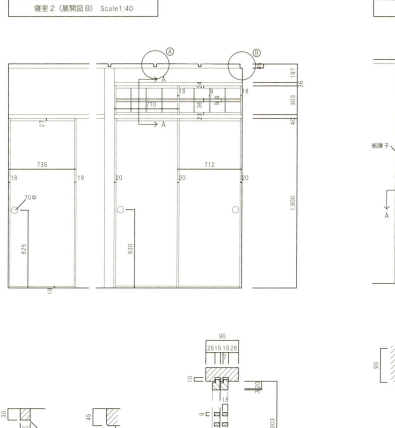

寝室2（展開図B） Scale1:40   寝室2（展開図C） Scale1:40

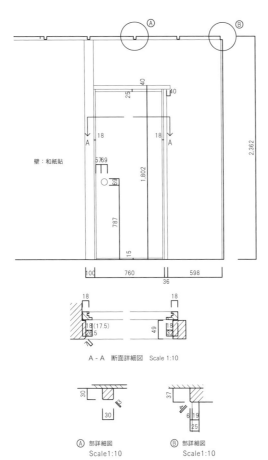
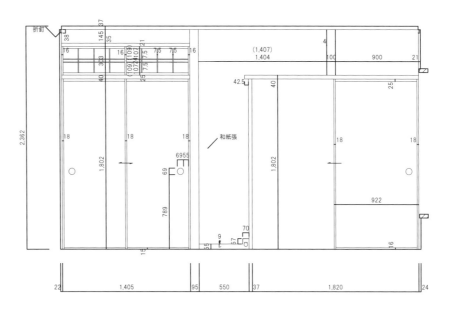

A-A 断面詳細図　Scale 1:10

Ⓐ 部詳細図　Scale1:10　　Ⓑ 部詳細図　Scale1:10

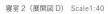
寝室2（展開図D） Scale1:40

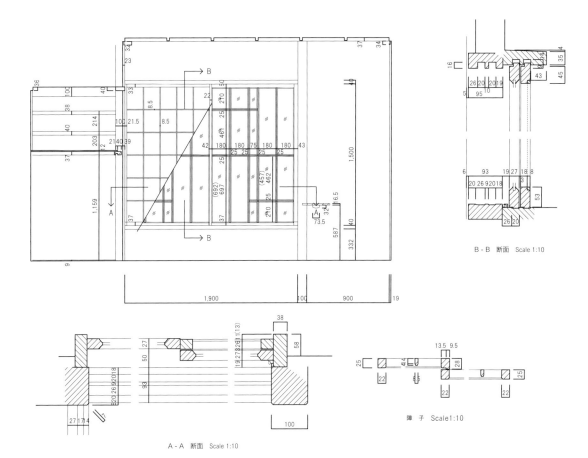

B-B 断面 Scale 1:10

A-A 断面 Scale 1:10

障子 Scale1:10

展開図（本屋／寝室・納戸・便所・外部便所）

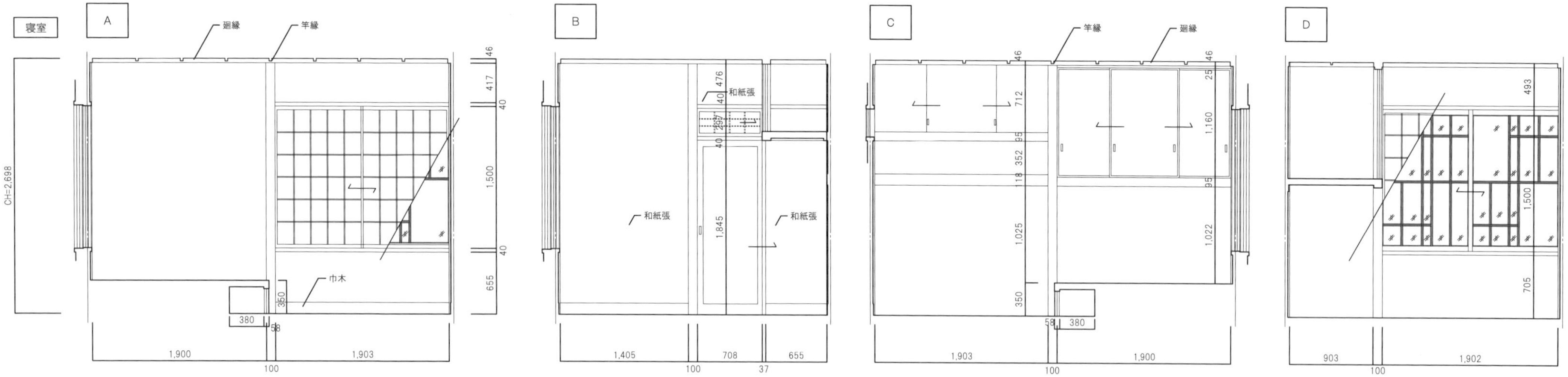

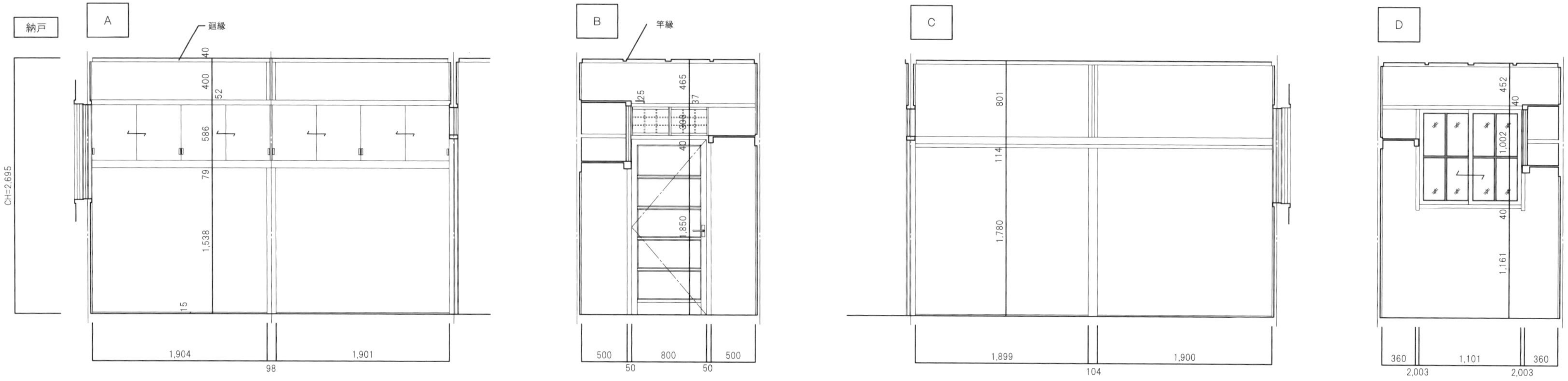

Scale 1:60

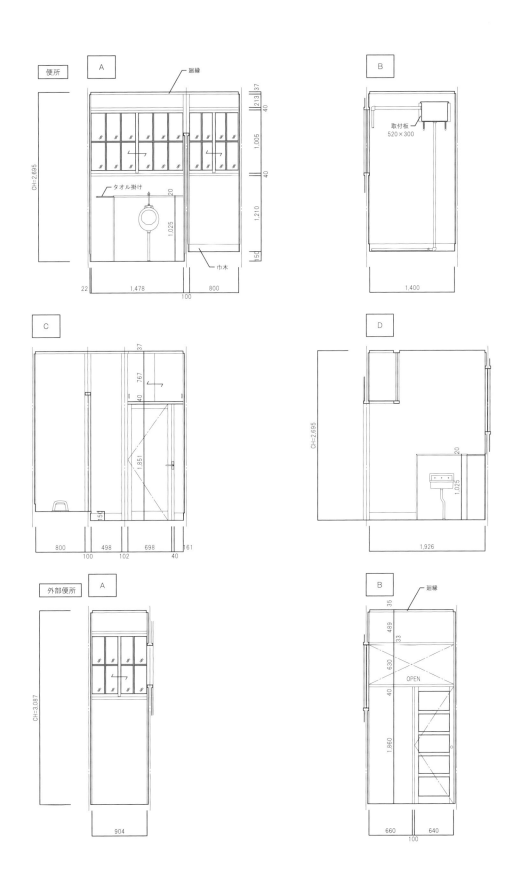
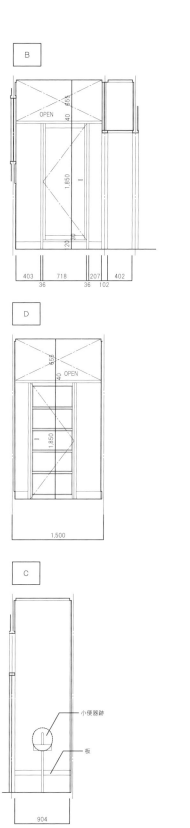

便所

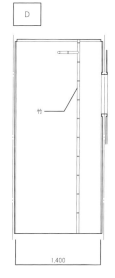

Scale 1:60

展開図（本屋／脱衣室・浴室）

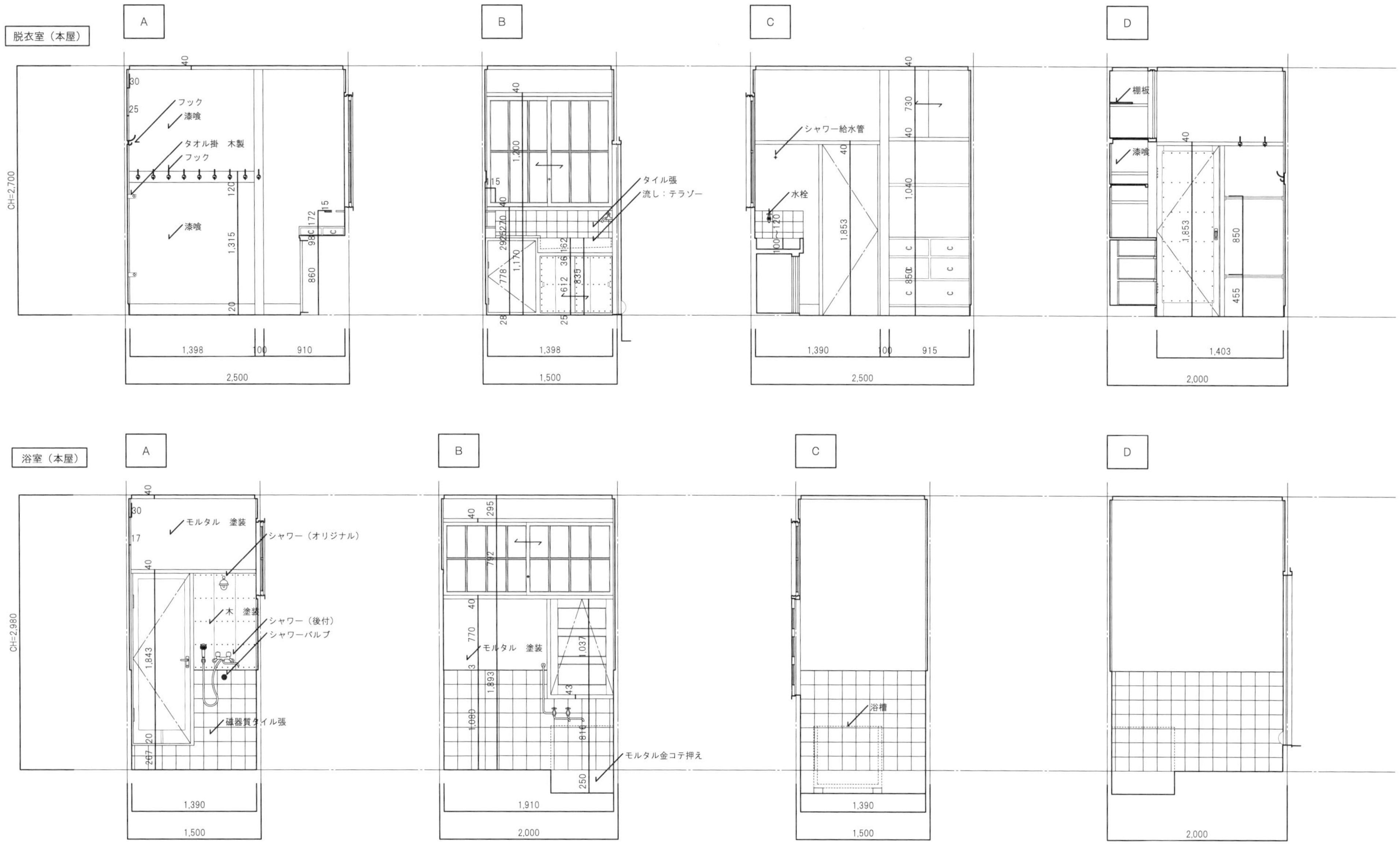

Scale 1:60

部分詳細図（本屋／脱衣室）

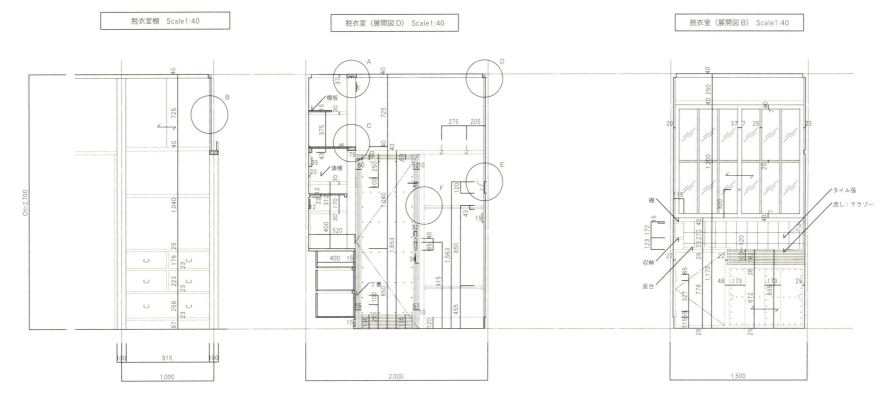

脱衣室流し

部分詳細図（本屋／脱衣室）

A部詳細図 Scale1:20

D部詳細図 Scale1:20

脱衣室収納姿図 Scale1:20
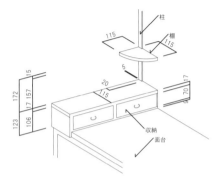

B部詳細図 Scale1:20

E部詳細図 Scale1:20

脱衣室流し詳細図 Scale1:20
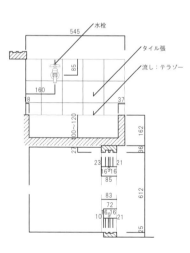

C部詳細図 Scale1:20
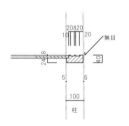

F部詳細図 Scale1:20
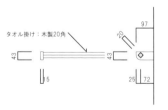

脱衣所

家具詳細図（本屋）

枕付肘掛椅子　Scale1:20

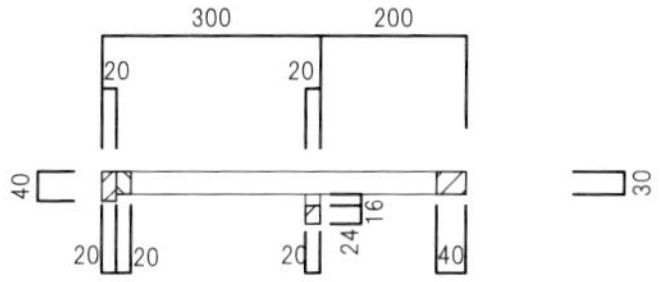

座面の断面　Scale1:20

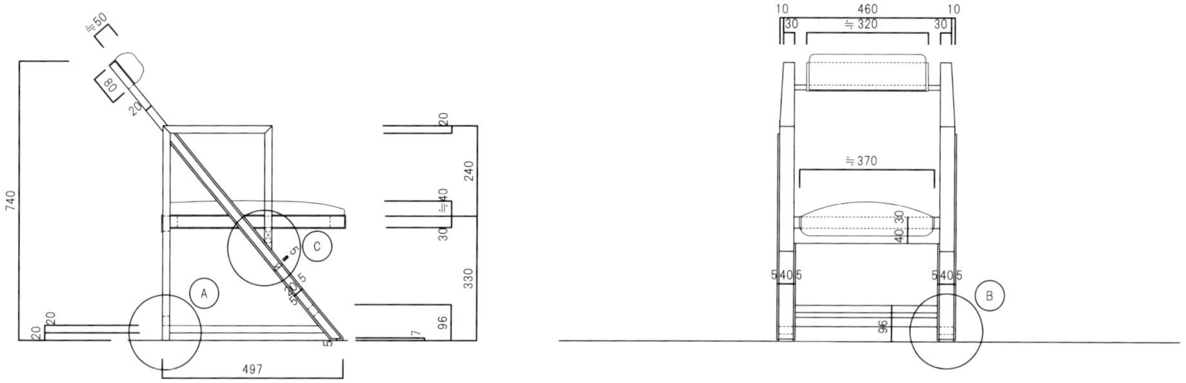

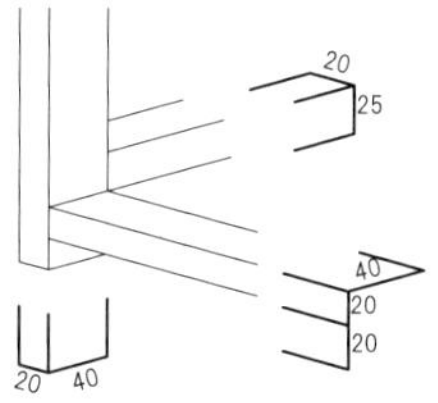

A　部詳細図　Scale1:10

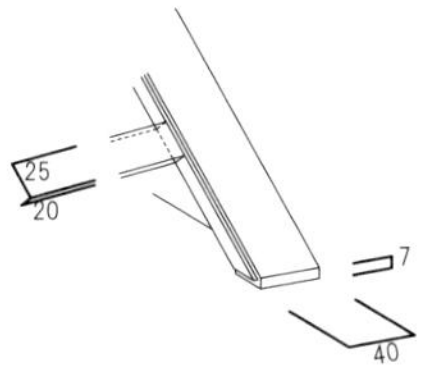

B　部詳細図　Scale1:10

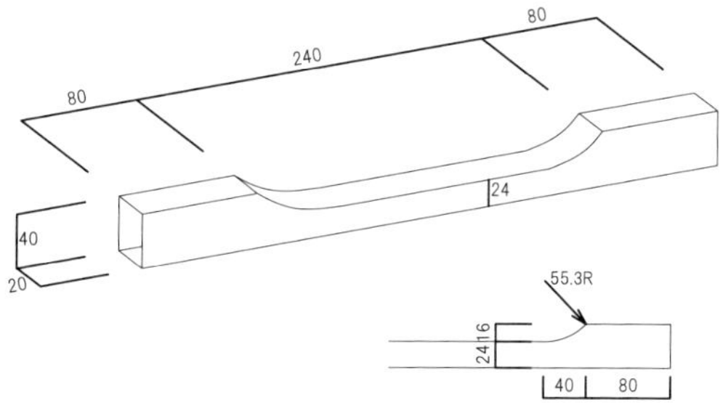

C　部詳細図　Scale1:10

217

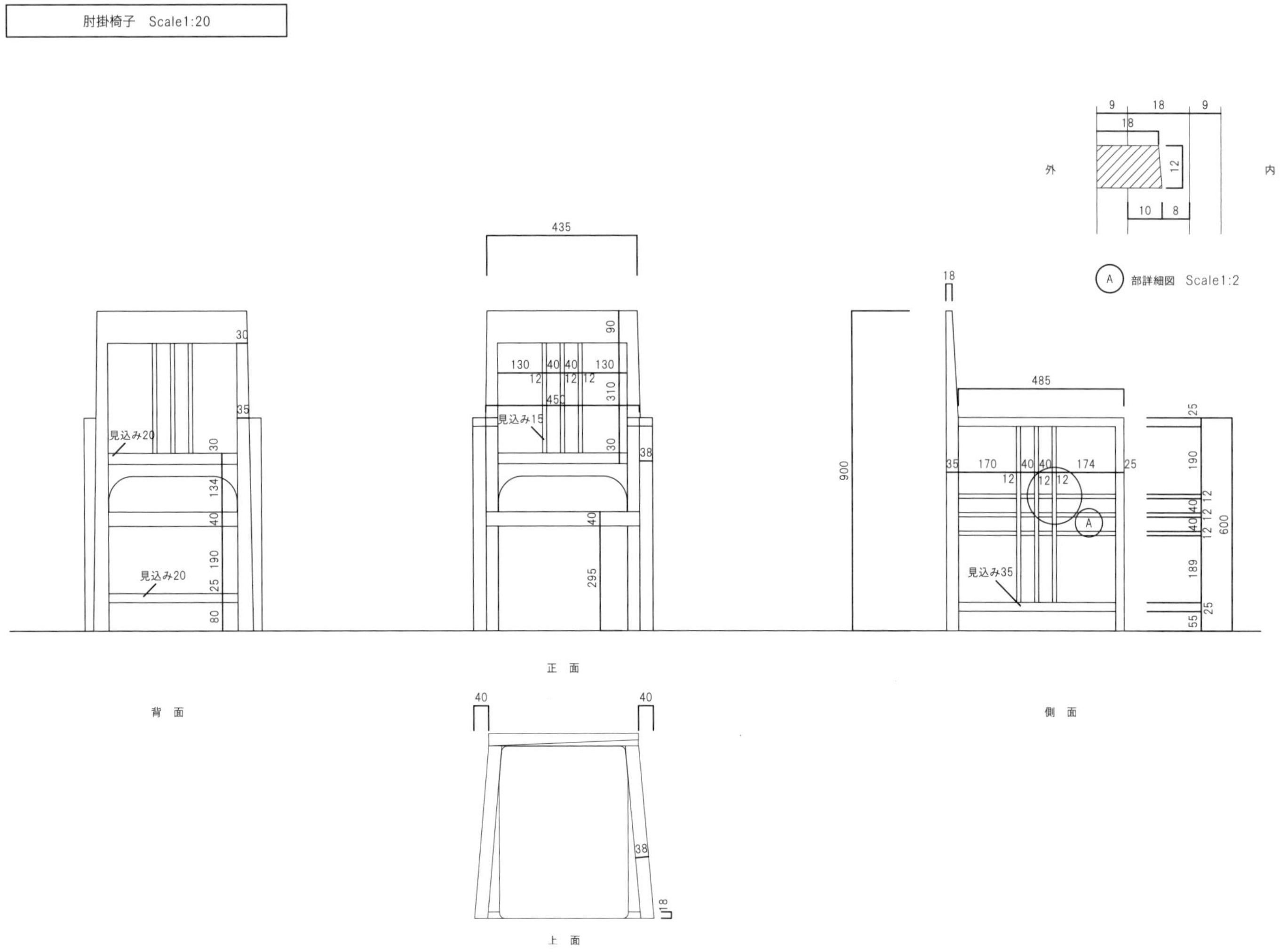

家具詳細図（本屋）

肘掛椅子　Scale1:20

A部詳細図　Scale1:2

背面　　　　正面　　　　側面

上面

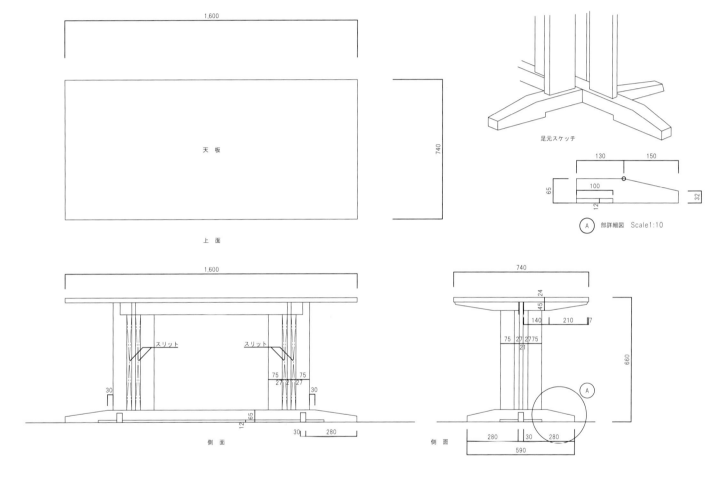

家具詳細図（本屋）

テーブル2 Scale1:20

上面

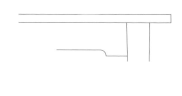

側面

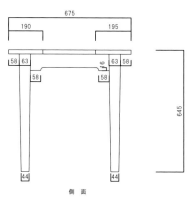

側面

平面図（閑室）

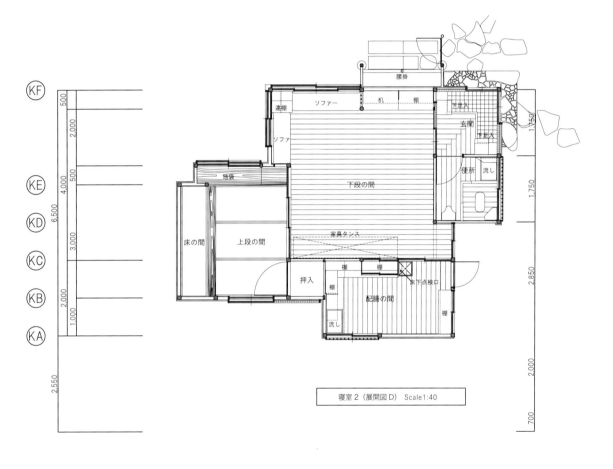
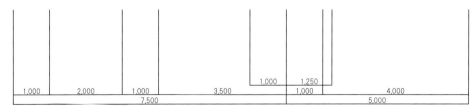

寝室2（展開図D） Scale1:40

＊後に取り付けられた家具タンスは撤去された。

Scale1:100

天井伏図（閑室）

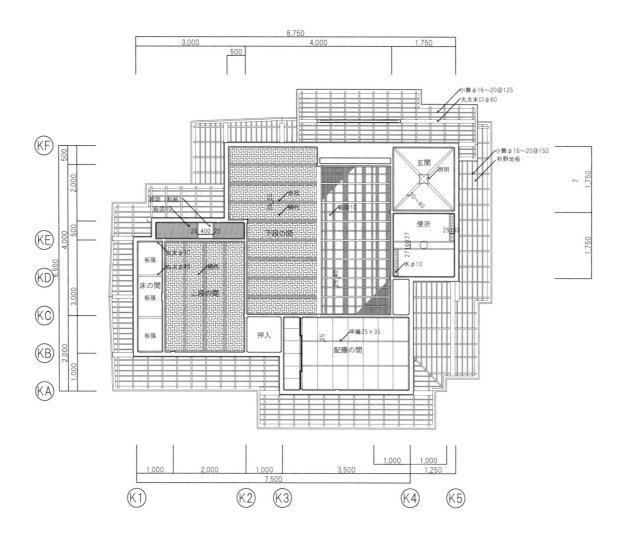

Scale 1:100

屋根伏図（閑室）

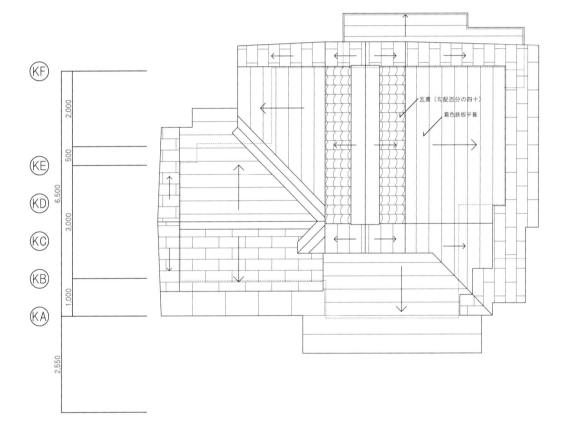

Scale1:100

立面図（閑室）

東立面図

南立面図

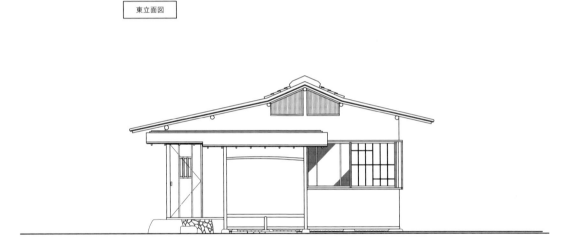
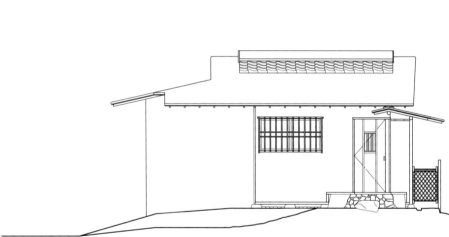

Scale1:100

西立面図

北立面図

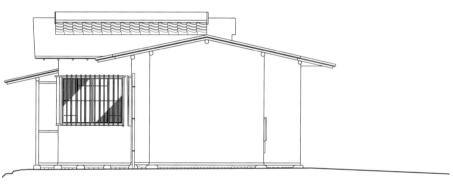

225

Scale1:100

断面図（閑室）

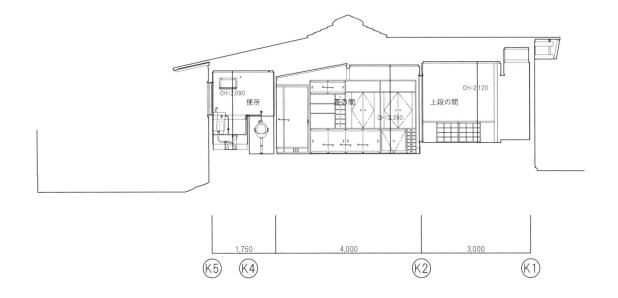
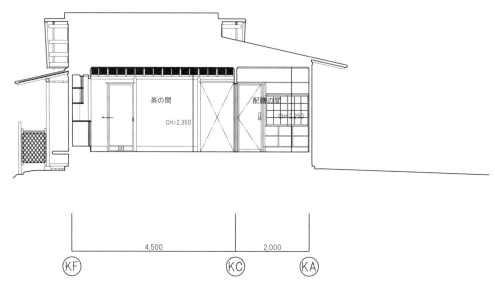

Scale1:100

部分詳細図（閑室）

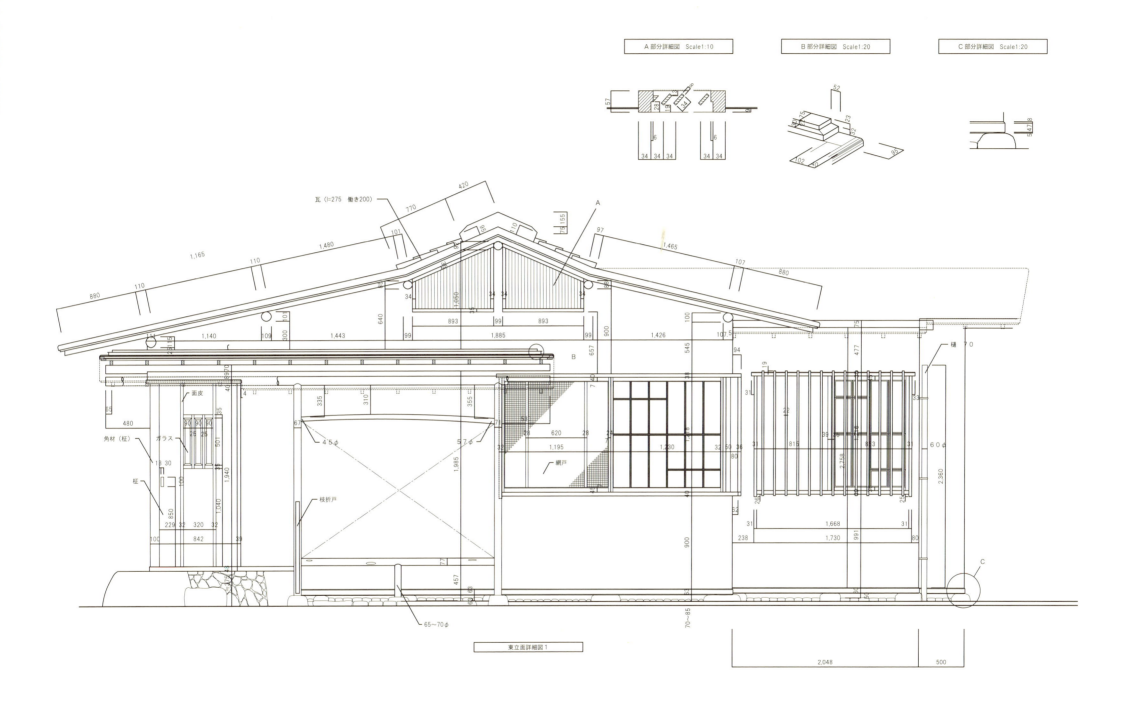

部分詳細図（閑室）

南立面詳細図

Scale 1:40

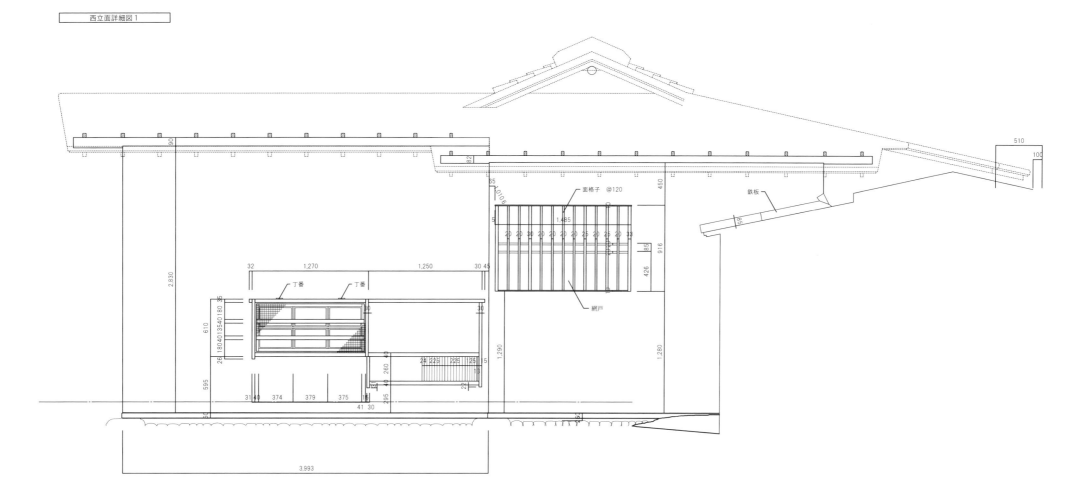

部分詳細図（閑室）

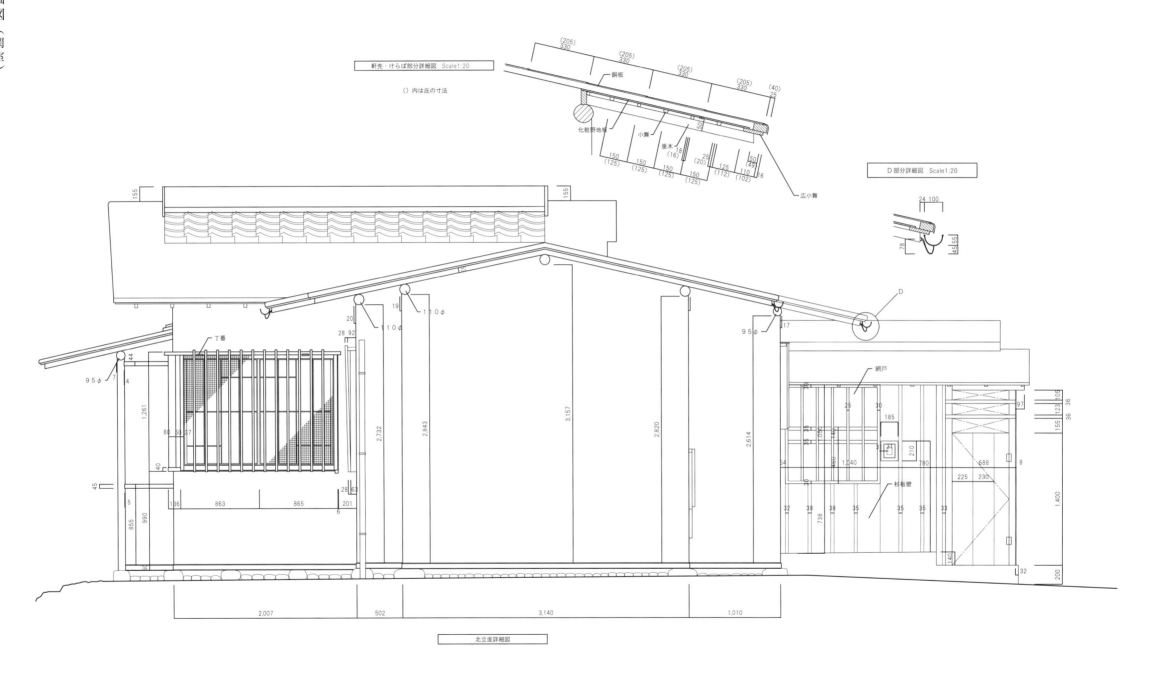

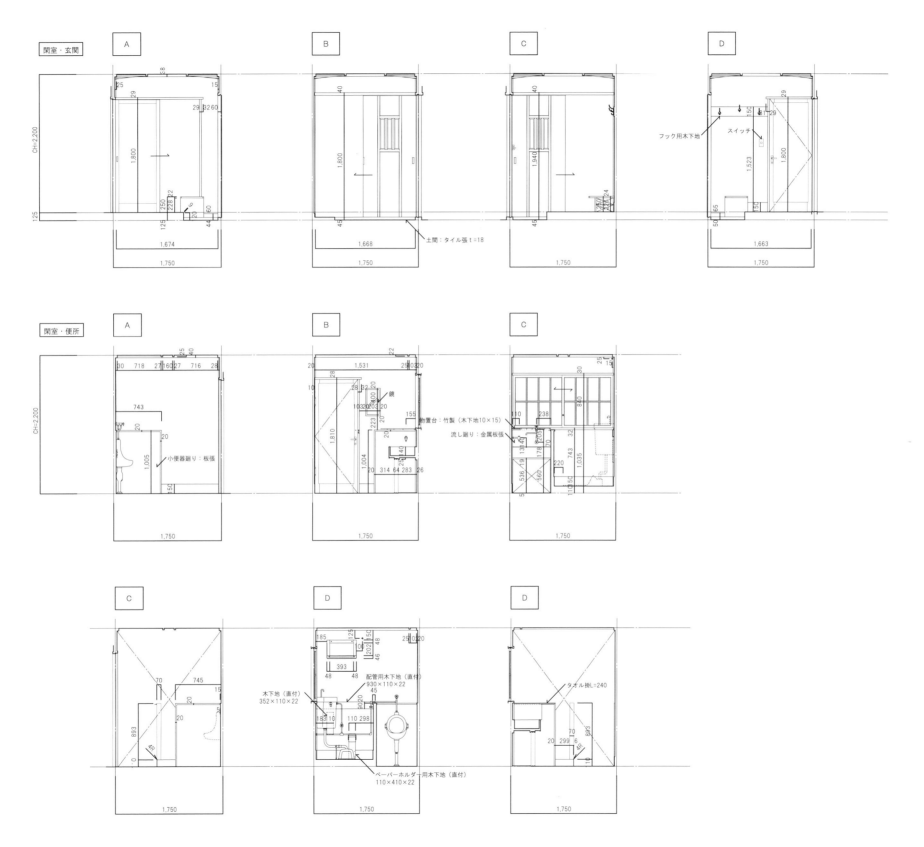

展開図（閑室／下段の間・上段の間）

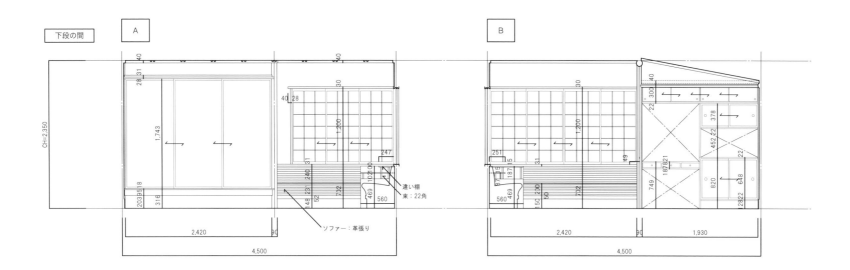

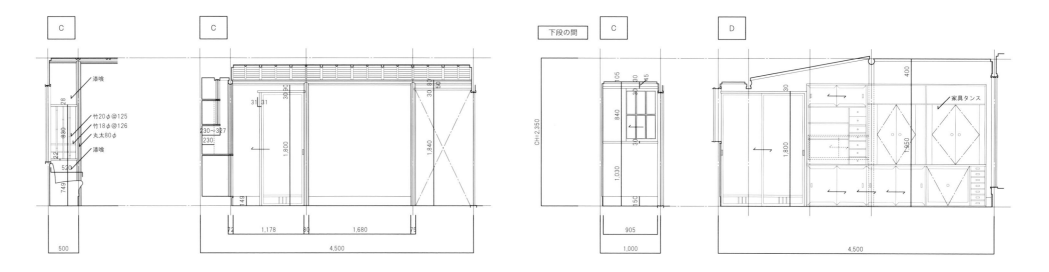

＊後に取り付けられた家具タンスは撤去された。

Scale 1:60

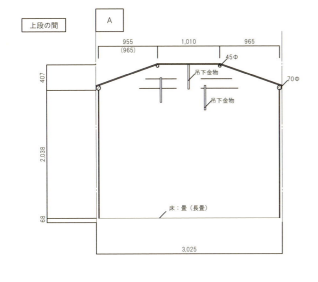
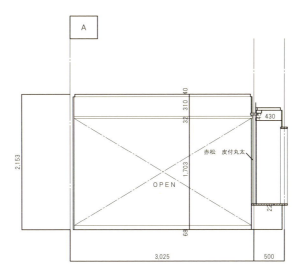
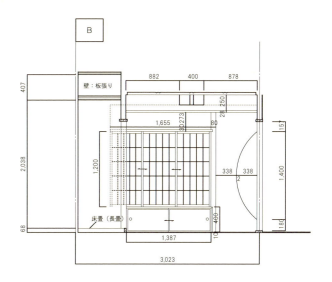
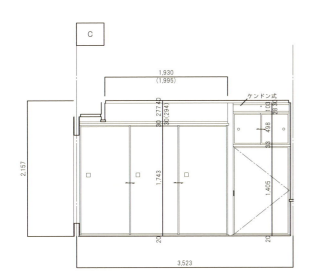
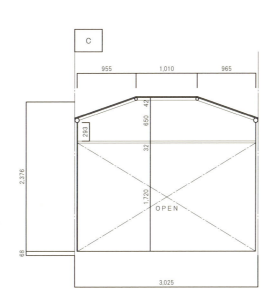
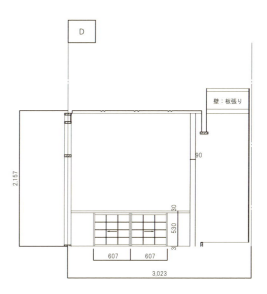

Scale 1:60

部分詳細図（閑室・上段の間）

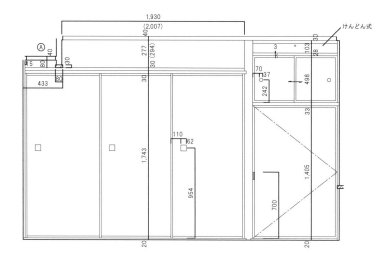
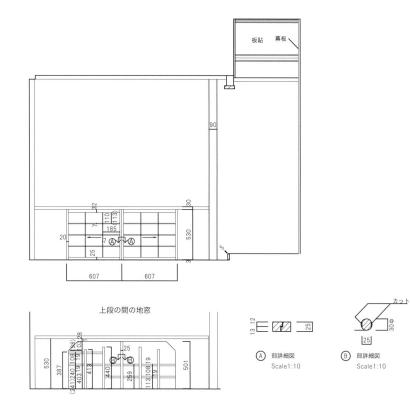

Scale1:40

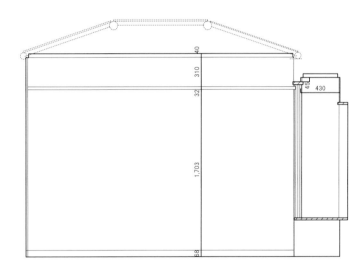
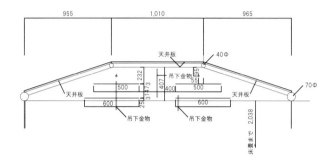

上段の間雲板

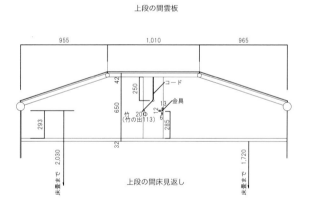

上段の間床見返し

Scale1:40

展開図（閑室／配膳の間）

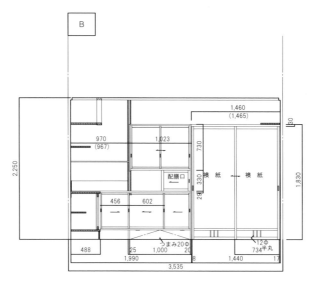
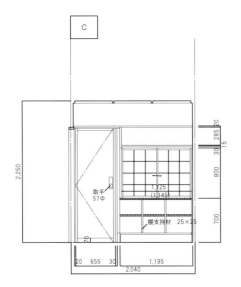
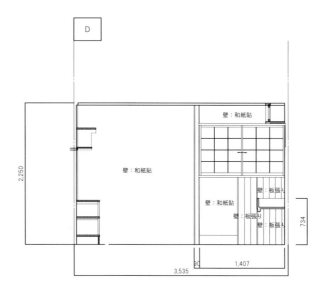

Scale1:60

部分詳細図（閑室・配膳の間）

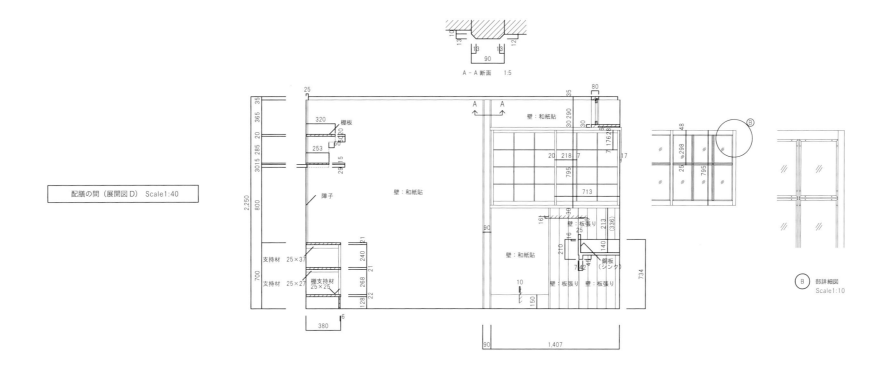

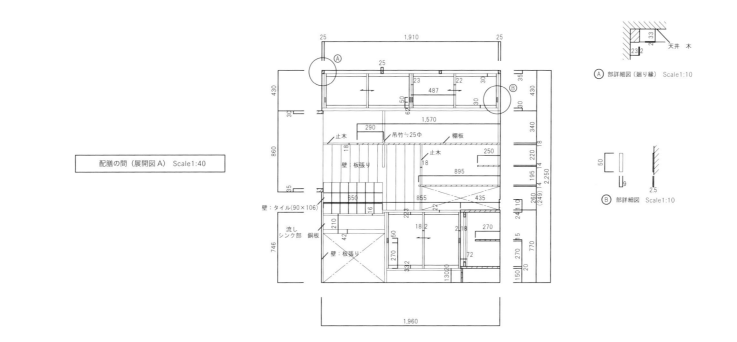

部分詳細図（閑室／配膳の間）

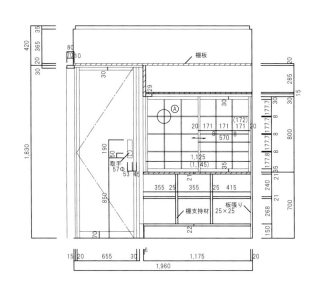

部分詳細図（閑室／各室）

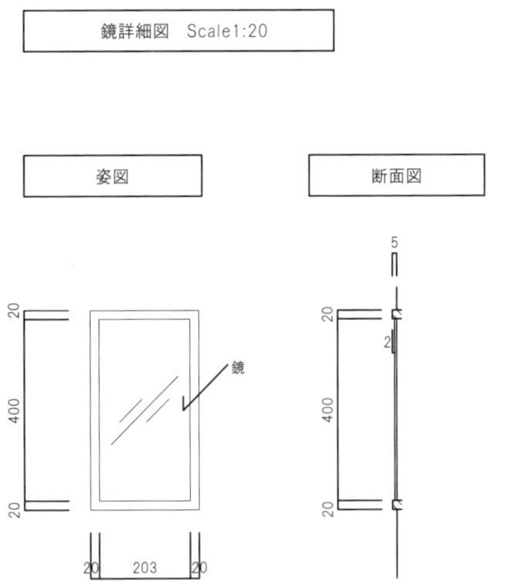

鏡詳細図 Scale1:20
姿図
断面図
鏡
20
400
20
203
5
2

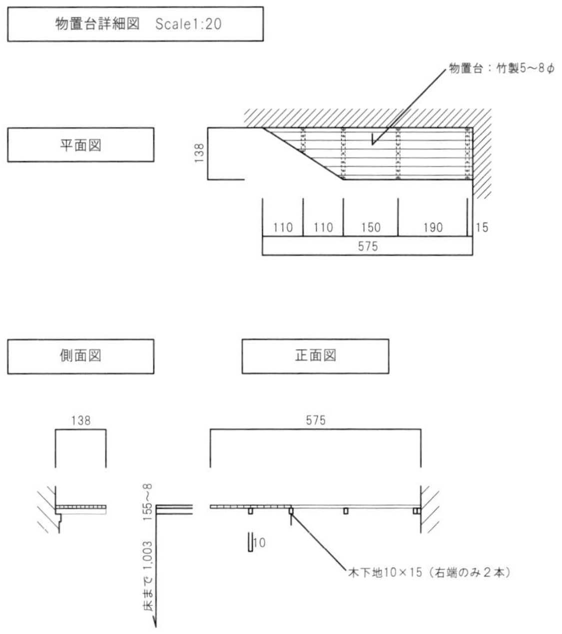

物置台詳細図 Scale1:20
平面図
物置台：竹製5～8φ
138
110
110
150
190
15
575
側面図
正面図
138
575
155～8
床まで 1,003
10
木下地10×15（右端のみ２本）

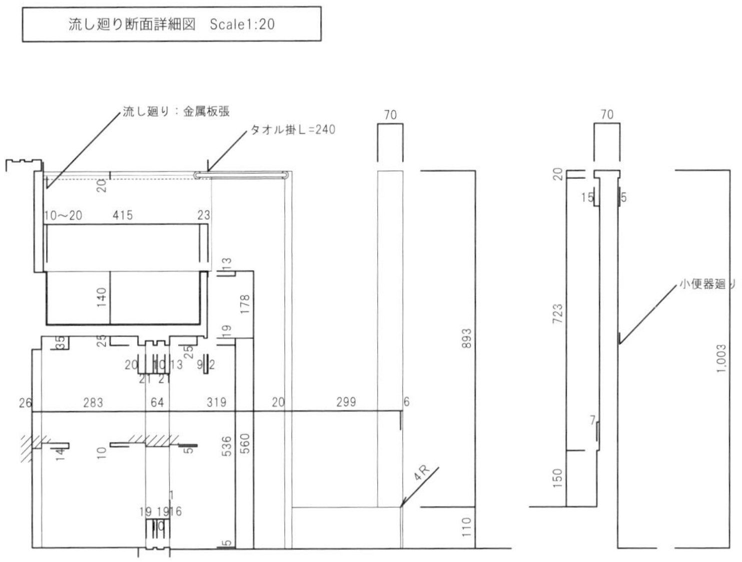

流し廻り断面詳細図 Scale1:20
流し廻り：金属板張
タオル掛L=240
10～20
415
23
140
178
283
64
319
299
536
560
893
4R
110
723
150
1,003
小便器廻り：板張
70

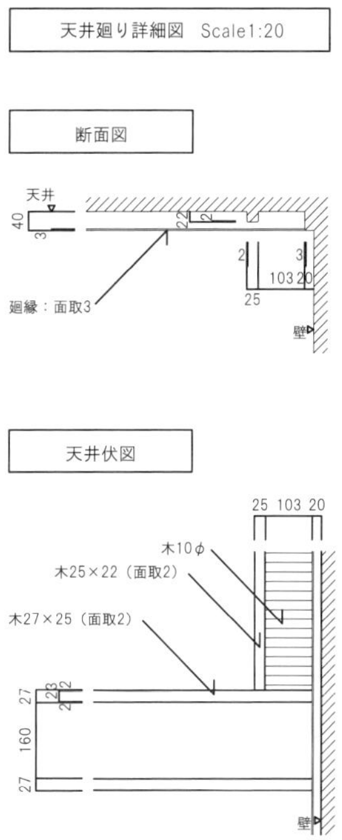

天井廻り詳細図 Scale1:20
断面図
天井
40
廻縁：面取3
103
25
壁
天井伏図
25 103 20
木10φ
木25×22（面取2）
木27×25（面取2）
27
160
27
壁

家具詳細図（閑室）

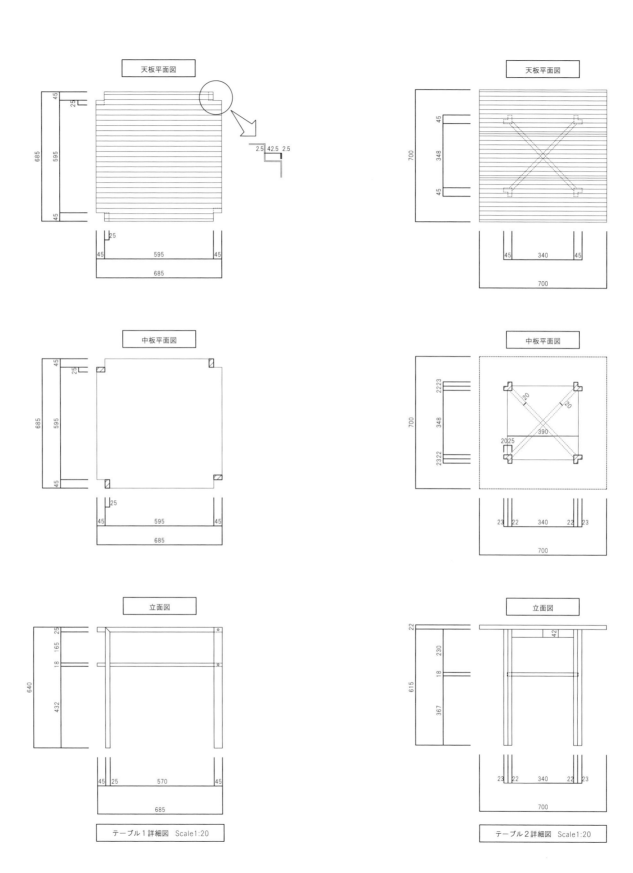

閑室・下段の間家具詳細図

Ⓐ 部詳細図　Scale1:10

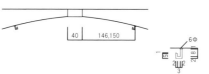

吊金具詳細図　Scale1:4

玄関照明詳細図　Scale1:10

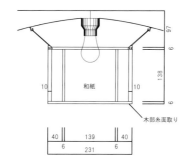

和紙

木部糸面取り

平面図（茶室）

平面図

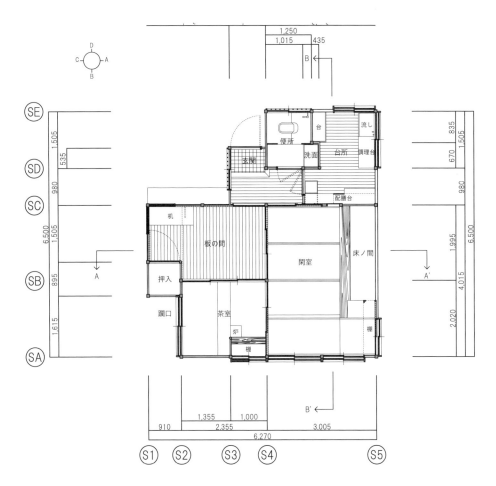

Scale1:100

天井伏図（茶室）

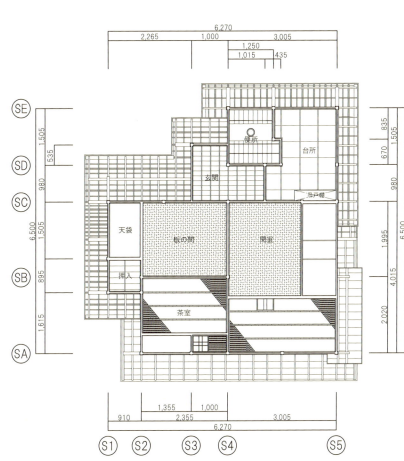

Scale1:100

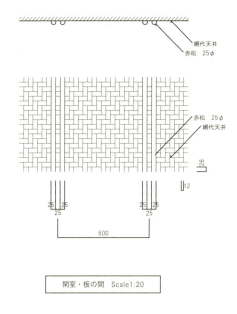

閑室・板の間　Scale1:20

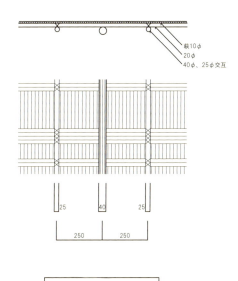

茶室・閑室　Scale1:20

屋根伏図（茶室）

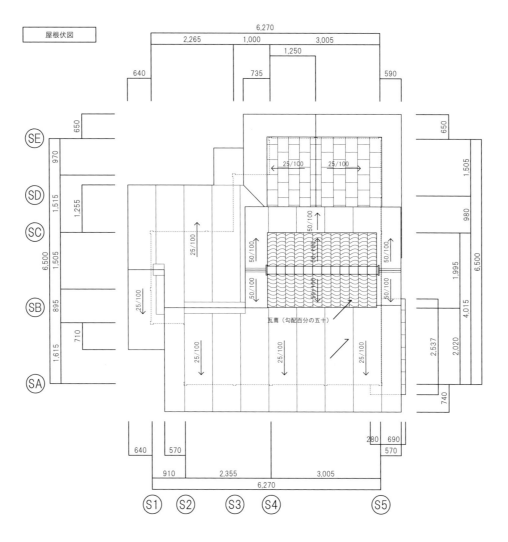

Scale 1:100

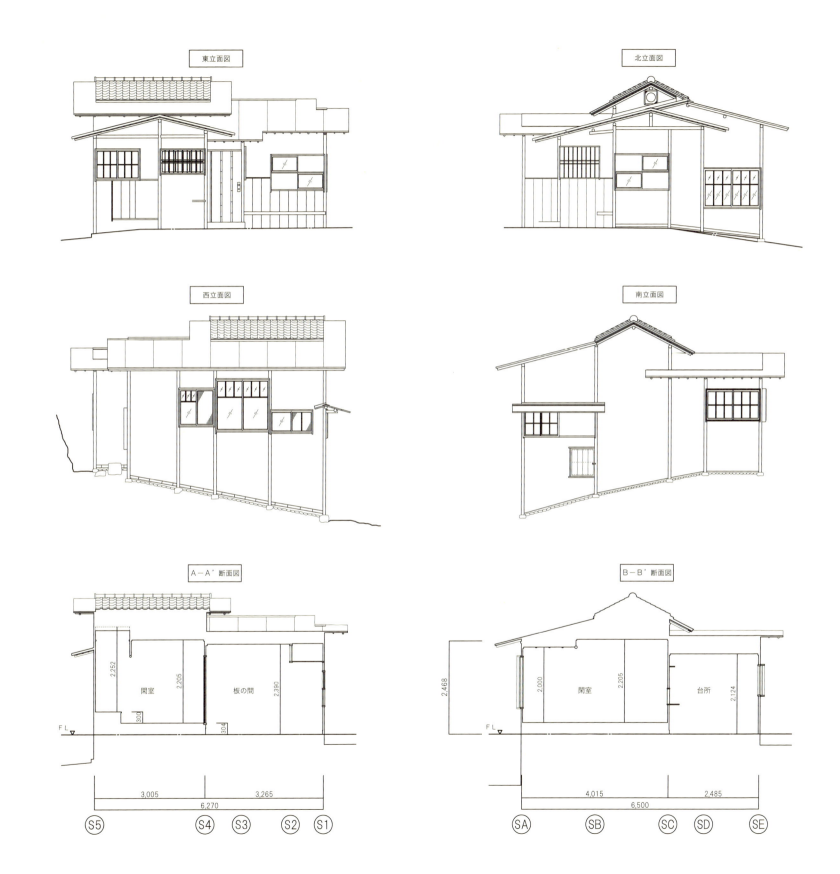

立面詳細図（茶室）

東立面

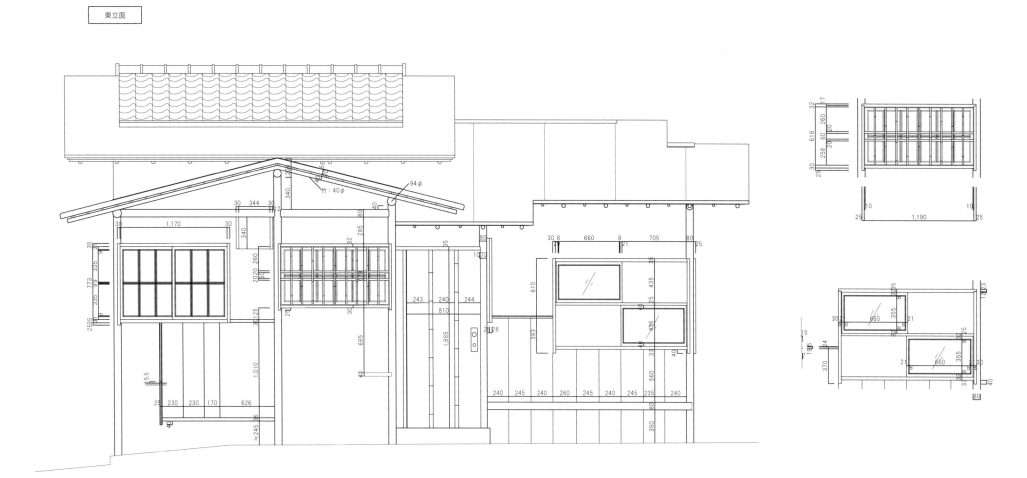

Scale1:40

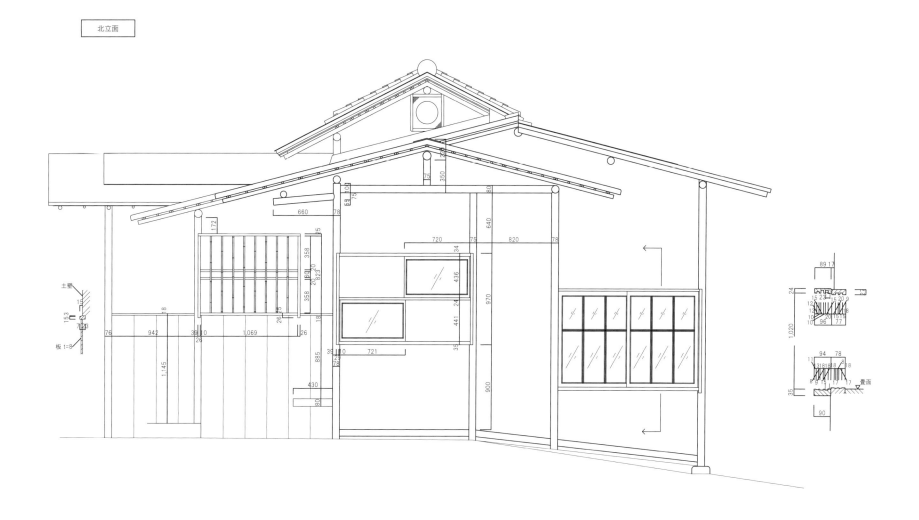

立面詳細図（茶室）

西立面

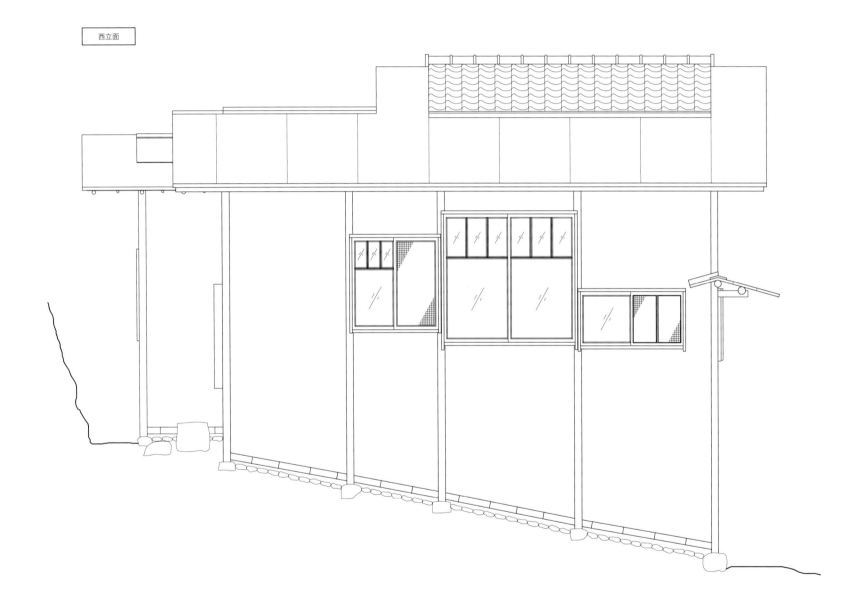

248

Scale 1:40

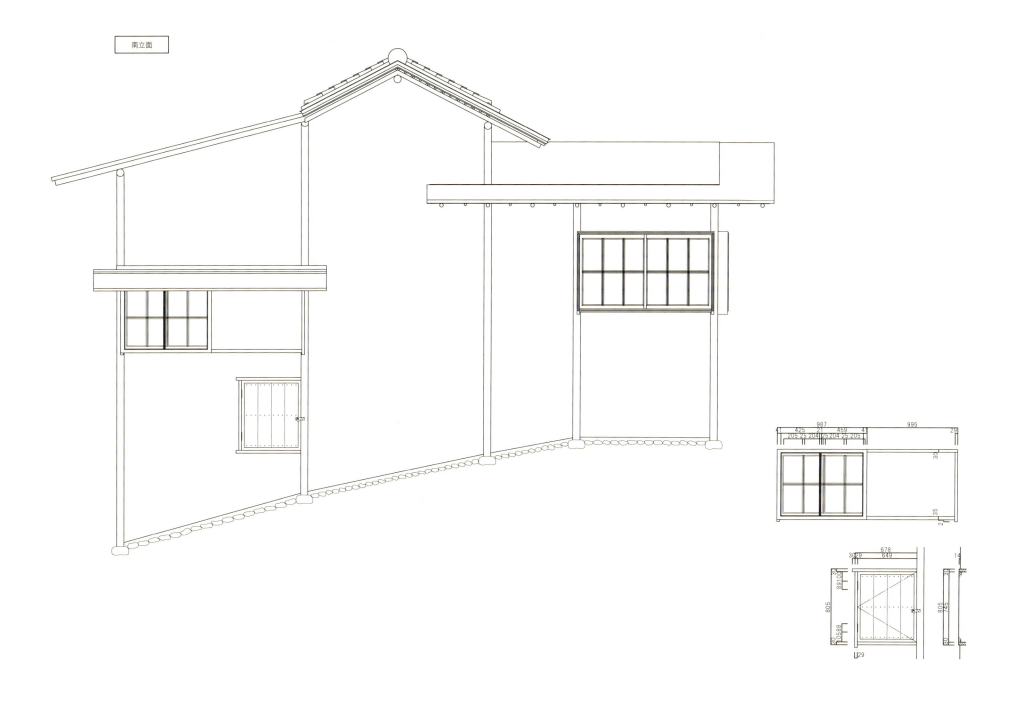

展開図（茶室／玄関・便所・台所）

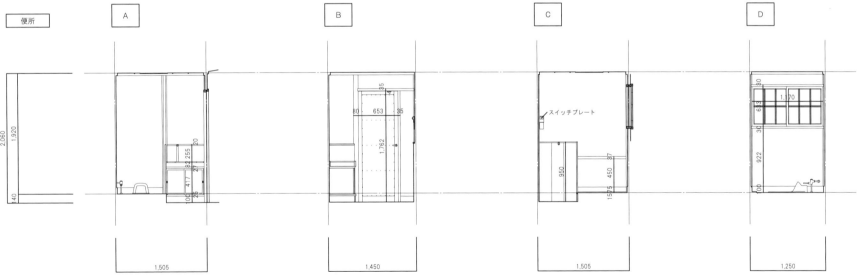

Scale 1:60

台所

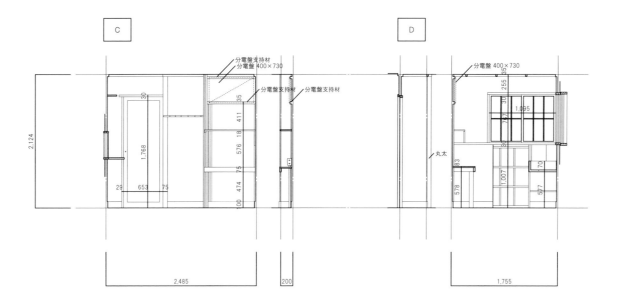

Scale1:60

展開図（茶室／閑室）

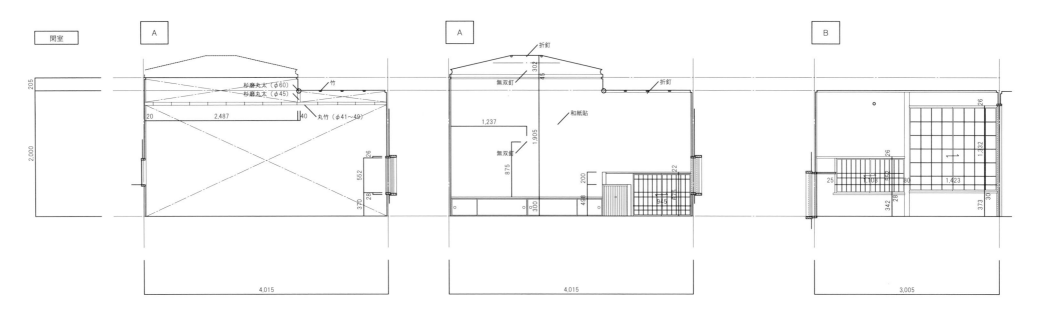
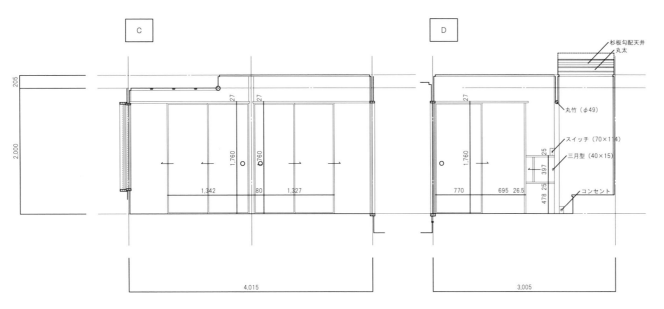

Scale 1:60

部分詳細図（茶室／閑室）

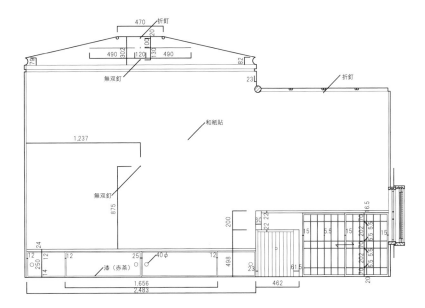
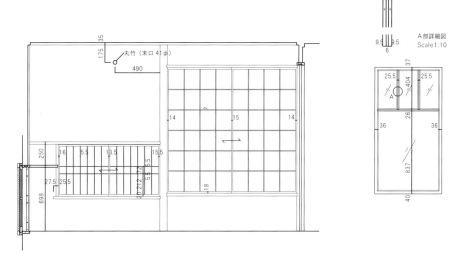
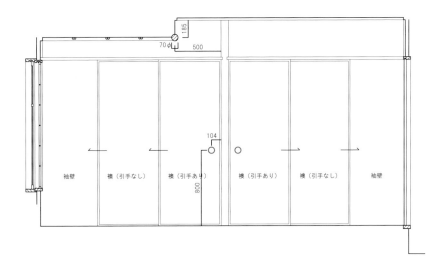
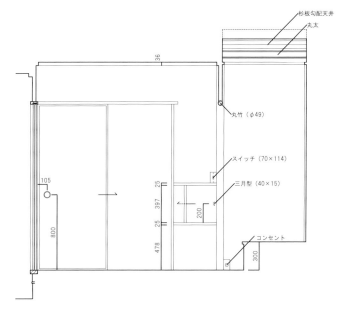

Scale1:40

展開図（茶室／板の間）

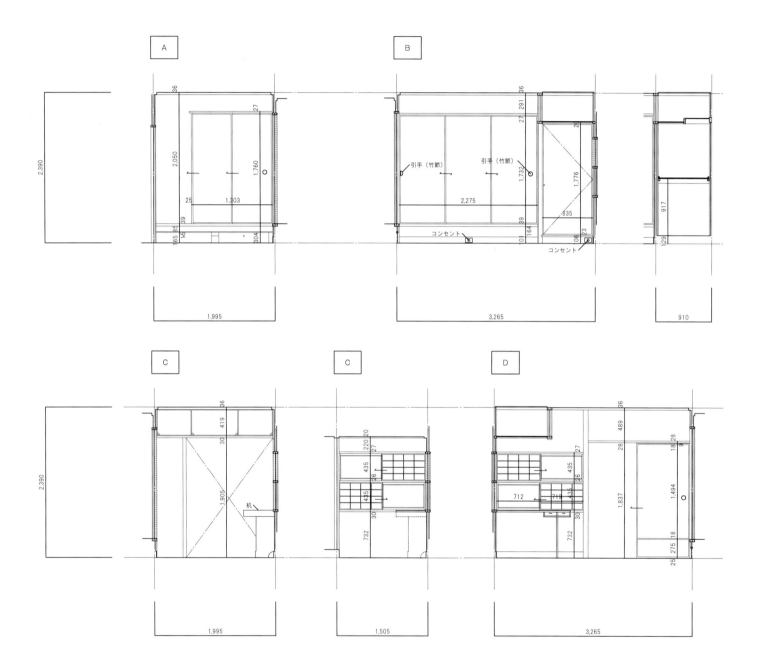

Scale1:60

部分詳細図（茶室／水屋）

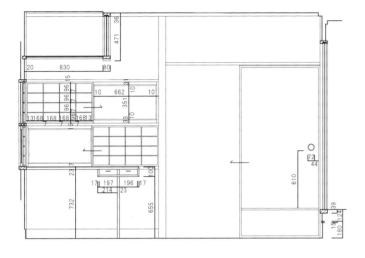
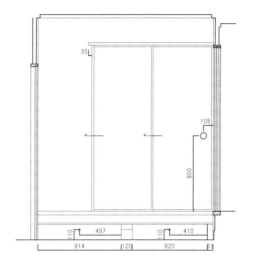
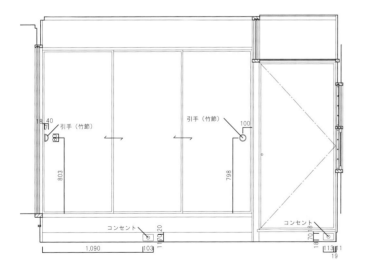
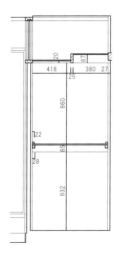
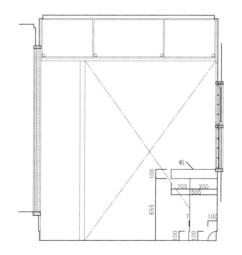

Scale 1:40

展開図（茶室／茶室）

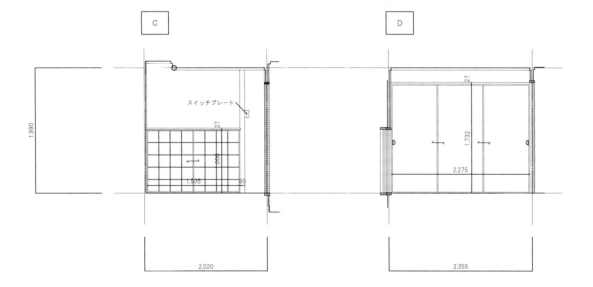

Scale 1:60

部分詳細図（茶室／茶室）

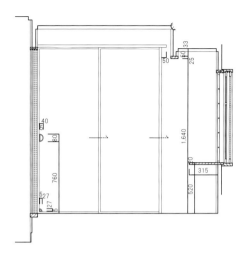
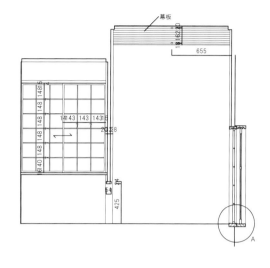
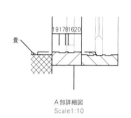

A部詳細図
Scale1:10

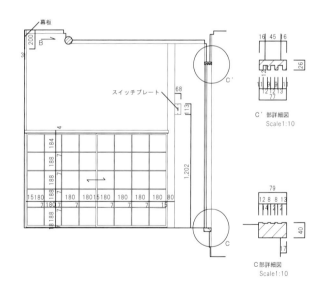
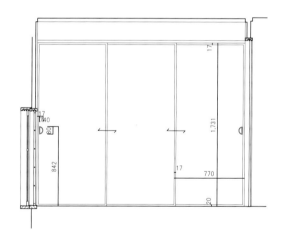

C'部詳細図
Scale1:10

C部詳細図
Scale1:10

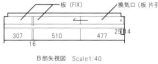

B部矢視図　Scale1:40

Scale1:60

藤井厚二 年譜

『ふくやま美術館開館15周年記念展 武田五一・田辺淳吉・藤井厚二 日本を意匠した近代建築家たち−』
（ふくやま美術館）所収「藤井厚二年譜（谷藤史彦編）」他、「聴竹居と藤井厚二展」リーフレット（ギャラリーA'編）、『近代日本総合年表 第三版』（岩波書店）などを参考に、新たな事実を加筆して作成

年代	年齢	年譜	藤井の作品と同時代の建築 『建築物』（建築家）＊未確認または年代未確認	社会の動き ★建築関連
1888（明治21）年	0歳	12月8日、広島県深安郡福山町字深沖町（現在の福山市宝川）に、「くろがねや」の藤井与一右衛門と元の次男として生まれる。11代続く「くろがねや」は造酒屋の他、製塩、金融業なども営んでいた。	『岩崎家深川別邸』（ジョサイア・コンドル）	ドイツで初のガソリンエンジン自動車（1886）
1898（明治31）年	10歳	父・与一右衛門が亡くなる。藤井は10歳。兄・祐吉が12歳で家督を継ぐ。		エッフェル塔（1889）
1907（明治40）年	19歳	広島県福山中学校（現誠之館高校）を卒業し、9月、第六高等学校に入学する。		★セセッション（ウイーン分離派）の活動始まる（1892）
1910（明治43）年	22歳	7月、第六高等学校を卒業。同月、東京帝国大学工科大学建築学科に入学。学生時代は、学習院に通う妹・快、母・元とともに東京・小石川に住む。日本画家・結城素明に絵を習う。		第1回近代オリンピック（1896）★日本建築学会討論会で「様式論争」（1910）
1911（明治44）年	23歳		『芝川邸』（武田五一）	
1912（明治45）年	24歳		『西本願寺・伝道院』（伊東忠太）	
1913（大正2）年	25歳	7月、東京帝国大学工科大学建築学科を卒業する。10月、合名会社竹中工務店に入社し、神戸に勤務。同社で最初の帝大卒の社員となる。		
1914（大正3）年	26歳	神戸市葺合区熊内に第1回住宅を完成させ、母親と住む。	第1回住宅（神戸市）※	
1916（大正5）年	28歳		大阪朝日新聞社（大阪市）	
1917（大正6）年	29歳		大阪朝日新聞社（大阪市）／橋本汽船ビルヂング（神戸市）	
1918（大正7）年	30歳	千家壽子（明治31−平成5年）と結婚。父は第80代出雲大社大宮司・東京府知事・千家尊福。兄に詩人の千家元麿がいる。5月、竹中工務店を退社（翌年11月初めまで残務と引き継ぎで出社）。	村山邸・書院棟（神戸市・現存）／十合呉服店（大阪市）	第一次世界大戦終わる
1919（大正8）年	31歳	11月8日、私費による欧米6か国への視察旅行、横浜港から出発。		★バウハウス開校
1920（大正9）年	32歳	8月14日、欧米6か国への視察旅行から帰国する。12月2日、京都帝国大学工学部講師を嘱託される。意匠製図を担当。12月10日、京都帝国大学中央大講堂設計事務を嘱託される。冬、京都府乙訓郡大山崎町に第2回住宅を完成させ、移り住む。	第2回住宅（大山崎町）	★日本初の近代建築運動「分離派建築会」結成
1921（大正10）年	33歳	5月、京都帝国大学助教授に任ぜられる。9月13日、長女福子が生れる。『住宅に就いて』（小冊子）。	斉藤邸（京都市）／賀屋邸倉庫（京都市）／明海ビルヂング（神戸市）／深瀬邸＊（京都市・現存）／坂本邸＊	
1922（大正11）年	34歳	春、京都府乙訓郡大山崎町に第3回住宅を建てる。	第3回住宅（大山崎町）／有馬文化村住宅群（神戸市）／森田邸＊（京都市）／山中邸＊（芦屋市）／石崎邸＊（京都市・現存）	
1923（大正12）年	35歳	夏、実験住宅において、1年をかけて気温などのデータを収集する。10月13日、次女・章子が生れる。	永井邸（大阪府・現存）／宇治町役場＊（宇治市）／鈴木邸＊／浜部邸＊（京都市・現存）『帝国ホテル』（フランク・ロイド・ライト）	関東大震災起こる

※『住宅に就いて』（1921）による

年代	年齢	年譜	藤井の作品と同時代の建築『建築物』（建築家）＊未確認または年代未確認	社会の動き ★建築関連
1924（大正13）年	36歳	京都府乙訓郡大山崎町に第4回住宅を建てる。	第4回住宅（大山崎町）／戸田邸（京都市）／久保邸＊（京都市）／太田邸＊（京都市・現存） 『レーモンド自邸』（アントニン・レーモンド）／『シュレーダー邸』（ヘリット・トーマス・リートフェルト）	メートル法実施 ★文部省外郭団体が『住宅生活の改善』刊行
1925（大正14）年	37歳	11月、博士論文「我国住宅建築の改善に関する研究」を『国民衛生』に連載（昭和2年3月まで）。	三戸邸＊（京都市）	
1926（大正15）年	38歳	4月1日、工学博士の学位を受ける。 5月30日、京都帝国大学教授に任ぜられる。建築学第四講座「建築設備」を担当。	奥村邸（京都市・現存）／喜多源逸邸（京都市・現存）／大覚寺心経殿＊（京都市・現存）／瀬戸邸（津市） 『紫烟荘』（堀口捨己）／『バウハウス校舎』（ワルター・グロピウス）	
1927（昭和2）年	39歳	妻・壽子に次いで去風流八世・西川一草亭に入門し、花を習う。	池田邸（京都市・現存）	★「日本インターナショナル建築会」結成
1928（昭和3）年	40歳	京都府乙訓郡大山崎町に第5回住宅「聴竹居」を建てる。 衛生工業協会大会で「日本趣味」をテーマに講演する。 新建築主催『住宅展覧会』に出品。 12月、岩波書店より『日本の住宅』を出版。	聴竹居・第5回住宅（大山崎町・現存）／聴竹居閑室（大山崎町・現存）／杉本邸（京都市・一部現存）	★「近代建築国際会議（CIAM）」結成
1929（昭和4）年	41歳	5月、岩波書店より『聴竹居図案集』を出版。 長男・裕三が生れる（昭和18年没）。	大澤邸（京都市）／山田邸（京都市）	世界恐慌始まる
1930（昭和5）年	42歳	1月、明治書房より『THE JAPANESE DWELLING-HOUSE』を発行。	八木市造邸（寝屋川市・現存）／喜多愿吉邸（寝屋川市）／聴竹居茶室＊（大山崎町・現存）／藤井邸＊（大山崎町から茶室のみ移築） 『トゥーゲントハット邸』（ミース・ファン・デル・ローエ）	
1931（昭和6）年	43歳	春、『住宅に就いて三』（小冊子）。 4月、『瓶史』陽春号に「挿花」「床の間」掲載。田中平安堂より『鉄筋混凝土の住宅』発行。	濱口邸（京都市）／内田邸＊（京都市）／本庄邸（京都市） 『サヴォア邸』（ル・コルビュジエ）	満州事変
1932（昭和7）年	44歳	4月、田中平安堂より『続聴竹居図案集（木造住宅図版）』発行。 4月、田中平安堂より『聴竹居作品集 二』（藤焼）発行。 岩波書店より『日本の住宅』（普及版）出版。	清野邸（京都市）／田中邸（京都市）／貴志邸（京都市）／高木邸（京都市・現存）／大阪女高医専病院（大阪市）	★モダンアーキテクチャー展開催（ニューヨーク近代美術館）
1933（昭和8）年	45歳	5月9日、ブルーノ・タウトが「聴竹居」を訪ねる。 10月、『建築学研究』に「床の間に就いて」掲載。	汐見邸（京都市・一部移築）／小松邸＊（京都市） 『夏の家』（アントニン・レーモンド）／『東京中央郵便局』（吉田鉄郎）	日本、国際連盟脱退
1934（昭和9）年	46歳	10月、満州（現中国東北区）に出かける。6日／下関。7日／釜山、京城。9日／外金剛山。10日／平壌、大連。12日／旅順。13日／新京。15日／ハルピン、奉天。20日／門司。 田中平安堂より『床の間』発行。	小川邸（京都市・現存）／岩本邸（京都市） 『築地本願寺』（伊東忠太）／『明治生命館』（岡田信一郎・捷五郎）	
1935（昭和10）年	47歳	『建築学研究』に、横山尊雄とともに「日本人に対する建築諸設備の寸法的研究」（第14巻88〜90号）を1938年まで発表。	金生堂＊（京都市）／堀野邸＊（京都市） 『土浦亀城邸』（土浦亀城）	
1936（昭和11）年	48歳		八木芳之助邸（京都市・現存）／島津邸＊（広島市） 『日向別邸』（ブルーノ・タウト）／『落水荘』（フランク・ロイド・ライト）	2・26事件
1937（昭和12）年	49歳	夏、直腸がんを告げられる。 自家用車で東海道五十三次を旅行、兄・与一右衛門と有馬温泉に遊び、6月、入院・手術。 一時回復し、教壇に立つ。 遺作となる「扇葉荘」竣工。『扇葉荘小景』を妻、藤井壽子発行（1940年、新築社より「扇葉荘」出版）。	清野邸（京都市）／瀬戸邸＊（京都市）／扇葉荘（京都市） 『パリ万国博覧日本館』（坂倉準三）	
1938（昭和13）年		3月、再入院。 7月17日、逝去。正四位勲三等。戒名淳風厚道居士。二尊院に眠る。		国家総動員法公布

Chronological Record of Koji Fujii

This record was prepared in reference to *Chronological Record of Koji Fujii* in the collection of Exhibition at Fukuyama Museum of Art in Commemoration of the 15th Anniversary on Modern Architects who designed Japan, Goichi Takeda, Junkichi Tanabe, and Koji Fujii, compiled by Fumihiko Tanifuji, Exhibition Leaflet of *Chochikukyo and Koji Fujii*, compiled by GALLERY A[4], and *3rd Version of Comprehensive Chronology of Modern Japan* by Iwanami-shoten among others. Recent findings are also reflected in the update chronological record.

Year	Age	Chronology	Fujii's Works & Other Works in the Same Year Name of Building (Architect in charge)/* Year the building built is yet to be confirmed or unknown	World Events ★ Event related to architecture
1888	0	December 8, in Fukanaka-cho, Fukuyama-machi-aza, Fukayasu-gun, (currently, Takaragawa, Fukuyama City), Hiroshima Prefecture, Koji was born as the second son of Yoichiemon and Gen Fujii. Kuroganaya, a Japanese sake brewery lasted over 10 generations, was also involved in salt manufacturing and financial service among other business.	Iwasaki Family Fukagawa Villa, Western House by (Josiah Conder)	First gasoline engine automobile in Germany (1886)
1898	10	Yoichiemon, his father died. Koji was 10 years' old. Yukichi, Koji's elder brother, succeeded his father as the head of a family.		The Eiffel Tower (1889)
1907	19	Koji graduated from Hiroshima Prefectural Fukuyama Junior High School, a predecessor of Seishikan High School. In September, he joined The 6th High School.		★ Sezession (Wiener Secession) Movement started (1892)
1910	22	July, he graduated from The 6th High School and was enrolled at Department of Architecture, Faculty of Engineering, Tokyo Imperial University. During his school days, Koji lived in Koishikawa, Tokyo with Kokoro, younger sister who was the student of Gakushuuin and Gen, mother. Koji learnt painting from Somei Yuki, an artist of Japanese painting		First Modern Olympic Games (1896) ★ Argument on Modal at Discussion Panel of AIJ (Architectural Institute of Japan) (1910)
1911	23		The Shibakawa Residence (Goichi Takeda)	
1912	24		Nishi-Honganji Dendoin (Chuta Ito)	
1913	25	July, Koji graduated from Faculty of Architecture, Engineering Department, Tokyo Imperial University. October, Koji joined Takenaka & Co. and worked in Kobe; the first full time design architect who graduated from the Imperial University.		
1914	26	Koji built the 1st house, Kumochi, Fukiai-ku, Kobe and moved in with his mother.	1st house, Kobe✱	
1916	28		Osaka Asahi Shinbun Office, Osaka	
1917	29		Osaka Asahi Shinbun Office, Osaka; Hashimoto Shipping Building, Kobe	
1918	30	Koji married Hisako Senge (1898 – 1993). Chikako's father was the 80th chief priest of Izumo Taisha Shrine & Tokyo Prefectural Governor, Takefuku Senge. Her elder brother, Motomaro was a poet. May, Koji left Takenaka & Co. (though he kept in close contact with the office to do the follow-up work until early November.)	Sogo Department Store, Osaka; The Ryuhei Murayama Residence, Drawing Room Annex, Kobe, preserved	The First World War ended.
1919	31	November 8, Koji left port of Yokohama visit 6 countries in the west on his own expenses.		★ Bauhaus opened.
1920	32	August 14, Koji returned from the visit to six Western countries. December 21, Koji was asked to be a lecturer of Department of Engineering, Kyoto Imperial University in charge of interior drawings. December 10, Kyoto Imperial University commissioned design work of the Central Grand Auditorium of the University. Winter, Koji built the 2nd house in Oyamazaki-cho, Otokuni-gun, Kyoto and moved in.	2nd House, Oyamazaki-cho	★ The first contemporary architectural movement in Japan, Association of The Secession School, was established.
1921	33	May, Koji assumed the assistant professor of the University. September 13, Fukuko, the eldest daughter, was born. Koji issued a leaflet entitled *Jutaku-ni-tsuite* (About Houses.)	The Saito Residence, Kyoto; Stock house of the Kaya Residence, Kyoto; Meikai Building, Kobe; *The Fukase Residence, Kyoto, preserved; *The Sakamoto Residence	
1922	34	Spring Koji built the 3rd house in Oyamazaki-cho, Otokuni-gun, Kyoto.	3rd House, Oyamazaki-cho; Group of Houses in Arima Cultural Village, Kobe; *The Morita Residence, Kyoto; *The Yamanaka Residence, Ashiya; The Ishizaki Residence, Kyoto, preserved;	
1923	35	Summer Koji collected the data on temperature, etc. at the experiment house for a year. October 13, Akiko, the second daughter, was born.	The Nagai Residence, Osaka, preserved; *Uji Town House, Uji; *The Suzuki Residence; *The Hamabe Residence, Kyoto, preserved; The Imperial Hotel (Frank Lloyd Wright)	Great Kanto Earthquake hit Tokyo area.

✱ by *Jutaku-ni-tsuite* (1921)

Year	Age	Chronology	Fujii's Works & Other Works in the Same Year Name of Building (Architect in charge)/* Year the building built is yet to be confirmed or unknown	World Events ★ Event related to architecture
1924	36	Koji built the 4th house in Oyamazaki-cho, Otokuni-gun, Kyoto.	4th House, Oyamazaki-cho, The Toda Residence, Kyoto; *The Kubo Residence, Kyoto; *The Ohta Residence, Kyoto, preserved Raymond Residence by (Antonin Raymond); The Schroder Residence (Gerrit Thomas Rietveld)	Applied meter measurement. ★Affiliated forum of Ministry of Education published *Jutaku Seikatsu-no Kaizen* (Improvement of Living in Houses)
1925	37	November until March 1927, Koji contributed his doctor thesis entitled Research to Improve Domestic Architecture in Japan to *Kokumin Esei* (National Hygine) .	*The Sannohe Residence, Kyoto	
1926	38	April 1, Koji was presented with the doctor of engineering. May 30, Koji was promoted to Professor in charge of 4th course of architectural studies on architectural facility.	The Okumura Residence, Kyoto, preserved; The Residence of Genitsu Kita, Kyoto, preserved; *Shingyo-den Hall, Daikakuji Temple, Kyoto, preserved; The Seto residence, Tsu Shien-so (Sutemi Horiguchi); Bauhaus School (Walter Groperiis)	
1927	39	Following Hisako, Koji joined the Kyofu-sect of the flower arrangement, led by the 8th Nishikawa Issotei.	The Ikeda Residence, Kyoto, preserved	★ Japan International Architecture Association was established.
1928	40	Koji built Chochikukyo, the 5th house, in Oyamazaki-cho, Otokuni-gun, Kyoto. Koji talked about the Japanese taste/flavor at Annual Convention of Hygienic Industry. Koji exhibited at the Housing Exhibition hosted by *Shinkenchiku*. December Koji published *Nippon-no-Jutaku* (Dwelling-houses in Japan) from *Iwanami Shoten*	Chochikukyo, 5th house, Oyamazaki-cho; Kanshitsu (Room of Quiet) in Chochikukyo, preserved, Oyamazaki-cho; The Sugimoto Residence, Kyoto, partially preserved	★ Congrès International d'Architecture Moderne (CIAM) was established.
1929	41	May, Koji published *Chohiukyo Zuhan-shu* (Drawing Document of Chochikyo) from *Iwanami Shoten* Yuzo, the eldest son, was born (died in 1943)	The Osawa Residence, Kyoto; The Yamada Residence, Kyoto;	World Economic Depression started.
1930	42	January, Koji published "THE JAPANESE DWELLING-HOUSES" from *Meiji Shobo*.	The Residence of Ichizo Yagi, Neyagawa, prserved; The Residence of Genkichi Kita, Kyoto; *Tea Room of Chochikukyo Shimo Kanshitsu, Oyamazaki-cho, preserved; *The Fujii Residence, Tea Room was relocated from Oyamazaki-cho Villa Tugendhat (Ludwig Mies van der Rohe)	
1931	43	Spring, Koji issued a leaflet of *Jutaku-ni-tsuite III* (About Houses). April Koji posted *Pressed Flowers and Alcove to Heishi* (Flower Arrangement). Koji published *Tekkin-konkurito-no-Jutaku* (House in Reinforced Concrete) from *Tanaka Heian-do*.	The Hamaguchi Residence, Kyoto; *The Uchida Residence, Kyoto; The Honjo Residence, Kyoto; Villa Savoye (Le Corbusier)	Manchuria Civil War broke out.
1932	44	April, Koji published *Zoku Chochikukyo Sakuhin-shu* (2nd series of Collection of Design Document), drawings & sketches of wooden houses, from *Tanaka-Heian-do*. April, Koji published *Chochikukyo Sakuhin-shu* (Collection of Artifact) on Fuji-pottery from *Tanaka-Heian-do*. *Iwanai-shoten* published *Nippon-no-Jutaku* (Dwelling-houses in Japan) in paperback version.	The Kiyono Residence, Kyoto; The Tanaka Residence, Kyoto; The Kishi Residence, Kyoto; The Takagi Residence, Kyototo, preserved; Osaka Women's Medical Collage, Osaka	★MOMA hosted Modern Architecture Exhibition.
1933	45	May 9, Bruno Taut visited Chochikukyo. October, Koji contributed *Tokono-ma ni-tsuite* (About alcove) to *Kenchikugaku Kenkyu* (Research on Architectural Study).	The Shiomi Residence, Kyoto, partially relocated; *The Komatsu Residence, Kyoto/Summer House (Antonin Raymond); Tokyo Central Post Office (Tetsuro Yoshida)	Japan withdrew from League of Nations.
1934	46	October, Koji visited Manchuria (North East District, China): On 6th; Shimonoseki, 7th; Busan, Keijo (Seoul), 9th; Uekumugan, 10th: Pyongyang, Dalian, 12th; Lushun, 13th; Xingjing, 15th; Harbin, Mukden, 20th; Moji Published *Tokonoma-ni-tsuite* (About Alcoves) by *Tanaka-Heian-do*.	The Ogawa Residence, Kyoto, preserved; The Imamoto Residence, Kyoto Tsukiji Honganji Temple (Chuta Ito); Meiji Seimei Building (Okada Brothers, Shinichiro & Shogoro)	
1935	47	From 1935 to 1938, Koji co-wrote with Takeo Yokoyama on proportional study of architectural Equipment/facility for the Japanese Issue 88 – 90, Series No. 14.	*Kinsei-do, Kyoto; *The Horino Residence, Kyoto The Residence of Kameki Tsuchiura (Kameki Tsuchiura)	
1936	48		The Residence of Yoshinosuke Yagi, Kyoto, preserved; *The Shimazu Residence, Hiroshima Hyuga Villa (Bruno Taut); Kaufmann House (Frank Lloyd Write)	February 26 Incident, Tokyo
1937	49	Summer Rectal cancer was discovered. Koji drove through 53 stations along Tokaido (along the Pacific Ocean). Together with Yoichiemon, his big brother visited Arima-onsen, Kobe. In June, he was hospitalized for operation. He recovered once so that he resumed teaching. Senyo-so, his last work, was built. Kojii's wife, Hisako, published *Koji Fujii's Senyo-so Shokei* (landscape painting of Senyoso). 1940 *Shinkenchikusha* published *Senyo-so*.	The Kiyono Residence, Kyoto; *The Seto Residence, Kyoto, The Senyo-so, Kyoto Japananese Pavillione, Paris World Exposition (Junzo Itakura)	
1938		March, Koji was sent to hospital again. July 17, he died. He received the Third Order of Merit. He rests in a tomb in Nison-in Temple under the posthumous Buddhist name of Junpukodo-koji.		National Mobilization Law, Japan, came into force.

藤井厚二「其の国の建築を代表するものは住宅建築である」── あとがきにかえて

　藤井厚二は、完成形とした「聴竹居」を実例に日本の気候風土と日本人のライフスタイルや感性に適応した「日本の住宅」の思想を紹介する英文の著書「THE JAPANESE DWELLING-HOUSE」を1930（昭和5）年に発行、世界発信している。それから88年、激動の昭和の時代を越え平成を迎えて30年になる今、昭和の住宅として初めて重要文化財に指定された「聴竹居」は、20世紀の日本を代表する世界的な住宅遺産として注目されている。

　今回、このような形で「聴竹居」と「日本の住宅」の思想を再び世界発信する機会を与えて頂いた平凡社の坂田修治さんに先ずは感謝したい。さらに編集者の酒井香代さん、素晴らしい装丁とデザインの書籍にして頂いた大原大次郎さんと世界発信にとって何より大切な翻訳をして頂いた福島真紀子さん、そして、ご寄稿頂いた藤森照信さん、深澤直人さん、堀部安嗣さんにも心から感謝したい。

　最後に謝辞を述べておきたい。先ずは、私の所属する竹中工務店。ここまで「聴竹居」に長く取り組んで来られたのも、会社が常にあたたかく見守ってくれたからだ。さらに、聴竹居倶楽部。2008年の設立以降10年にわたりより近くで「聴竹居」をあたたかく見守り、育んできてくれた。そして、常に価値観を共有し身近で応援し続けてくれた両親と家族。本当にありがとう。

　　　　松隈 章　　新緑に包まれた京都・大山崎「聴竹居」にて　2018年春

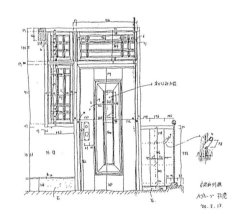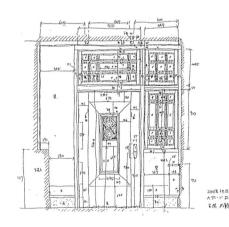

2000年実測調査時のスケッチより（松隈 章）

Domestic architecture represents architecture of the country/region by Koji Fujii

　Koji Fujii released his idea of the Japanese dwelling-house which fits the climate and natural features of Japan and the life style and taste of the Japanese people, referring to Chochikukyo as the completion of his idea, to the world in THE JAPANESE DWELLING-HOUSE published in English in 1930. It is 88 years since then. Chochikukyo had survived drastically-changed Showa era and 30 years of Heisei era and was designated as the national important cultural asset, the first among dwelling houses built in Showa era. Chochikukyo is now entertaining an attention as a world-famous domestic architecture representing Japan in the 20th century.

　First of all, I would like to extend my sincere appreciation to Mr. Shuji Sakata, HEIBONSHA, to allow this opportunity to share Chochikukyo and Fujii's idea of the Japanese dwelling-house with the world again. My appreciation goes to Ms. Kayo Sakai, an editor, Mr. Daijiro Ohara, who finished the book in excellent binding and design, and Ms. Makiko Fukushima, in charge of translation into English which is an important process to share the idea internationally. My sincere appreciation also goes to three contributors, Messrs. Terunobu Fujimori, Naoto Fukasawa, and Yasushi Horiba.

　Last but not the least, I would like to thank Takenaka Corporation, which I work for, for the generous support to date, which has enabled me to involve in the preservation/use of Chochikukyo. Furthermore, since 2008, Chochikukyo Club has been and is always with Chochikukyo to nurture it in the community. Let me close my concluding remarks with the following words to my parent and family who share a sense of value, "Thank you very much for all of your support"

　　　　　　　　　　　　　　　　Akira Matsukuma
　　　　　　　　　　　　　　　　Spring 2018 at Chochikukyo

図版・写真

2	南の立面／『聴竹居図案集』(1929年　岩波書店)より転載	
23	配置／『聴竹居図案集』(1929年　岩波書店)より転載	
31	食事室から見た居室／『聴竹居図案集』(1929年　岩波書店)より転載	
49	配置／『聴竹居図案集』(1929年　岩波書店)より転載	
59	透視図／京都大学大学院工学研究科建築学専攻所蔵	
59、60	茶室再現ＣＧ　竹中工務店	
61	北の立面と西の立面／『聴竹居図案集』(1929年　岩波書店)より転載	
71	間取／『聴竹居図案集』(1929年　岩波書店)より転載	
97	八木邸北立面図（酒徳金之助）／酒徳氏所蔵	
107～117	「藤井厚二の生涯」	

肖像写真　小西家蔵

福山誠之館高校記念館　撮影協力／広島県立誠之館高校同窓会

三川合流写真　淀川資料館所蔵

第1回～第4回住宅平面図・写真／『日本の住宅』(1928年　岩波書店)より転載

第5回住宅写真／『聴竹居図案集』(1929年　岩波書店)より転載

その他の写真、図面、資料／竹中工務店所蔵

参考文献

藤井厚二『日本の住宅』(1928年岩波書店)

藤井厚二『聴竹居圖案集』(1929年　岩波書店)

藤井厚二『THE JAPANESE DWELLING-HOUSE』(1930年　明治書房)

藤井厚二『続聴竹居圖案集』(1932年　田中平安堂)

藤井厚二『床の間』(1934年　田中平安堂)

小能林宏城「大山崎の校閲」『昭和住宅史』(1976年　新建築社)

石田潤一郎「『日本趣味』の空間 ── 藤井厚二論序説」『日本の眼と空間 ── もうひとつのモダン・デザイン』(1990年　セゾン美術館編)

藤岡洋保「主要作品解説・聴竹居」「建築家論　藤井厚二」『新建築創刊65周年記念号　建築20世紀』(1991年　新建築社)

藤岡洋保「聴竹居の今日的意味」『SOLAR CAT』20（1995年）

竹中工務店編『芝川邸と武田五一展』(1996年)

大川三雄＋川向正人＋初田亨＋吉田鋼市『図説　近代建築の系譜』(1997年　彰国社)

竹中工務店「特集　聴竹居」季刊『アプローチ』冬号（2000年）

竹中工務店設計部編『「聴竹居」実測図集−環境と共生する住宅』(2001年　彰国社)

ふくやま美術館編『開館15周年記念展　武田五一・田辺淳吉・藤井厚二　日本を意匠した建築家たち』(2004年　ふくやま美術館)

小泉和子『「日本の住宅」という実験−風土をデザインした藤井厚二』(2008年　農山漁村文化協会)

『日本の住宅　藤井厚二』住宅建築文献集成　第3巻（2009年　柏書房）

編集協力

株式会社 竹中工務店

一般社団法人 聴竹居倶楽部

協力（順不同・敬称略）

小西章子

小西伸一

八木重一

八木圭子

村山龍平邸和館／公益財団法人香雪美術館

京都大学大学院工学研究科吉田建築系図書室

京都工芸繊維大学大学院工芸科学研究科建築研究科

広島県立福山誠之館高等学校　同窓会

ふくやま美術館

小倉山二尊教院華台寺（二尊院）

柏書房

ゆまに書房

聴竹居
日本人の理想の住まい
Chochikukyo, An ideal dwelling in Japan.

2018年5月18日　初版第1刷発行

著　者　松隈 章
写　真　古川泰造
発行者　下中美都
発行所　株式会社平凡社
　　　　〒101-0051
　　　　東京都千代田区神田神保町3-29
　　　　電話　03-3230-6583（編集）
　　　　　　　03-3230-6573（営業）
　　　　振替　00180-0-29639
　　　　ホームページ　http://www.heibonsha.co.jp/
印刷所　株式会社東京印書館
製本所　大口製本印刷株式会社

©Akira Matsukuma, Taizo Furukawa 2018 Printed in Japan
ISBN978-4-582-54463-3 C0052
NDC分類番号521.85
B4変型判（36.4cm）　総ページ264

落丁・乱丁本はお取り替えいたしますので、
小社読者サービス係まで直接お送りください（送料小社負担）。

松隈 章（まつくま・あきら）

株式会社竹中工務店設計本部所属、公益財団法人ギャラリー A⁴（エークワッド）企画マネージャー兼務。一般社団法人聴竹居倶楽部・代表理事。1957年、兵庫県生まれ。北海道大学工学部建築工学科卒業後、竹中工務店に入社。設計業務の傍ら近代建築の保存活動やギャラリー A⁴ での企画展をはじめとする数多くの建築展に携わる。近著に、『聴竹居――藤井厚二の木造モダニズム建築』(2015年、平凡社) の執筆、『竹中工務店 建築写真集』全5巻・復刻版 (2015年、ゆまに書房) の企画・編集・解題・解説、展覧会図録『竹中工務店 400年の夢――時をきざむ建築の文化史』(2016年、世田谷美術館) の編集・執筆、『竹中工務店 住まいの空間』(2016年、建築画報社) の企画・編集・寄稿、『木造モダニズム建築の傑作 聴竹居――発見と再生の22年』(2018年、ぴあ) の執筆などがある。

古川泰造（ふるかわ・たいぞう）

1957年、大阪府生まれ。大阪写真専門学院卒業。スタジオ勤務、フリーランスを経て1982年より竹中工務店で建築写真の撮影に携わる。さらにギャラリー A⁴ の企画展、木造モダニズム建築の撮り下ろし撮影を手がけ、「『聴竹居』と藤井厚二展」「『札幌聖ミカエル教会』とアントニン・レーモンド展」「日土小学校と松村正恒展」「甦った西本願寺『伝道院』と伊藤忠太展」「三里塚教会物語と吉村順三展」などの展覧会のための建築家の作品撮影および、『竹中工務店 住まいの空間』(2016年、建築画報社) で撮影を担当。2018年3月、竹中工務店を退職。4月、フォト・アトリエ・F 設立。

挿花
藤本三喜子（17、25、27、30、36、43、44、51、73頁）

翻訳
福島真紀子

装幀
大原大次郎

編集
酒井香代
坂田修治